W9-CJM-277

WITHDRAWN
No longer the property of the
Boston Public Library.
Sale of this material benefits the Library

Georg Jensen
A Tradition of Splendid Silver

GEORG JENSEN

A Tradition
of Splendid Silver

Janet Drucker

Schiffer Publishing Ltd

4880 Lower Valley Road, Atglen, PA 19310 USA

To Byrd, my husband, whose guidance, support, help in research, and faith in my ability made this book possible. I am eternally grateful to him.

FINE ARTS DEPT.

F - A MAY - 6 1998
NK7198
.G38
D78
1997

SEP 2 1998

Library of Congress Cataloging-in-Publication Data

Drucker, Janet.

    Georg Jensen: a tradition of splendid silver/Janet Drucker.
      p. cm.
    Includes bibliographical references and index.
    ISBN 0-88740-978-4
    1. Georg Jensen sølvsmedie, A/s. 2. Jensen, Georg Arthur, 1866-1935. 3. Silverwork--Denmark--History--20th century--Themes, motives. I. Jensen, Georg Arthur, 1866-1935. II. Title.
NK7198.G38D78 1997
739.2'3722--dc21   97-11059
                           CIP

Copyright © 1997 by Janet Drucker.

All rights reserved. No part of this work may be reproduced or used in any form or by any means--graphic, electronic, or mechanical, including photocopying or information storage and retrieval systems--without written permission from the copyright holder.

Designed by "Sue"

ISBN: 0-88740-978-4
Printed in Hong Kong

Frontispiece: Silver caviar dish with glass liner inscribed with Georg Jensen's signature on the back. Horn and silver serving spoon in Cactus. Private collection.

Published by Schiffer Publishing Ltd.
4880 Lower Valley Road
Atglen, PA 19310
Phone: (610) 593-1777; Fax: (610) 593-2002
E-mail: schifferbk@aol.com
Please write for a free catalog.
This book may be purchased from the publisher.
Please include $3.95 for shipping.
Try your bookstore first.

We are interested in hearing from authors
with book ideas on related subjects.

Acknowledgments

This book would not have been possible without the help of many dedicated individuals. I would like to extend my heartfelt thanks to:

Eva Bærentzen, Henning Andersen, Rolf Kronstadt, Jan Møller, and Michael Von Essen from Georg Jensen/Royal Copenhagen in Denmark;

Ana Maria McGinnis, Ivar Ipsen, Josephine Dillon, Deborah Rehr, Karin Slatem, and Dana Mitchell Milonski from Georg Jensen/Royal Copenhagen in the United States;

Anita Rasmussen, Vice Consul Cultural Affairs, Royal Danish Consulate General in New York;

My friend Lolo Hallstrom, the "Jensen Lady in London," for her help and encouragement;

Dr. Melissa Hardie of the Newlyn Art Gallery, and Sonia and David Newell-Smith of Tadema Gallery in London;

David Beasley, Librarian, and Melanie Lock, Assistant Librarian, Goldsmith's Hall in London;

Anne Shannon for sharing her enthusiasm for my project and her assistance in research;

Penny Jones Napier, Janet Zapata, Leah Gordon, Elyse Zorn Karin, Susan Peabody Oakes of the Oakes Studio, Gloria Lieberman of Skinner's, Inc.;

Jens Bille, Ea Jensen, Mr. and Mrs. Ib Jensen;

Erik Fries, Eric Petersen, Karin Slatem, Jens Bille, Søren Jensen for translations;

Janet and Scott Lehrer, Linda Morgan, Robert Friedeau and Rosemary Schulze, Ed and Lisa Guari, Doris and Bill Einbinder, Dr. Barry Goozner, Fern Elkind, Emma and Jay Lewis, Kitty and Martin Jacobs, Laurie Phillips, Gail Roeshman Selig, Lee Ellen Friedland, Janet Laws and Steve Mey, Lis Rusch, John Rusch, Klaus Olesen, Charles Hoblitz Ole S. Pedersen, Marcia Ewing-Current, Debra and David Rosensaft, JoAnn Schrier, Robert and Barbara Paul, Steve and Barbara Herman, Janet Morrison Clarke, Geraldine Wolf, Freema Gluck, Yvette Scobie, and the many others who choose to remain anonymous;

Special thanks to Douglas Congdon-Martin and to Nancy Schiffer;

Barbara Rosenbaum for her skills and encouragement;

Kathleen Carmody, for organizational skills that kept me on track;

David Taylor, for his encouragement and editorial assistance;

A very special thank you to William Drucker, my son, who shares my devotion to the work of Georg Jensen, for his patience and photography that made the completion of this book a reality.

And, finally, to my family, especially to Carol, Abby and Rhonda who cheered me on with their reassurance and support.

This work could not have been undertaken without the pioneering efforts of the following authors in documenting Jensen's life and work: Jørgen E. R. Møller, L. C. Nielsen, Ivan Munk Olsen, Chr. Ditlev Reventlow, and Walter Schwartz.

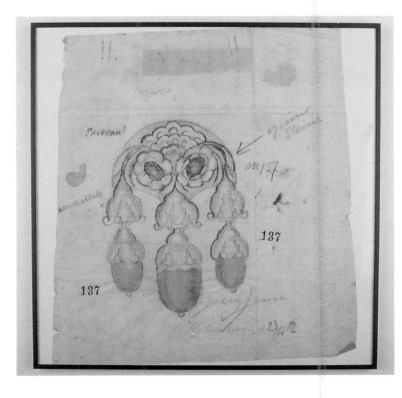

Original drawing for brooch no. 137 by Georg Jensen, see page 91. Courtesy Georg Jensen/Royal Copenhagen.

Georg Jensen at 60 years of age. Courtesy of Georg Jensen/Royal Copenhagen.

Signature of Georg Jensen (life 1866-1935) taken from a brochure of 1966 commemorating the hundredth anniversary of his birth.

1866-1966

CONTENTS

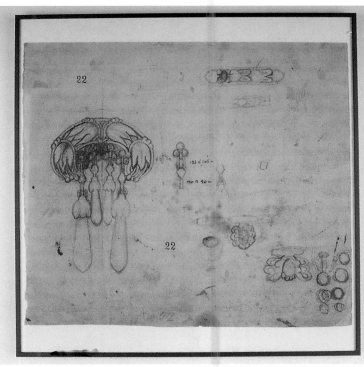

Original drawing for brooch no. 22 by Georg Jensen, see page 74. Courtesy Georg Jensen/Royal Copenhagen.

Footed covered bowl, fork and bracelet.
Courtesy of Georg Jensen/Royal Copenhagen.

Preface

My love affair with Georg Jensen silver developed from a search for beautiful yet affordable jewelry. Twenty years ago, when I began to deal in antique jewelry, diamonds and gold were out of the question. Not only were they too costly, they didn't appeal to me aesthetically. Then I found my first piece of Georg Jensen silver. I knew immediately there was something magical about it, and to my further delight, I discovered I could afford to buy it.

The memory of finding that first piece of Jensen silver is indelible. It was brooch number 100B, sometimes referred to as the tulip pin. Though less than two inches long, it perfectly conveyed the curvaceous beauty of a flower, maybe a tulip. I realized that the sculptural, handmade appearance of the brooch was what first captured my attention. Then I noticed the amazing skill of the execution. The hammered surface seemed unique, even mysterious. It looked as though it had been meticulously beaten to impart a series of tiny hexagonal hammer marks. I could almost hear and feel the methodical pounding of the silversmith's hammer. These two factors -- splendid form and the "handmade" look -- convinced me that I had discovered a treasure.

When I turned the tulip pin over, I saw impressed marks: "Georg Jensen" within a beaded oval, "925 Sterling" and "100B." At the time, I did not understand the significance of the marks. When another tulip pin with the same number, 100B, appeared, with different accompanying marks, I realized there were questions I needed to answer: What did the marks mean? Why did they sometimes differ from piece to piece? How could reading them help me to "decode" Jensen silver?

I soon learned the answers to these questions, which inevitably led to further questions. I wanted to know such things as: who designed the piece, how many examples were produced, what different stones were used, and how one design related to others within the Jensen canon. I began searching for answers in books, company catalogs, exhibition records, museum collections, and anywhere else I could find information. With each answered question, I gradually learned more not only about Jensen silver, but also about the fascinating man Georg Jensen -- artist, sculptor, designer, silversmith, businessman, and family man.

Simultaneously, my involvement with other Jensen silver products grew as well. Though I initially bought and sold only Jensen jewelry, I soon found I could not stop there. I began to deal in Jensen flatware and serving pieces as well. Customers asked for other specific items, and I went out to find them. Before long, I was handling almost anything with the Jensen hallmark. What began as an attraction to Jensen's "wearable and affordable art" jewelry grew to encompass virtually the totality of his work and the work of the designers employed by the firm he founded.

I now know that the features that so entranced me about the first Jensen brooch I encountered were consistent with the overall style or "look" of Jensen jewelry. And I know too, that my reaction was not at all unusual. For example, when working at antique shows, I often observe people who stop in front of my display case, point, and say excitedly, "That's Jensen!" Then, some will spontaneously tell me stories about a favorite Jensen pin or a bracelet, the special Jensen piece a relative brought back from a trip abroad, or a family tradition of collecting and cherishing Jensen silver. When I hear their comments and stories, I recognize the same enthusiasm I felt when I first encountered Jensen silver. Even after many years of buying and selling Jensen silver, I still feel it. Apparently, my level of enthusiasm is so obvious that I'm sometimes asked: "Are you a dealer or a collector?" Some antique dealers become dispassionate about their wares -- and adopt a "professional" attitude, some might say -- but I've learned, when it comes to Jensen, that that is impossible for me. Perhaps it is a bit paradoxical for a dealer to sell what he or she dearly loves to collect, but for me any sense of loss I feel from the sale of a treasured piece is more than compensated for by the joy of introducing a newcomer to the wonders of Jensen silver, or sharing the appreciation of a beautiful piece with an experienced collector.

The Road to Raadvad

In August, 1995, after more than 20 years of collecting and selling Jensen silver, I fulfilled a long-standing dream by visiting the place where Georg Jensen grew up and started his workshop. I traveled to Denmark with a plan to visit Raadvad -- the place where he spent his childhood -- and thus directly experience the environment that was the inspiration for his artistic expression. And so, on a Sunday morning, I took an hour train trip from Copenhagen to the small town of Raadvad, near Lyngby. I arrived at the train station at six o'clock in the morning. At first glance I seemed to be the only person up and about, but soon I spotted two taxis waiting nearby. Luckily for me, one of the drivers spoke English, and

Water wheel at the cutlery factory in Raadvad where Georg Jensen's father worked.

Raadvad, Denmark.

Plaque marking the birthplace of Georg Jensen.

Raadvad street that leads to the factory.

The timeless quality of Raadvad.

The landscape of Raadvad near the location of Jensen's home as a boy.

understood where I wanted to go -- the home of Georg Jensen. After a short ride through the beautiful countryside, I spotted a plaque identifying Jensen's exact birthplace and called out for the driver to "Stop!"

It is difficult to convey the excitement I felt as I stepped out of the taxi onto the road that runs through the small industrial village of Raadvaad and the forest known as Jaegersborg Deer Park. The house with the plaque I spotted is not the original Jensen home; it is simply on the site of Jensen's home. Across the road, there is a picture-perfect lake framed by lush, flourishing foliage. The patterns on the water's shimmering surface that day reminded me of the hammer marks on the tulip pin which I had found so mysterious and enticing. Having read Jensen's reminiscences of his boyhood, I could easily conjure up the image of young Georg playing on the shore and digging up the clay he would later use to fashion his first sculptures. And when I closed my eyes, I could see him walking down the road, exploring the marshes and looking at the flowers and other natural forms he would later memorialize over and over in his work. When I saw some old factory buildings and the waterways that provided them with hydraulic power, I could visualize the way the landscape had been when Georg's father worked as a grinder at the Raadvad Knife Manufactory -- the place where Georg had shown his first clay figures to beguiled workmen. Other scenes helped me fill in a picture of the past: old houses, the peaceful forest and well-born horseback riders galloping along the paths just as others had done in his day. On that Sunday, it seemed as though I had arrived not only in the physical place where Jensen spent his formative years, but also in the emotional space that nurtured the gentle spirit of one of the most accomplished and respected artists of his time.

This book presents information I learned on that wonderful journey which began with a pair of little silver tulips, and carried me down the road to Raadvad. Along the way, I have served as collector, dealer, and researcher and watched others also appreciate Georg Jensen silver. Its artistry reflects the brilliance of Georg Jensen and the steadfast devotion to his legacy of incomparable design and craftsmanship as maintained by the company that bears his name.

In Denmark and other European countries, a *goldsmith* is one who makes jewelry, a *silversmith* is one who raises silver to make hollowware, and a *cutler* is one who makes flatware. For defininitive purposes, hollowware refers to bowls, vases, desk implements, etc., anything that is not flatware. In the United States, *jewelers* make gold as well as silver jewelry. Georg Jensen is referred to as a silversmith in this text, although we know he made flatware, hollowware and gold jewelry as well. Jensen referred to himself as a silversmith sculptor.

Small tulip pin #100B designed by Georg Jensen. Courtesy of Georg Jensen/Royal Copenhagen.

Tongs, footed gravy bowl and bird pin.
Courtesy of Georg Jensen/Royal
Copenhagen.

Chapter 1
Setting the Scene

Crosscurrents of the Arts and Crafts Movement

and Art Noveau at the Beginning

of the 20th Century

At first glance, the story of Georg Jensen appears simple: an artistically gifted Danish boy from a working-class family who loved nature and aspired to become a sculptor, grew up to become a silversmith, founded a company, and designed and made jewelry, flatware and hollowware that earned him international acclaim and significantly influenced the direction of decorative arts. All these things are true; however, Jensen's fascinating story is not so simple. In order to properly understand his life and his accomplishments, one most take a broader view that goes beyond the useful but narrowly focused biographical material available. That is, certain social, cultural, and economic trends that developed before and during his lifetime must be taken into account in order to understand how his artistic and philosophical values were shaped and why his accomplishments are so worthy of recognition. It is useful, therefore, to review the historical events that rocked the foundations of Western culture in the turbulent century that surrounded Jensen's birth in 1866.

Of paramount importance is the fact that the first two decades of Jensen's life coincided with the emergence of a powerful artistic movement--the Arts and Crafts movement. Dedicated to the proposition that good craftsmanship is of great value to society, proponents of the Arts and Crafts philosophy taught that crafts and decorative arts deserve to be recognized as important as fine arts. What flowed from that movement, and eventually engaged Jensen and a host of other extraordinary designers and craftsmen, was an unprecedented explosion of activity within the realm of decorative arts in Europe and America. A corresponding expansion of popular interest in the consumption of decorative arts of all kinds resulted, as well as the search for and promotion of national styles in the fine and decorative arts.

The Industrial Revolution heralded mass production and the promise of increased goods and services at affordable prices. Subsequently, goods manufacturers could provide consistent quality and a greater selection of products. Not only did the availability and costs of these products help to make life more comfortable for the average man and woman, but the new manufacturers also provided them with increased employment opportunities. Workers began to flock from the countryside to the cities to work in the new factories. In addition, these industrial workers only needed to learn one specific skill in the manufacturing process. It was no longer necessary for the worker to own his own tools, market his own product, or in any way be associated with the finished product. When the concept of division of labor had been implemented in the production of goods, the worker's dignity and pride in producing a quality item was greatly reduced.

Exciting ideas and inventions were also changing the world. Charles Darwin's theory of the survival of the species created a great stir, while his studies of flora and fauna brought about a new interest in nature and human development. Steam power was replaced by the combustion engine. The electric light brought about a fundamental change in the nature of work since a productive workday was no longer limited to the hours of sunlight; factories could run day and night. This was truly a time of expanding productivity.

However, as the years went by, the development of new and better machinery resulted in reduced labor needs and in frequent periods of unemployment for many workers.

While there is no question that industrial and scientific progress opened new doors, these very changes also spawned a new breed of social reformers who saw the increasing use of machinery as a harbinger of ugliness and second-rate workmanship. Perhaps the most prominent catalysts for an artistic movement which came to be known as Arts and Crafts were two Englishmen: art critic/philosopher John Ruskin (1819-1900) and artist/designer William Morris (1834-1896). Both men were ardent social reformers who believed that changes in society that resulted from the Industrial Revolution and other factors were contributing to a general decline in their nation's moral well being. Specifically, they felt that the availability of cheap, poorly designed, poorly made, mass-produced goods fashioned from inferior materials were deleterious and led to the corruption of traditional values. Their belief was that superior furnishings and other products were those which were well designed, well made by craftsmen who took pride in their work, fashioned from high-quality materials, and were likely to last for a long time. Believing that art was a vehicle for the improvement they sought for everyday life, Ruskin and Morris championed a return to a medieval model of craft production. This, they believed, would revive "honest craftsmanship," accentuate the "truth" of materials, and refocus attention on vernacular expression--especially the Gothic style, which they took to be the best of all English styles. As well, they celebrated craftsmanship by hand while rejecting the use of machines for the creation of art. Fundamentally, "through the practice of craftsmanship, (Ruskin and Morris) hoped to reunite art and labor, mental effort and manual achievement, work and play, countering the fragmentation of social life endemic to the emerging corporate order." (Boris.) William Morris is significant not only for the arts and crafts ideals he formulated and espoused, but also for the way he endeavored to put those ideals into practice--to live, one might say, an arts and crafts life. In order to demonstrate the validity of his beliefs in the superiority of goods produced by hand, in 1861 he established a company--Morris, Marshall, Faulkner and Co., Fine Art Workmen in Painting, Carving, Furniture, and Metals--that designed and produced a wide variety of products, including furniture, wallpaper, fabrics, books, and stained glass. Morris not only designed many of the firm's products but also worked alongside other craftsmen in creating them. Since he sought to resurrect old techniques, he often taught them to his workers. At the same time, since he believed that art should be a source of joy for the maker as well as the user, he attempted to give his workers as much latitude for individual expression as possible. "Dressed in a workman's blouse, his hands stained with dyes, Morris shared the labor and understood the culture of his men." (Boris) Ironically, because Morris would not compromise on the quality of materials and craftsmanship, his firm's beautiful products were expensive and, therefore, only the wealthy could afford to buy them. Thus, while he was successful in drawing public attention to the desirability of improving the quality of design, by the nature of the time and expense required to create exemplary hand-made items, he was not personally successful in putting art in the hands of a large number of people. The products remained too costly for the audience Morris was trying to reach.

The philosophies of Ruskin and Morris, however, helped give rise to a new sense of artistic beauty, and many English painters, sculptors and other artists came to believe that it was their moral duty to improve the lives of ordinary people through their art. Thus, the artistic process was not seen to be separate from social responsibility. Many artists believed they could help provide the antidote to what they saw as the scourge of the industrial era; poor quality, machine-made products that were flooding the market. Some joined craft guilds that aimed to produce beautiful, affordable products while simultaneously providing a spiritually uplifting experiences for the artists. Some of the guilds provided technical training to amateurs and in so doing were among the first schools to offer broad technical and vocational training. Another significant result of the arts and crafts movement in England was the growing opportunity for women to become artisans; they were trained in the workshops to produce jewelry, embroidery, ceramics and other hand-made goods.

One of the most influential English designers involved in the English arts and crafts movement was Charles Robert Ashbee (1863-1924), a contemporary of Georg Jensen. Ashbee was a silversmith and jeweler who founded the Guild of Handicrafts, a cooperative group of craftsmen, in 1888. Ashbee was one of the first designers to produce Arts and Crafts jewelry. In addition, the Guild produced domestic metalwares as well as copper and pewter items. Ashbee's work is of particular significance to our understanding of Georg Jensen, not only because he was also a silversmith and leading figure in the English arts and crafts scene, but also because Ashbee exhibited some of his own work in Copenhagen in 1899. The jewelry designs he displayed were a striking departure from Danish jewelry designs. Specifically, his pieces were open and loose in design, depicting natural forms, and were set with non-precious colored stones. Danish jewelry of the period, on the other hand, tended to replicate stilted classical forms and were set with precious stones. One brooch in particular by Ashbee seems to have strongly influenced Danish jewelers (see page 70). The design, with central, oval opal surrounded by scroll wire work in an oxidized setting of naturalistic leaves, is more in keeping with the skønvirke aesthetic than with the celtic inspiration of other English jewelry of the time.

One of Jensen's other contemporaries, who also had a profound impact on the decorative arts in his own country and abroad, was the brilliant Scottish architect and designer Charles Rennie Mackintosh (1868-1928). Mackintosh's designs were among the boldest and most original of the era, and his work strongly influenced Josef Hoffmann (1870-1918) in Austria who, along with others, founded the Weiner Werkstätte. Hoffmann and Mackintosh became colleagues as well as friends, and Mackintosh was better known in Austria than in England at the turn of the century.

Pendant and necklace by Theodor Fahrner.

Pendant with malachite and pearl by Theodor Fahrner.

Elsewhere, others who were also inspired by various aspects of the English arts and crafts movement developed their own interpretations of the new style. In France, the style was called Art Nouveau. Within the areas of jewelry and silver manufacture, the most prominent proponent of Art Nouveau was René Lalique (1860-1945) whose exquisite jewelry often reflected insects, birds, flowers, leaves and other naturalistic forms. Lalique used diamonds and other colored gemstones in conjunction with materials of less value like horn and mother-of-pearl, ivory, and carved glass. His peerless use of plique-à-jour enameling and singular color pallete of cool greens combined with the new subject matter established Lalique as a harbinger of the "art nouveau" style. Also in France, new periodicals of commentary and critical revues surfaced at the turn of the century. The illustrated monthly journal *La Revue de la bijouterie, joaillerie, orfeverie* was devoted, for the first time, entirely to jewelry design. It was founded in 1900 and continued until 1905. (Becker.)

In Germany, the new style was called Jugendstil, a name taken from a German art magazine called *Jugend* which was established in 1896. Here artists attempted to introduce and integrate artistry to all aspects of life in the home and workplace, including the designs for houses, furniture, lights, door handles, etc. A major influence in this effort was Hermann Obrist (1863-1927) whose textile embroidery designs were based on naturalism and the flowing lines of plants. One extoardinary design by Obrist, called Whiplash, came to be an international symbol of the art nouveau style.

A characteristic of Jugendstil philosophy, as opposed to Arts and Crafts philosophy in England, was the belief that hand and machine work could be combined in the production of decorative arts. Theodor Fahrner (1859-1919) is perhaps the most significant manufacturer in Germany to successfully utilize the Jugendstil philosophy in his business. His firm, in Pforzheim, was a major manufacturer of art jewelry, and it exported large quantities to England, France and the United States. Around the turn of the century, Fahrner instituted cooperation between artist-designers and the manufacturing process to create 'artist-manufactured' jewelry in the new style. Typically, the pieces were made of silver and were decorated with colored stones, enamelling, mother-of-pearl and other less costly materials. With respect to design, his jewelry was sometimes figurative and sometimes abstract geometric forms with stones uniquely faceted and set. Because he used designs from independent artists, the variety of styles is exciting and varied. He won acclaim at the Paris World's Fair in 1900 for his industrially produced jewelry. René Lalique, too, won acclaim at the Fair for his work. Although Lalique's were diametrically contrasting with Fahrner's in their production methods, they shared the credo that the value of a piece of jewelry is based on design rather than materials. Pforzheim jewelers went to Paris and returned with ideas and inspiration (Becker). Their highly skilled manufacturing techniques were sometimes sought, in turn, by the Parisian jewelers.

Three brooches of naturalistic motifs made by Theodor Fahrner (with citrine) of Germany, Edward Oakes (with colored stones) of the United States, and Georg Jensen (in silver) of Denmark.

Fahrner's jewelry also was pictured in respected journals that had world wide circulation, e.g. a special supplement of *The Studio* in 1901-1902 on German comtemporary jewelry. Fahrner's firm produced designs of some of the most prominent artists of the day, including those of the Darmstadt Art Colony which was established in 1899. An important distinction, in the operation of both Liberty & Co. in London and Fahrner in Pforzheim, was their common search for the best designers. Fahrner, in respect for the designers' work, allowed for the initial signatures of many designer to be placed alongside the Fahrner company mark on jewelry. Liberty only used the company mark. Therefore, a designer such as Patriz Huber is acknowledged on Fahrner jewelry with his initials PH. In 1914, Theodor Fahrner exhibited in Mälmo, along with Georg Jensen.

In Belgium, another contemporary of Georg Jensen was architect/designer/painter Henry van de Velde, (1863-1957). After first working as a painter, he channeled his energies toward architecture, decorative arts, and the study of theories of design. In pursuit of these goals, he not only designed houses and their furnishings, but also traveled extensively in order to undertake commissions, exhibit his work, and meet artists and entrepreneurs on the leading edge of the new style. In 1898 he opened his own decorating firm in Brussels, and undertook work in France and Germany. He was most influential through his writings, which advocated the union of the fine and decorative arts. In 1905, he visited Georg Jensen in Copenhagen.

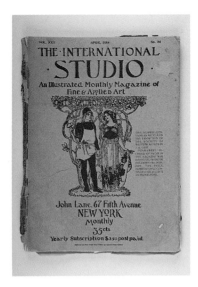

Cover illustration for *THE FRA, Exponent of the American Philosophy*, June 1913. Elbert Hubbard, Editor and Publisher, East Aurora, New York.

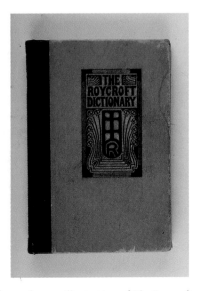

Embossed cover illustration of *The Roycroft Dictionary* published by Elbert Hubbard, 1914.

THE ARTS & CRAFTS MOVEMENT IN AMERICA

During the 1890s, elements of the English arts and craft movement began to influence thinking in the United States. News of the movement was brought to America by Americans who had been exposed to it in England, and also by periodicals such as *International Studio*--the American edition of *The Studio*, the journal of record for the English arts and crafts movement. Although Americans tended not to embrace the political underpinnings of the English movement, they were eager to embrace some of its other aspects, expecially the goals of improving craftsmanship, bettering people's aesthetic environments, making art as satisfying to the producer as to the consumer, and trying to identify a national style that reflected the character of the American people. Jewelry worn in America, until the last quarter of the nineteenth century, was primarily of European origin, including cameos, Victorian brooches, mosaics, and coral. The import duty placed on jewelry by the American government in 1850 helped to stir American jewelry manufacturers to find "their own style." Craft workshops and small cooperatives developed around the 1880s. In Boston, Chicago, Minneapolis, Detroit, New York, and Providence, Rhode Island, arts and crafts societies were formed. Most important, the distinguishing characteristic of the Arts and Crafts movement was that it was really about "art" and "beauty," and how people's lives could be enhanced by bringing both together in daily life.

The two earliest and best-known American proponents of the arts and crafts movement were Elbert Hubbard (1856-1915) and Gustav Stickley (1857-1952). Both were inspired by the example of William Morris. Hubbard, who claimed to have met Morris in England, founded a small press in 1895 and later established a community of artisans called the Roycrofters, in East Aurora, New York. The Roycrofters engaged in the hand production of books, furniture, and metalwork in the Arts and Crafts style. Similarly inspired by a trip to Europe, furniture designer Gustav Stickley opened Craftsman Workshops in New York in 1898, and began making oak furniture in the "mission" style, which he believed reflected the arts and crafts ideals of high quality and craftsmanship in an American manner. In 1901, Stickley also founded a magazine, *The Craftsman*, through which he disseminated his philosophy and provided practical advice about architecture and home furnishings; he devoted several issues to the writings of Morris and Ruskin. *The Craftsman* became the best known American periodical devoted to the Arts and Crafts philosophy.

Many other people also figured prominently in the early years of the American arts and crafts movement. Jane Addams was a social reformer who visited Ashbee's guild and school at Toynbee Hall in London during the 1880s. She founded the settlement house Hull House, in Chicago, in 1889. Louis Comfort Tiffany (1848-1933) established workshops in New York City that produced jewelry, metalwork, bronzes, ceramics, and "favrile" glass. He was listed in the *Directory of the Society of Arts and Crafts, Boston, Exhibition Record 1897-1927* as a glass designer and worker and exhibited in the first exhibition, in Copley Hall, Boston, in 1897 and in 1899.

Within the fields of jewelry and metalwork, numerous others made important contributions. Clara Barck Welles (1868-1965) of Chicago opened the Kalo workshop in 1900 in Chicago. Metalsmith Robert Jarvie (1865-1941), also from Chicago, opened the Jarvie Shop in 1904. In the Boston area, jewelers Margaret Rogers (1868-1949) and Edward Everett Oakes (1891-1960), both members and award winners of Boston's Society of Arts and Crafts, produced intricate, hand made jewelry of gold and silver that exhibited the kinds of naturalistic motifs which characterize the American Arts and Crafts style and quality.

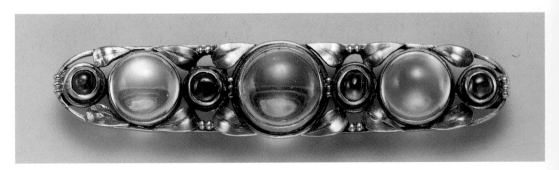

Gold, moonstone and sapphire bar pin attributed to Margaret Rogers. Private collection.

Examples of ceramic work by the sculptor Thorvald Bindesbøll.

Skønvirke (1900-1925): A New Style For Denmark

When Edward the VII, the future British King, married Alexandra, the Danish Princess, in 1864, this was a merger of cultures. Their marriage may have been the stimulus for Danish artists becoming more aware of British tastes and the writings of Morris and Ruskin. A generation later, the contact grew into a new style.

In Denmark, aspects of the Arts and Crafts philosphy and style were expressed in a distinctively Danish way. By 1907, the Danish term for the style was coined "skønvirke," which literally means "beautiful work."

Another salient feature of the skønvirke period, which spanned 1900 to 1925, was the recasting of roles for artists (who traditionally created new designs) and craftsmen (who did the handwork to execute the designs); distinction between the two roles, which previously had been quite clear, was now blurred. During the first decade of the 20th century, artists frequently made the items they designed and craftsmen created new designs; the notion of an individual being both artist and craftsperson found acceptance.

A preeminent example of the melding of these roles was the remarkable Danish artist Thorvald Bindesbøll (1846-1908). Though trained as an architect, Bindesbøll became an exceptional and imaginative designer as well as craftsman, and demonstrated his expertise through the creation of a wide range of products: bookbindings, ceramics, and jewelry. Clearly, by helping to erase the barriers between artists and craftsmen, Bindesbøll and others helped to bring about greater freedom of artistic expression and to promote cooperation among the designers and makers, and so paved the way for the endorsement of the new role of artist/craftsman.

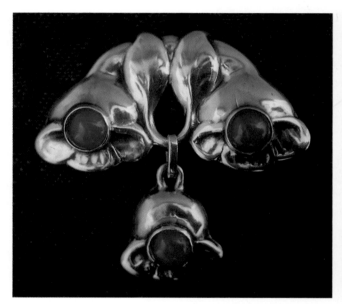

Brooch in the Skønvirke style, circa 1900. Collection of Marsha Ewing-Current.

Although Danish artists and craftsmen were aware of the stylistic directions of England, France, and Germany, there are characteristics that set their work apart. With respect to jewelry, the Danish skønvirke style was different from the others in several ways: first, the use of enamelling was extremely rare; second, a desire persisted to make their work reasonably priced, highly artistic, and technically exact; and third, many Danish jewelers were trained as sculptors and therefore possessed knowledge of the artistic possibilities of the metals with which they worked (Thage.).

Georg Jensen's career as an independent silversmith began as the skønvirke period was developing. The silver work of Mogens Ballin (1871-1914), Siegfried Wagner (1874-1952), and a few others were defining skønvirke metalwork. For Georg Jensen, all this served as a useful foundation for a career that would propel Danish silverwork to the highest ranks in international decorative arts.

The decorative art for which Denmark first achieved international acclaim was porcelain tablewares. At the 1900 World Exhibition in Paris, works by the Royal Copenhagen Manufactory and other firms earned high praise; Royal Copenhagen was awarded a grand prize.

At the turn of the century and for many years to come, Danish manufacturers of porcelain, silver, and virtually all other decorative arts benefited greatly from the economic strategy of the national government. In a report published by the Danish Ministry for Foreign Affairs and the Danish Statistical Department in 1924, Ivar Egebjerg, Secretary of the Danish Chamber of Commerce or Manufacturers described this strategy in the excerpt on page 20.

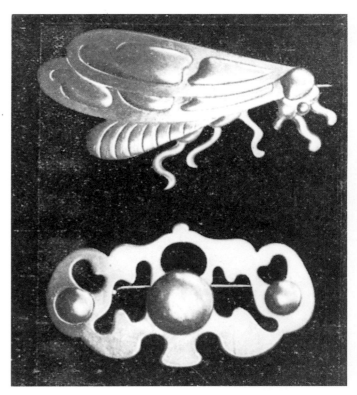

Two brooches designed by Erik Magnussen.

Brooch with green agate and three drops in the Skønvirke style.

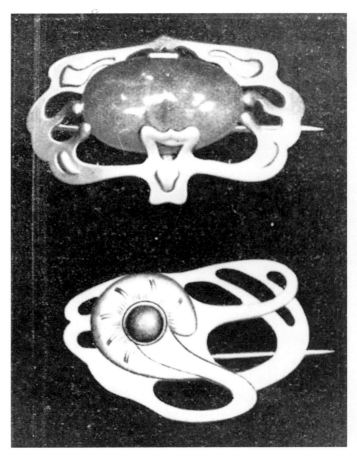

Two brooches designed by Erik Magnussen.

Bust of Georg Jensen in the Georg Jensen Museum, Copenhagen.

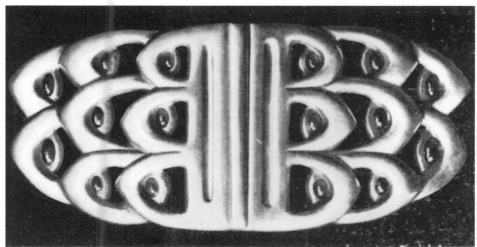

Belt buckle from the Mogens Ballin workshop.

Brooch from the Mogens Ballin workshop.

Brooch from the Mogens Ballin workshop.

Brooch by Mogens Ballin. Collection of Gail Roeshman Selig.

When the Danish community was faced by the necessity of creating an export trade in industrial goods, endeavors were concentrated principally upon applied arts and crafts. The beautiful work which is the outcome of the characteristically Danish taste, and which bears the stamp of centuries of tradition among an artisan class the work or which was marked by individual taste, offered a field in which workers could find personal satisfaction, while at the same time the article produced could be sold in the larger countries without involving the necessity of abundant capital and power of economic expansion which modern industry demands .... Danish applied art not only caters for the class which has the greatest purchasing power; it seeks its customers everywhere, and it does not regard the making of articles of luxury, but the production of useful articles of beauty, as its principal object. (Ivar Egebjerg, "The Export Industries of Denmark," 1924.)

Clearly, this was an asute strategy for a country with few raw materials or much in the way of industrial capacity, but with a significant number of skilled artisans inculcated with a traditionally Danish way of perfecting their craft or other work. In addition, this passage also echoes many of the themes--such as the satisfaction of the worker, and the creation of beauty above luxury--advanced by the arts and crafts movement.

Danish silver manufacturing gained stature at the turn of the century, but some years passed before the contributions of Georg Jensen and his contemporaries vaulted its reputation to an equal or greater level than that of the Danish porcelain industry. When artists, painters and sculptors alike were attracted to the beauty of silver, and jewelers including the firms Tostrup, David Andersen, Dragsted, Michelsen, and Georg Jensen developed, a distinct Danish style in silver emerged. The combination of the long-standing tradition of excellent craftsmanship and the cooperation of artists trained in diverse disciplines led to the development of the modern Danish silver style.

The social, cultural and economic context for Georg Jensen's career suggests sources for his philosophy of art and work, and the inspirations for the aesthetic choices he made. Jensen and other supremely talented artists and craftsmen from many countries shaped a new field of design and elevated decorative arts to a level approaching fine arts.

Mixed stone pendant designed by Kay Bojesen in the Skønvirke style, circa 1900-1910. Collection of Linda Morgan.

Brooch #223 with green agate designed by Georg Jensen.

Chapter 2
Georg Jensen: His Life up to 1900

Clippings of His Life

While aware of the international Arts & Crafts movement, Georg Jensen remained singular in his drive to create beautiful works in silver. Unlike Morris and Ruskin, Jensen had no social message and advocated no particular moral philosophy. Jensen was interested in conveying a message of beauty and skill in craftsmanship in affordable products that could be worn and used in daily life. The story of Georg Jensen-- the man, the artist, the company, and the style-- is a fascinating tale.

When Georg Jensen died on October 2, 1935, at the age of 69, the world's leading newspapers and magazines noted his death. *The New York Herald Tribune* called him "the greatest silversmith of the last 300 years." Clearly, Jensen's achievements as an artist and craftsman were recognized around the world; in fact, he was acclaimed long before his death. However, despite his notoriety, relatively little is generally known about the man Georg Jensen, and most of what has been written appears in the Danish language.

Recollections of His Youth

Little information exists about Jensen's personal life. He seems to have been reticent about his origins, as an autobiographical article appears to bear out. Published in a Danish decorative arts journal, it appeared on the occasion of Jensen's sixtieth birthday when his success and fame had long been achieved. Yet, even when the master artist would be forgiven for indulging in some measure of self-congratulation, Jensen told his life story modestly and took less than three and a half pages to do it. ("Af et Tres-Aarigt Kunstnerliv: Erindringer Fra Min Barndom og Udviking" ["Memoirs of My Childhood and Growth as an Artist"], *Samleren* [*The Collector*], 1926.) Jensen's autobiography is mainly a straight-forward description of his training and artistic milestones, but does provide a few glimpses of the gentle man who, as a child, loved to dream and took inspiration from the natural environment. He fondly and lyrically recalled Raadvad, the small town of his birth:

> Raadvad was a paradise on earth, the loveliest of woods with magnificent oaks and beech trees, with its large mill pond from which the stream that drove the water mill divided itself into two arms and flowered further through the low-lying meadows, with the mysterious alder thicket, where the crows gathered together in large flocks just after sunset and screamed out so that they could be heard from a great distance... As children we agreed it was the Parliament of the birds discussing world affairs. [translated from the Danish][1]

A path leading through Deer Park in Raadvad

[1]This autobiographical article, the only material available on Jensen's life, was not enough. In 1958, Jørgen E.R. Møller, the president of Georg Jensen & Wendel A/S from 1951-1979, commissioned Danish author Walter Schwartz to write a book about Møller's famous uncle, Georg Jensen. The Schwartz book is appropriately titled *Georg Jensen -- An Artist -- His Time and Family*. Since the Schwartz book was printed in Danish, the information was unavailable to the non-Danish speaking public. To fill this gap, Jørgen Møller retold excerpts of the Schwartz book in English in *Georg Jensen the Danish Silversmith*, which was published in 1984.

The landscape of Raadvad looking out from the entrance to Jensen's childhood home.

Bust of Georg Jensen's father, the first sculpture done by Georg Jensen.

While Jensen described an idyllic childhood, his early years were, in reality, far from worry free. He was born in 1866 into a large, working-class family that struggled to make ends meet. His father, Jørgen, worked as a laborer at one of Raadvad's cutlery factories and his mother, Marthine, worked as a housekeeper for a wealthy family. Certainly, these are not the circumstances, particularly in mid-nineteenth century rural Denmark, from which one would predict a great artist would arise.

Jensen seems to have had an exceptionally happy childhood; at least that is how he chose to recall it some 50 years later. He writes of his boyhood affinity for the local country-side; and for those of us who strive to understand his character and artistic inspirations, these passages are especially intriguing. For example, he recounts a walk through the forest when, on the way to get milk for his mother, he discovers a field mouse and proceeds to play with it. Through this vivid recollection, one can perceive his love of the quietude of the forest, the smell of leaves and grasses, and the antics of mice and other tiny creatures. And when Jensen recalls that his father was not angry at him for tarrying on his errand in order to play with the mouse, since "he too was a little boy once," one obtains the impression that his father, and his mother, too, were loving and supportive. Jensen alludes to his closeness to his father in other ways. For example, he mentions accompanying him on his morning walks to work at the cutlery factory.

Significantly, one of Jensen's earliest attempts at artistic expression was literally fashioned from the substance of Raadvad. Young Jensen made little sculptures from blue clay he found in the marshlands near his home. One of his first figures was of Gorm, the Danish king from the eighth century, posed heroically with one foot on a canon. He kept Gorm in a cigar-box museum, along with other little figures he had crafted. Among the first to be shown the collection were workers in the local brickyard. They appreciated the boy's work, and praised him by saying the figures were as good as those that adorned the facades of some of the finest houses in Copenhagen. (Jørgen E.R. Møller, *Georg Jensen the Danish Silversmith*, p. 5.)

Like many other boys of his era, Jensen went to work at an early age. By thirteen, he was working at the same factory where his father worked, beginning as an apprentice golder, a maker of wooden forms used for metal casting. It is highly likely that his experience in the factory shaped his perspectives on such things as craftsmanship, machines, metal-working processes, and treatment of workers.

A YOUNG MAN'S ASPIRATIONS

Jensen's parents recognized his creativity and the artistic ability he demonstrated through his clay figures and, later, in the factory. They believed he had talent that should be nurtured. In 1880, shortly after the family moved to Copenhagen, he was apprenticed to a goldsmith, A. Andersen, who had a workshop at number 5 St. Pederstræde. He also attended a technical school called De Massmanske Søndagsskoler where he studied drawing and perspective under an architect named Schmidt. This arrangement -- a common one under the Danish education system at the time -- permitted apprentices such as Jensen to broaden their training as artisans. At about the same time, Jensen made his first serious sculpture -- a bust of his father.

While attending the technical school, Jensen became acquainted with another student, Christian Joachim Petersen, and they soon became close friends. They often walked to the technical school together, joking and talking about their artistic aspirations. Their daily walks took them through a park that was a venue for important Danish sculpture, and this prompted them to discuss the work of established sculptors as well as their own artistic attempts. When Jensen finished the bust of his father, seeking further encouragement, he told Joachim about it. Jensen also told his friend that he wanted to show the bust to Professor Stein of the Royal Academy of Art. Although Joachim teased him for the audacity of his plan, Jensen was undeterred, and, summoning courage, he found a way to show his work to the professor. Professor Stein was aware Jensen was a goldsmith's apprentice, not an art student, he kindly agreed to examine his sculpture. Stein was impressed by Jensen's talent, and encouraged him to continue sculpting and provided a further boost to Jensen by permitting Jensen to prepare for the entrance exam to the Royal Academy of Fine Art by sculpting in his atelier. Thus, Jensen's dream of becoming a sculptor began to seem like a real possibility.

While he worked at becoming a sculptor, Jensen continued his training as a silversmith. In 1884, when he was 18 years old, Jensen completed his four-year apprenticeship, and thereupon received his journeyman certificate as a goldsmith. At this stage in his career, Jensen was able to support himself through his silversmithing.

Jensen did what he could to develop his skill as a sculptor in his spare time. The hours he spent in the atelier of Professor Stein modeling his work were finally rewarded when, in 1887, he was accepted as a student of sculpture in the Royal Academy of Art. During the time he was at the Royal Academy, Jensen completed his second sculpture, "En Høstkarl" (The Harvester), a realistic depiction of a farmer at work in the fields. In 1891, the year before he completed his training as a sculptor, this sculpture was exhibited in the Charlottenborg Spring Exhibit, and, later, in Munich. It now stands in the courtyard of the Georg Jensen Silversmithy in Copenhagen. With the exposure he received through the exhibit, the door to the art world seemed to open for Jensen, and it appeared that his career as a sculptor was launched. In 1892, he graduated from the Royal Academy of Art as a sculptor and did not see himself as an artist craftsman at all, in spite of his acknowledged skill as a silversmith. His graduation from the Academy and his success with "The Harvester" persuaded Jensen to concentrate on his sculpture rather than goldsmithing. Jensen's continued interest to pursue his career as a sculptor led him away from his craft of a silversmith and to the ceramics venture with his friend Joachim.

Høstkarl (The Harvester) sculpture by Georg Jensen, 1891.

Georg Jensen at a Royal Academy sculpture class (1887-1892).

Georg Jensen at 25 years of age. Courtesy of
Georg Jensen/Royal Copenhagen.

Adult Years

In 1891, while still a student at the Royal Academy, Jensen married Marie Christiane Antonette Wulff. Later that year, their son Vidar was born. Four years later, another son, Jørgen, arrived. Still endeavoring to become a sculptor, Jensen was finding it difficult to support his growing family. Though he received acclaim for "The Harvester", it did not sell, and his next sculpture, "Foraaret" (Spring), the depiction of a young girl, was rejected for the Royal Academy's annual exhibition for 1897.

The rejection of "Foraaret" proved to be a cloud with a silver lining for Jensen was invited to participate in an exhibition called "den Frie Udstilling" (The Free Exhibition), an exhibition in Copenhagen that featured the work of non-mainstream painters and sculptors whose works had been rejected by the Academy. Not only did Jensen's involvement with this alternative exhibition provide the encouragement Jensen needed to continue with his sculpture, it also enabled him to meet the celebrated painter/designer Johan Rohde who organized the exhibition with the painter Joakim Skovgaard. Johan Rohde would become Jensen's close friend, and one of the most influential artist/designers to collaborate with Georg Jensen.

1897 also brought great sorrow to Jensen when Antonette, his wife of only six years, died. Unable to earn a living from sculpting, he was now a widower with two small sons to care for. At 31 years of age, he took a short trip to France and Italy for the first time, and there met many contemporary artists. The trip gave Jensen new impressions about art and craftsmanship. Of course, he still dreamed of success as a sculptor, but he returned home with the impetus to seek another way to earn a living. He earlier had collaborated with Joachim in a ceramics business, and it seemed natural to return to it now.

In order to earn a living to support his family, Jensen worked at various jobs. One job was at the Aluminia Faience Works doing ordinary work like making jugs and basins. He also worked at the Terra Cotta Factory where he modeled figures. For a short time he was a modeler at the Bing & Grøndahl porcelain factory in Copenhagen. This experience, Jensen later wrote, "opened his eyes" to the variety of forms that could be used in ceramics and other decorative arts. After his long day, he and Joachim would work together, searching for the creation in ceramics that would be the artistic expression that they both sought.

In 1898, the two men soon hatched a plan to sell their ceramic work in order to support their families and hopefully receive recognition for their artistry. Unfortunately, it became clear that their financial profits were much less than they had anticipated. While the ceramics venture was not a financial success, it did yield some recognition for Jensen and Joachim through their joint work "Pigen på Krukken" (The Maid on the Jar), an earthenware jug with a small female figure perched on the rim. The jug was coarse in appearance and the use of the female figure was one of the few times to appear in Jensen's work.

Recognition As A Ceramist

The ceramic jug "Pigen på Krukken" was chosen for the arts and crafts exhibit in the Danish pavilion in the 1900 World Exhibition in Paris. It was a great honor to have gained the attention of the Director of the Danish Museum of Decorative Art, Pietro Krohn, who chose to include the ceramic jug. Prior to their exhibition in Paris, the selections were shown to the Danish public and given favorable reviews in the press. Other pieces by Jensen and Joachim were shown independently and their sales were very good. They received an honorable mention for their combined work in ceramics. Jensen was awarded a travel grant of 2,500-kroner. Jensen's career seemed to be on an upswing.

Jensen's travel grant provided him with a golden opportunity to tour the continent and visit the leading art centers of Europe during a time of incredible artistic ferment. He embarked on a two-year tour in 1899. In Paris, he witnessed Art Nouveau in full flower. In France and Italy, he met artists who were making great strides in the field of applied arts and were being recognized for their accomplishments, earning a living from their work, and creating objects that were not only useful, but beautiful.

In Paris, he met many artists and shared time and conversations about their work. Danish painter Ejnar Nielsen traveled with Jensen and painted a portrait of him in a somber, almost surrealistic style. Jensen's face and hands reflect the only lightness in the painting as Nielsen captured Jensen's serious and pensive nature. The portrait now hangs in the Museum of Decorative Art in Copenhagen. It was used by the Danish postal authority in 1966 to commemorate the centennary of Jensen's birth.

Perhaps the experiences gained in this travel led Jensen to believe that he, too, could channel his artistic skills into applied art and bridge the gulf that existed between fine art and decorative art. Objects of usefulness in everyday life took on new meaning. Utilitarian objects could be designed and valued for their artistic quality.

Foraaret (Spring) by Georg Jensen, 1897.

Pigen på Krukken (The Maid on the Jar) ceramic work by Georg Jensen and Joachim Petersen, 1899.

Jensen's trip to Paris and Italy ultimately changed his direction as an artist. In addition, the periodicals *Jugend* and *Pan* carried the message of the arts and crafts revival philosophy. Imbued with ideals of functionalism and beauty, he was enthused about returning home and renewing his work in ceramics with Joachim.

Georg Jensen in his workshop.

FIRST
DAY
COVER

1866—1966

GEORG JENSEN

KØBENHAVN V
31. AUG. 1966
POSTENS FILATELI
FRIMÆRKETS UDGIVELSESDAG

KØBENH
31. AUG. 1966
POSTENS FILATELI
FRIMÆRKETS UDGIVELSESDAG

Georg Jensen
Sølvsmedie A/S
Ragnagade 7
København Ø.

Official Danish postage stamp issued on the 31st of August, 1966, commemorating the centenary of the birth of Georg Jensen. The design of the stamp is based on a portrait of Georg Jensen painted by Ejnar Nielsen in 1900 in Paris.

An example of a Bronze Age necklet, part of the exhibition The Arts of Denmark, 1960-61.

Chapter 3
Georg Jensen: His Life from 1900 to 1935, and the Growth of the Company

Inspiration From His Travels

In 1901, when Jensen returned to Denmark from his foreign travels, he brought with him a renewed zeal for making beautiful things that would enrich people's daily lives. Jensen settled in Birkerød, 15 miles north of Copenhagen, where Joachim Petersen also lived, to resume the ceramic work they had begun earlier. It was necessary for Jensen to continue with silversmithing because the ceramics business did not provide enough money to support his family. And so he worked as a silversmith in Copenhagen during the day, and returned to Birkerød to work with Joachim in the evening in their ceramics business. He made jewelry for himself and often for friends who admired his work and offered him encouragement to continue his silversmithing.

Silver brooch from the Mogens Ballin workshop.

The continued efforts to build a ceramics business for the two aspiring artists were economically futile. Predictably, because of the great amount of time Jensen spent traveling back and forth between Birkerød and Copenhagen, he was unable to keep up with the demands of the new venture, and was forced to give up the ceramics business. This turn of events offered an opportunity to Jensen that no one could have forseen. The success of Jensen's silver work during this time was an affirmation of his skill, and offered him an outlet for his creative talent and the possibility of financial reward. In addition, the encouragement Jensen had recieved when Pietro Krohn of the Museum of Applied Art acquired pieces of his silver jewelry alluded to his future success. Although he left his ceramic collaboration with Joachim, who went on to become head of the Aluminia Faience Works (later a subsidiary of Royal Copenhagen Porcelain), the two fellow art students in boyhood, remained good friends.

Jensen Returns to Silver in the Mogens Ballin Workshop

Having decided to continue with silversmithing, Jensen found employment with a number of Copenhagen silversmiths. One of them, Mogens Ballin (1871-1914), exerted an especially strong influence on Jensen, even though Ballin was five years his junior. Ballin, born into a prosperous Copenhagen family, began his artistic training in painting at the age of 17. He later went to Paris where, among other things, he became familiar with Gauguin and other contemporary artists. Following a religious conversion and a brief stay in a monastery, Ballin returned to Copenhagen and resumed his artistic career.

Espousing principles that were in accord with the philosophy of the Arts and Crafts movement, Ballin aspired to found a studio that would foster the revival of artisan skills. In addition, he wanted to enrich the lives of common men and women by providing them with artful, yet affordable, objects of various kinds. Ballin wrote:

"I want to make everyday objects with a lovely form, of bronze, pewter, polished copper, and other cheap metals. It is my intention to make things which even the smallest purse can afford. Art for the people and not refined art for rich parvenus. As you see, I am building on some of the ideas of the English: William Morris, John Ruskin, and their fellows have shown me the way..." (Thage)

Ballin put this philosophy into action. Though trained as a painter and not as a metal artisan, he established a workshop where silver and other inexpensive metals, as well as affordable colored stones, were used as the raw materials for jewelry. In addition, tin was used to make vases, bowls, lamps, jugs, and other utilitarian objects. Like his idol, William Morris, Ballin learned how to do the work himself, and labored alongside the silversmiths he employed. Much of his workshop's jewelry exhibited naturalistic forms, including the shapes of flowers, fruit and insects.

Belt buckle from the Mogens Ballin workshop.

One of the principal designers at the Ballin workshop was Sigfried Wagner (1874-1952). Like Georg Jensen, he trained as a sculptor at the Royal Academy of Fine Art and had also worked at the Bing & Grøndahl Porcelain factory. Wagner's sculptural sense and skill as a designer were major assets for the workshop, a fact acknowledged by art journals of the period. It is highly likely that Wagner, who, along with Ballin, had already achieved international recognition for his work, also significantly influenced Jensen's approach to decorative arts.

Belt buckle from the Mogens Ballin workshop.

In 1901, Georg Jensen began working at Ballin's workshop as a journeyman. Within a short period of time, he was named foreman of the shop. During his employment here, he was encouraged to develop his own designs. Ballin went one large step further by permitting Jensen to exhibit his jewelry designs under his own name. This is especially remarkable, since, at the time, works displayed in exhibitions were invariably sold under the name of the workshop where they were produced and the individual designers were not generally acknowledged. In 1901, while working at the Ballin workshop, Jensen created a silver belt buckle depicting Adam and Eve in the garden of Eden; it is thought to be one of his earliest pieces of jewelry. Jensen received acclaim and recognition for the buckle and the director of the Museum of Decorative Art in Copenhagen, Emil Hannover, became an ardent admirer of Jensen's work. The buckle is in the musem's collection.

Tortoise comb decorated with silver and green agate designed by Georg Jensen. Collection of Anne Shannon.

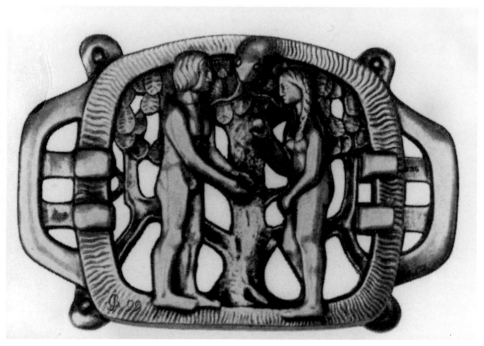

Adam and Eve buckle designed by Georg Jensen.

THE JENSEN WORKSHOP BEGINS, 1904

Heartened considerably by the positive reactions to his work, Jensen decided to leave the Ballin workshop and establish a workshop of his own. No small emphasis should be placed on the very "normal" need for Jensen to support himself and his family. Jensen wrote in his memoir, "Pressures of circumstance force me to take up my old craft." With financial assistance from a private businessman, Jensen opened a small workshop at 36 Bredgade in Copenhagen, on April 19, 1904, where he produced jewelry, and subsequently hollowware and flatware. The workshop was a retail shop as well where Jensen displayed his work in a portable case that was mounted on the wall outside the front of the shop during the day, and taken in at the close of business. When objects from the case were sold, they were replaced with others. Lettering painted on the shop's front door stated simply "Georg Jensen Sculptor, Silversmith." This self description clearly reveals that Jensen had not abandoned his identity as a sculptor; indeed, it took precedence over that of silversmith. Finally, he had established a vehicle for his creative energy.

Although opening the workshop marked the beginning of a new venture for Jensen, he was by no means a neophyte in the world of fine and applied art. Jensen had spent years developing his skill as a sculptor and a ceramist, and almost twenty years as a silversmith, when he began the Bredgade workshop, he was 38 years of age.

The staff at the workshop included an apprentice and a helper, in addition to Jensen. The apprentice was Henry Pilstrup (1890-1967) who was fourteen years of age when he started with Jensen and Pilstrup remained with the Georg Jensen firm until his retirement in 1957, long after Jensen had died. Not only did Jensen allow his workers artistic freedom, but he also encouraged their independent work. Jensen, an ardent advocate of Pilstrup, took great care to attribute and credit him with the work he accomplished. Pilstrup, years later, related the following description of Jensen at his workshop: "When he arrived in the morning he pulled a pile of designs out of his pocket, they had been drawn on whatever piece of paper he could lay his hands on, sometimes he had drawn on torn off wrapping paper. He worked quickly, in an afternoon he could fill up a sheet of sketches, all the while he sat singing his own songs to his own melodies." (Erik Lasson.) Jensen affected the look of an artist, as early photos of the workshop attest. He habitually wore a long white smock and a flowing cravat.

Evening bag with embroidery by Marie Møller, sister-in-law of Georg Jensen, brooch and earrings no. 14. Courtesy of Georg Jensen Museum Copenhagen.

Georg Jensen's first workshop at 36 Bredgade in Copenhagen, circa 1909. From left, an unknown worker, Inger Møller, Kay Bojesen, Georg Jensen, and Alba Mathilde Lykke. Courtesy of Georg Jensen Royal Copenhagen.

At the turn of the century, emerging art styles had already impacted the well-to-do citizens of Copenhagen and many were familiar with the new Art Nouveau movement, as well as the Arts and Crafts Movement. Women were interested in learning handicrafts as a pastime, since it was looked upon as a worthwhile endeavor for young ladies. Chasing, a part of the silversmith's craft, was less strenuous than hammering silver, and several prominent families with young ladies sought-out Jensen's workshop as a learning place for their daughters. Jensen gave instruction in the art of chasing for a fee of 25 kroner per month. This additional income on a regular basis was welcome in these early years of business. For most of the students, this activity was only a hollow experience, but there were a few who showed true talent. Inger Møller, (1886-1979) one of these students, showed sufficient talent that Jensen took her on as an apprentice, and she went on to become an important Danish silversmith who operated her own workshop, from 1922 to 1966 in Copenhagen.

THE FIRST EXHIBITS

In 1904, Jensen again showed his work at an exhibition at the Danish Museum of Decorative Art. The items displayed, including his jewelry, were praised and enhanced the reputation of his workshop. The year 1904 was momentous for another reason as well; Jensen married Maren Pedersen, called "Magne," the housekeeper who had looked after him and his children since the death of his first wife. In 1905, Jensen held his first exhibition outside Denmark at the Folkwang Museum in Hagen, Germany. His success at this exhibition was amplified when the museum purchased a number of his pieces.

During the first few years in his workshop, Jensen's jewelry represented a majority of the production, since the financial investment in silver was less for jewelry than for hollowware or flatware. Also, jewelry sold more quickly than other items and could be stored in the cabinet drawers of the small workshop. Jensen expressed his plentiful ideas well in jewelry and received instant acclaim for it, which encouraged him. Each exquisite piece he made resulted in requests for more. Hatpins, buckles, brooches, rings, necklaces, and bracelets were made in many different designs and their rapid sale confirmed their appeal to the Danish women. Art critics, too, were quick to recognize the quality and beauty of Jensen's work.

Tortoise hair comb. Courtesy of Georg Jensen Museum Copenhagen.

As Henry Pilstrup had observed, Jensen was indeed an indefatigable and prolific designer. Ideas seemed to flow from him effortlessly, and before long his shop's production had expanded to include not only many new jewelry designs, but also flatware and hollowware, the latter including many spectacular bowls, candelabras and other pieces that world-famous museums purchased for their collections.

Though highly personal and individualistic, Jensen's designs were nurtured by his association with a coterie of artist friends with whom he often spent his evenings. Friends would bring sketches to Jensen and he would turn them into pieces of jewelry. In the earliest days of his workshop, Jensen purchased the "dove" design from Christian Møhl-Hansen, the Danish painter. This well known image was integrated into various pieces of jewelry including brooches, belt buckles, earrings, and bracelets. Ninety years later, this design, in one form or another, is in production and cherished by collectors.

Through collaboration with other artists, Jensen received stimulation for his own designs. Jensen's love for his work, his personal inspiration and his standards for artistic and skillful craftsmanship permeated his workshop. His open-minded collaboration established a model for design excellence that the Jensen firm has employed to the present.

One of the first artists to collaborate with Georg Jensen was Johan Rohde (1856-1935) who had invited Jensen to participate in the Free Exhibition in 1898. Though known primarily as a painter, Rohde also designed objects for his own use because he was not satisfied with the quality of commercially available home furnishings and silverware. His search for someone to execute his designs in silver led him to Jensen, and by 1906 the two worked together to produce Rohde's designs. Since Rohde was not trained as a silversmith, Jensen interpreted Rohde's drawings into the finished product.

Brooch designed by Christian Mohl-Hansen, circa 1907-1909. Georg Jensen Sølvsmedie, Gennem Fyrretyve Arr, 1904-1944.

Georg Jensen's Respect for Individual Craftsmen

Jensen's dedication to preserve craftsmanship, a Danish standard with a long history, was the basis for the quality and perfection in his jewelry and objects. In Jensen's modest workshop his ideas drawn on bits of paper were then brought to life. Most drawings for jewelry designs were made by Georg Jensen himself up to 1915. Johan Rohde, who sought out Jensen to fabricate his own designs, understood the creative process of Georg Jensen. The bond they formed was one of artistic understanding. Although their styles were quite different, Rohde's more simple, Jensen's more intricate, they shared an understanding of each other's vision. Johan Rohde's taste for simple unadorned forms of perfect proportion fit no particular time frame--they are for all times. Jensen's acknowledgement of Rohde's talent was a testament to his artistic vision. Rohde worked with Jensen from 1906 until his death in February, 1935, eight months before Jensen's own death.

The contrast between the two men was striking; Jensen came from a poor working class family, while Rohde came from an upper class family. Jensen, formally trained as a sculptor, was working as a silver craftsman, while Rohde was trained as a painter and was an established "fine" artist. Jensen was outgoing, passionate and rather impulsive; Rohde was reserved and methodical. Despite these differences, they worked together with virtually no conflict. It is likely that their easy working relationship was due, in large part, to a mutual respect for and understanding of each other's skills and sharing of artistic ideas. From the start of their collaboration, the two artists worked together in establishing the distinctive style and quality we recognize as "Jensen."

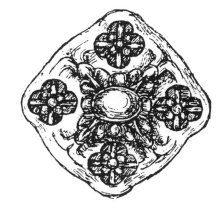

Brooch designed by Christian Mohl-Hansen, circa 1904-1907. Georg Jensen Sølvsmedie, Gennem Fyrretyve Arr, 1904-1944.

It was not until 1913 that Johan Rohde signed a contract to work solely as a designer for Jensen. Rohde was prolific in his drawings, and his work yielded a large quantity of exceptional pieces of jewelry, hollowware and flatware. Rohde's work reflected a style that was quite distinct from Jensen's; indeed, many of his pieces, especially an unornamented pitcher executed in 1920, was quintessential modern and well ahead of the time. Jensen believed the design was so advanced that the pitcher was not made until five years later. This Rohde pitcher, no. 432, produced for 70 years, remains in demand.

Although many other designers worked for the Jensen firm in later years, Rohde was the first designer of major significance and, certainly during Jensen's lifetime, the one whose contributions had the greatest artistic impact. Jensen was scrupulous about publicly crediting Rohde for the designs he produced and similarly crediting other designers who worked for the firm in later years, a laudable tradition of artistic recognition the Georg Jensen firm faithfully maintains.

From the onset of Georg Jensen's workshop, his skill and artistry attracted the best artists, painters, sculptors, and architects to his standards of quality workmanship and excellence in design. Jensen's understanding of silver and its possibilities for the silversmith allowed him great flexibility in the execution of the designs. The artistry of the smithy, staffed with silversmiths who Jensen trained to his own standards, produced work that immediately gained world recognition.

Johan Rohde.

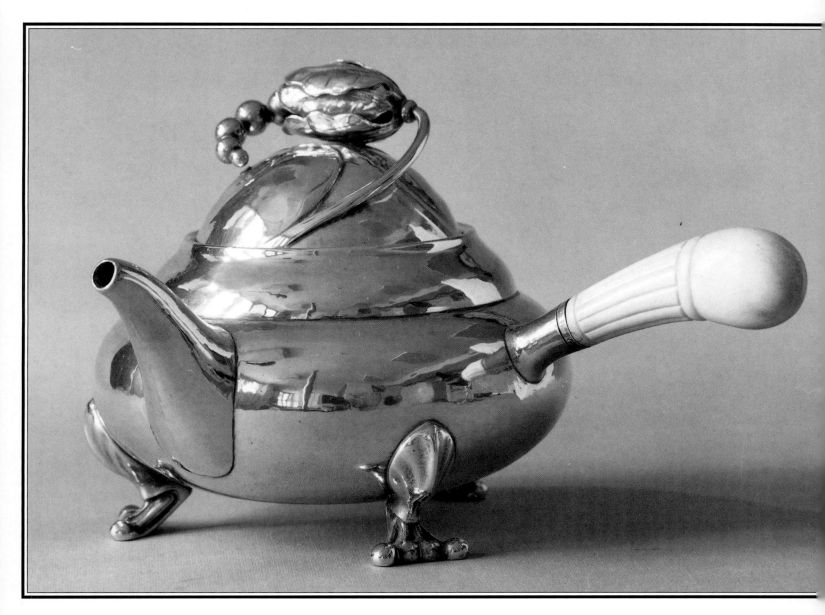

Teapot no. 2A, sterling silver, designed by Georg Jensen, 1905. Courtesy Statens Kunstmuseer, The National Swedish Art Museums, Stockhom.

Jensen's successes continued through 1905 and 1906. In 1905, one of his first piece of hollowware, a teapot in the Blossom/Magnolia pattern, was praised in the Danish press and later purchased by the Danish Museum of Decorative Art. In 1906, he brought out his first flatware pattern, known as the Continental/Antik pattern. With these and other successes, the world was looking bright for Georg Jensen.

This optimistic mood was tragically shattered in January, 1907, when his second wife, Magne, died of tuberculosis. Now widowed a second time and left with three children, including a young daughter, Jensen moved his family to Charlottlund, in the country, since his house in Copenhagen held too many sad memories.

Marriage to Johanne Nielsen

Later in the year, Jensen met Laura Julie Johanne Nielsen, known as "Johanne," and they were married on November 12, 1907. Jensen's marriage to Johanne proved to be important not only on a personal level, but on a business level as well. Johanne's large family was soon to be integral to the growth of Georg Jensen's company. Johanne's brother, Harald Nielsen, joined the Jensen workshop as an apprentice and it was not long before Jensen recognized his talent.

By 1908, the firm's staff had grown to eleven. Among them was a feeling of teamwork and a shared sense of pride in their work. This atmosphere, the epitome of the Arts and Crafts ambiance, was fostered by Jensen, who extended respect to all his workers. Many of his co-workers remained loyal to Georg Jensen and stayed with the firm throughout their career.

Although Jensen was sometimes referred to as the "lone survivor" of the Arts and Crafts movement, he did not adhere to the belief that use of machinery was a betrayal of Arts and Crafts ideals; on the contrary, later he provided his workers with machines they could use more efficiently to accomplish aspects of their work. The hammered surface, lovingly executed by the silversmith, removed every trace of machine involvement.

Georg Jensen and his wife Johanne.

Harald Nielsen was 17 when he apprenticed with Georg Jensen in 1909 at the height of Jensen's recognition. Nielsen, like Jensen, wanted to be an artist--a painter. His great ability was recognized by Jensen, and Nielsen, Rohde and Jensen were an asounding combination of talent and skill. Nielsen became close to the master Jensen and was able to visualize a drawing or the beginning of an object drawn by Jensen. As an apprentice, Nielsen exhibited great ability in drawing and shared Jensen's aesthetic sense and regard for exceptional quality. Nielsen later became an influential designer and, together with Johan Rohde and Georg Jensen, left an indelible mark on the Georg Jensen company. Nielson was named artistic director of the company after Jensen's death and continued the traditions that were established during their early years together.

One of Johanne's sisters married the sculptor Gundolph Albertus (1887-1970), and in 1911, Albertus also joined the firm. Albertus later became a designer and produced the well-known flatware pattern Cactus. In 1918, Albertus was named director of the newly established silversmithy, Georg Jensen Sølvsmedie A/S, and in 1926 became the assistant director of the company, a position which he held until 1954. Gundorph Albertus, who was trained as a sculptor and educated at the Royal Academy of Art, worked for some years as a silversmith in Munich and Paris. His forte was a great understanding of the artistic possibilities for silver and he maintained the high quality of workmanship. In the pamphlet *The Artists of Georg Jensen Silver*, Christian Ditlev Reventlow quotes Albertus, "The artistic design is not all important, the handiwork must be perfect, it must bring out all the artist's intentions, the whole spirit behind the drawing, and it can sometimes even improve on them."

Buckle with Pegasus on left and bird on right.

Melon set in Cactus pattern which was designed by Gundorph Albertus.

Another of Johanne's sisters became a bookkeeper with the firm, and in 1917 she married businessman Thorolf Møller. Møller would provide financing for the firm in 1919 when financial problems arose for Jensen. In 1924, Møller became the owner and president of the retail operation and P. A. Pedersen assumed control of the silversmithy.

Jensen's marriage to Johanne marked the beginning of a particularly creative and productive time. He was surrounded by family members who shared his love for his work, as well as pride in his accomplishments. During this period, the Georg Jensen firm was rightly referred to as a family business. National and international recognition for his work was growing. At the same time, he was enjoying a stable and fulfilling family life. He even took time to take trips with Johanne, visiting museums in France and Italy. During a visit to a museum at St. Germain, Jensen admired some "Roman bronze knives and the molds in which they were cast, all found together, and that early symbol of factory work strengthened his belief in machinery and its potentialities." (Ivan Munk Olsen, *Danish Art IV*.)

THE FIRST FOREIGN SHOP: BUSINESS EXPANDS

While Jensen's work was well received at home, the lion's share of his fame resulted from the recognition he received at major exhibitions held outside of Denmark. In 1909, Jensen exhibited his work at the Parisian galleries "Salon d'Automne" and "Art Décoratif," which later became famous when its name was used to describe the new arts of the 1920s, Art Deco. In 1910, Jensen's work won a gold medal at the World Exposition in Brussels.

Throughout Jensen's career, there were various self-appointed "emissaries" who carried Georg Jensen silver out into the world; one of them was the Danish art dealer Carl Dyhr. Folkwang Museum Director K.E. Osthaus was the first to exhibit Jensen's work in a museum abroad. After a successful exhibit at the Folkwang Museum in 1905, and subsequent traveling shows that introduced Jensen's work throughout Germany, Dyhr realized the potential market for Jensen

The Jensen store at Budapesterstrasse 43, Berlin. Destroyed in 1943. Georg Jensen Sølvsmedie, Gennem Fyrretyve Arr, 1904-1944.

silver there. Accordingly, Dyhr offered to move to Germany and open a store where Georg Jensen silver and Royal Copenhagen porcelain would be sold. The first Georg Jensen shop outside of Copenhagen, Der Dänische Silberschmeid (The Danish Silversmith), was opened in Berlin in 1909. This shop proved to be very successful and led to Germany becoming the firm's largest market. In fact, during the period from 1909 to 1915 (until the outbreak of World War I), the German market accounted for up to ninety percent of the firm's total sales. Orders were so plentiful that the workshop could not keep up with them. In 1912, the workshop moved to larger premises at Knippelsbrogade, Copenhagen. At the same time, a separate retail shop at 21 Bredgade was opened. Thus, in only eight years, Jensen's company had grown considerably and there was talk of further expansion to London, Paris and New York. The one constant during this period was Georg Jensen himself, who continued to assume full responsibility for every facet of the business, both artistic and financial. Unfortunately, his exceptional skill as an artist was not matched in his business acumen; in truth, he was not a very good businessman.

All signs seemed to indicate that expanding the business made sense. One of the few people who disagreed with Jensen's idea to enlarge the business was Johan Rohde. He thought the quality of the firm's work would suffer, and that the special spirit that had developed among its silversmiths would be lost. Rohde discouraged Jensen from expanding. Nevertheless, the firm seemed poised for growth. Jensen received worlwide attention in 1913 when he received the "Diplôme d'Honneur" award at the international exhibition in Gent.

In 1915, the firm made its first foray to North America when jewelry, flatware and hollowware were sent to the Panama Pacific International Exposition in San Francisco, California. There, the Jensen company garnered more gold medals, and almost all displayed work was purchased by the newspaper magnate and inveterate collector William Randolph Hearst. Additional details about this exposition are found in the section about the Panama Pacific Exposition in chapter four.

The interior of the Knippelsbro silversmithy, circa 1917. Georg Jensen Sølvsmedie, Gennem Fyrretyve Arr, 1904-1944.

Until 1915, it is safe to say that Jensen conceived and developed each drawing, except the ones he bought in. He directed the work and supervised the making of each piece of silver. His process of starting with a drawing and then crafting the piece was a shared experience. When Jensen gave the drawing to the silversmith it might have only been the beginning of an idea but once the silversmith completed the piece, the drawing was then finished. Another silversmith then took the drawing and was able to make a duplicate piece. The creative process itself finished the jewelry. The spirit of the craftsperson expressed itself in the process.

A story is told of how Jensen would give a drawing not fully detailed to a silversmith in his workshop. When the silversmith questioned Jensen for further instructions, Jensen responded by saying, "you know what I want just go ahead." Of course, when the piece was completed and shown to Jensen for his approval, his response was, "see, you knew just how I wanted it to look." Of course, Jensen knew each silversmith so well that he knew the capability of the craftsman to bring the idea to fruition. This confidence in his colleague's ability was evident because Jensen trained each apprentice from the beginning and showed them exactly what he expected. Every apprentice was able to start a piece and see it to completion. The same method of training for apprenticeship is continued in the smithy.

FINANCIAL DISTRESS

World War I dealt a serious blow to the Jensen company. The store in Berlin was forced to close, causing the firm's income to plunge sharply. The situation became so serious that, for a time, the staff was not paid regularly. Correspondence between Johan Rohde and Jensen regarding wages that Jensen owed to Rohde reveals that Jensen thought Rohde had agreed to wait until after the war to get paid, although he acknowledges how impossible this idea is. Jensen's sense of humor is revealed even in such troubled times. Further correspondence reveals that Jensen enclosed a check as payment to Rohde. Financial difficulties plagued the firm during the remainder of Jensen's life.

It was obvious that if the firm were to survive, new markets would have to be found to replace the revenues lost when the German market closed. It was fortunate that Jensen had shown his work at the Baltic Exhibition in Mälmo, Sweden, in 1914. At that exhibition, Stockholm art dealer Nils Wendel, who later became Jensen's partner, was so captivated by Jensen's work that he bought everything on display. Like Carl Dyhr, Wendel became another Jensen "emissary." He purchased more Jensen silver and promoted the pieces as works of art for sale in his gallery.

The Jensen store at Hamngatan 14, Stockholm. Georg Jensen Sølvsmedie, Gennem Fyrretyve Arr, 1904-1944.

Wendel was so successful that Swedish sales were able to fill the void created by the loss of the German market. Indeed, the firm's sales to Wendel's store in Stockholm eventually exceeded prior sales records in Berlin. Although the opening of the Swedish market was extremely positive at the time, it was not enough to solve the company's financial problems. Jensen still needed an infusion of capital to keep the expanded company afloat. He wouldn't consider the alternative of releasing loyal employees whom he considered members of his family. As he makes clear in the 1926 article in *Samleren*, he believed he had only two choices; to take on investors by selling stock, or to close the company. He ultimately chose the former and in 1916, Georg Jensen became a joint stock company known as Georg Jensen Sølvsmedie A/S with Jensen as president and artistic director and Nils Wendel as a major stockholder. For the moment, it seemed as though the financial problems for the company were resolved.

The following years were busy, and although successful, problems of production and finances would need to be dealt with again. In 1918, a larger workshop facility was found in Ragnagade, and there the smithy remained until 1988. An elegant, renovated retail store reopened at 21 Bredgade, also in 1918, created at great expense and appointed with furniture designed by Johan Rohde. Concurrent to the move to a larger factory in 1918, another Jensen retail store opened in Paris at a posh location on Rue St. Honoré, opposite the Place Vendôme. The cost of these expansions exerted severe financial pressure on the firm, and more capital was needed to keep the company solvent.

A corner of the Ragnagade smithy, circa 1924. Georg Jensen Sølvsmedie, Gennem Fyrretyve Arr, 1904-1944.

The interior of the smithy at Ragnagade, circa 1924. Georg Jensen Sølvsmedie, Gennem Fyrretyve Arr, 1904-1944.

A celebration at the Ragnagade silversmithy, 1924. Seated from left, bookkeeper Svend Nielsen, Georg Jensen, Miss A. Kjergaard, and Berlin dealer Carl Dyhr. Standing from left, Carl Jacobsen, foreman Henry Pilstrup, underdirector Gundorph Albertus, foreman Gustav Pedersen, and foreman Marius Thomassen. Georg Jensen Sølvsmedie, Gennem Fyrretyve Arr, 1904-1944.

The Jensen store at 239 Rue St. Honoré, Paris, circa 1930. Courtesy of Georg Jensen, New York.

Unique bracelet with rectangular carnelian made for Georg Jensen's fourth wife, Agnes. Collection of Ea Jensen, granddaughter of Georg Jensen.

In addition to this financial shortfall, personal tragedy struck Jensen again. Not long after the birth of his son Søren, his wife Johanne succumbed to the epidemic of Spanish influenza that swept Denmark in 1918. One can only imagine what a terrible blow this was for Jensen to have suffered the death of another wife. Financial problems were very pressing and Jensen's personal tragedy was a heavy burden for him.

Jensen married again in 1920 to Agnes Christiansen; they had a daughter, Mette, in 1921 and a son, Ib, in 1927.

Members of Johanne's family, the Nielsens, her brother-in-law Thorolf Møller, and good friend and admirer of Georg Jensen, P. A. Pedersen, again invested capital in the firm to carry it through its latest financial crisis. It seems abundantly clear that the development of new markets was the real, and perhaps only, key to the firm's financial stability. Consequently, a Georg Jensen store was opened in London in 1921; it was relocated in 1935 to the present Bond Street address.

The Jensen store at 15 New Bond Street, London. Georg Jensen Sølvsmedie, Gennem Fyrretyve Arr, 1904-1944.

The Jensen store at Ostergade 40,
Copenhagen. Georg Jensen Sølvsmedie,
Gennem Fyrretyve Arr, 1904-1944.

In 1922, Thorolf Møller, president of the retail division, and P.A. Pedersen, president of the smithy, approved Frederik Lunning's proposal to explore the potential for sales in the United States. Similar to Carl Dyhr in Germany and Nils Wendel in Sweden, Frederik Lunning was the third major emissary of Georg Jensen's work. The full details of Lunning's trip to the United States and subsequent activities there are discussed in more detail in chapter four.

Expansion resulted in changes in the company. Inevitably, its operations became more complex and administrative responsibilities were assigned to a number of managers; thus, Jensen's role was diminished. It was difficult for him to accept the changes that had occurred, and he was especially troubled by the firm's weighty financial problems. During the 1920s, Bredgade, which had been the major shopping street in Copenhagen, lost its status as Østergade, or Stroget, as it is called now, became the center of retail activity. In 1924, a new Georg Jensen retail store was opened at 29 Østergade, and the following year Georg Jensen & Wendel A/S was designated as silversmith to both the Danish and Swedish courts.

Awards

The work of the firm continued to be honored far beyond the Danish borders. In 1923, a small booklet advertising Royal Copenhagen porcelain and Georg Jensen silver printed an impressive list of awards Georg Jensen had received, including a Medaille d'Or in Brussel in 1910, a Diplôme d'Honneur in Gent in 1913, a Grand Prix at San Francisco in 1915, and a Grand Prix in Rio de Janeiro in 1923. Many company brochures for the New York, London and Copenhagen stores list his achievements.

In addition, printed material advertising silver for sale also listed the numerous museums that owned Georg Jensen silver. By the 1920s, Georg Jensen had received honors and accolades that established his importance in the art world; various museums had purchased his work in his early years as well as work designed in the 1920s. In light of the purchasing power of museums during this time, this was extraordinary. A partial list of museums that have Jensen silver in their collections is included at the end of this book.

Med hilsen fra

GEORG JENSEN
SØLVSMEDIE A/S

RAGNAGADE 7 KØBENHAVN Ø

Card from Georg Jensen Silversmiths.
Translation "with kind regards."
Private collection.

Wine cooler designed by Georg
Jensen with Paris marks.

THE PARIS WORKSHOP

His personal tragedies must have taken their toll on Jensen.
Late in 1924, at age 58, the disillusioned Jensen decided that a change
of scene would uplift his spirits, and so he went to Paris to work, the
place where he first basked in the warm glow of international acclaim. Coincidentally, his work was on display at the 1925 World
Exposition there, and he was awarded a Grand Prix. He took five silversmiths with him, since it was his intention to open a small workshop there. Research
has not revealed the identities of the workers who accompanied him. His efforts to recreate
the aura of his first workshop brought only disappointment. Little appears to be known
about this episode in his life. He opened a workshop, but it was short lived. Jensen and his
wife found it difficult to live in France, partly because neither he nor his wife spoke French,
and partly because of their unfamiliarity with French customs. Consequently, after a short
stay, the new workshop was abandoned and the Jensens returned to Copenhagen in 1926.
Once again, Georg Jensen became artistic director of the firm that carried his name.

In the autobiographical article in *Samleren*, Jensen made reference to his stay in Paris,
and to the large pieces of hollowware he made there, specifically two large wine coolers
exhibited in the 1926 Salon, one of which was purchased by a French millionaire and the
other by an American millionaire. This comment is the only reference to his work done
during his stay in Paris, although there are several pieces of jewelry referred to as Paris
designs (by Michael von Essen, Curator of the Georg Jensen Museum in Copenhagen) which
must have been made during his stay in France.

Next page:
Working drawing of bowl no. 740 by Georg
Jensen, circa 1930 dated September 12, 1952.
"Bowl 740. Among the posthumous sketches
of Georg Jensen we find a drawing from about
1930 showing the first rough outline of the
bowl. This and the corresponding candelabrum
were later on placed Lin Georg Jensen's
production as no. 740, and were to be his last
work before his death in 1935.

The photo shows the original workshop
drawing as coming from Georg Jensen's hand,
and was presumably finished about 1934. The
bowl was made up by a selected team of
silversmiths under the close supervision of
Georg Jensen himself. It has not been

attemped to make another bowl after the death
of Georg Jensen.

The bowl and the corresponding pair of
candelabra, which were made at the same time,
were sent to Paris and here exhibited in 1936-
37. From 1938 until the outbreak of the war
these three pieces were on several exhibits in
England, and during the war they were carefully
stored away. As soon as the war was over they
were returned to the Smithy here in
Copenhagen and the ravages of time and the
long storing were removed, and the bowl and
the candelabra restored to their original
brilliance.

It has often been pointed out that just
these three pieces, the last work of Denmark's
greatest silversmith, compriced [sic] all the
most outstanding features in the work of Georg
Jensen, and can be regarded as his 9th
Symphony in which his ability to construct a
form, that gives the impression of an over-
abundance of vitality not for a moment
colliding with the true artist's innate restraint,
reaches absolute perfection. The heavy
ornaments only stress the basic form which in
turn gives the ornamentations the full value of
the impression of solid handwrought silver."
Private collection.

The Jensen store at Paseo de Gracia 62, Barcelona. Georg Jensen Sølvsmedie, Gennem Fyrretyve Arr, 1904-1944.

Fruit bowl with grape motif, designed by Georg Jensen in 1918, used in numerous bowls, candlesticks and bottle trays at the end of the First World War. Courtesy of Dr. Melissa Hardie, Newlyn Art Gallery.

GEORG JENSEN IN HIS SIXTIES

In 1926, Jensen turned sixty and was feted with a birthday celebration by the firm's staff upon his return to Copenhagen. The company he had begun almost 25 years before now employed approximately 250 people and was acknowledged as one of the greatest artistic and industrial establishments in Denmark. To his fellow workers, and perhaps to the world at large, he was a native hero and a world-recognized artist/silversmith. Perhaps his international recognition was the impetus for the request to write about his life by the publication *Samleren*, mentioned previously.

Also in 1926, Jensen was excited by the opening of a new store in Berlin, with his longtime friend and business associate Carl Dyhr.

Information regarding Jensen's activities during the years 1926-1935 is scarce. It appears that Jensen continued his work as a silversmith apart from his role as Artistic Director of the company. Jensen moved to Hellerup and lived with his family in a home where he had his own workshop. The birth of his son Ib, in 1927, brought him great joy.

"The last ten years of Georg Jensen's life, from 1925 to 1935, became a period in which disappointments gave him long spells of bitterness and depression." (Møller, *Georg Jensen, The Danish Silversmith*) It is disheartening to imagine the despair this creative artist experienced toward the end of his life, in spite of his artistic achievements that brought a wealth of beauty and joy to the world. Jensen's work continued to be shown at major exhibitions, notably Barcelona's 1929 World Exposition where he won another Grand Prix.

RECOGNITION IN ENGLAND

Jensen's work was shown at the Newlyn Art Gallery in Cornwall, England, in 1927, 1928 and 1930. The Newlyn Art Gallery is a prominent institutional advocate of the Arts and Crafts movement, which "focuses on exhibitions which reflect the quality and diversity of local, national and international contemporary art practice." It is located in the same town as the Newlyn School of Applied Arts, which was founded in 1885. The following is a copy of the exhibition review from a local newspaper, *The Western Morning News*, of August 13, 1928.

> The silver is shown by Mr. O. Ramsden, R.M.S., and Mr. G. Jensen. Mr. Ramsden obtains a very rich effect with the judicious use of enamel, and one fine cup is let in with lapis. The minute decorations of Mr. Jensen's pieces tell of very careful molding. Among his exhibits is a miniature of a fruit bowl embellished with a hanging grape pattern, which was executed for the Crown Prince of Sweden. (Dr. Melissa Hardie, editor, Patten Press in association with Newlyn Art Gallery, Newmill, Penzance, Cornwall, England, 1995, p. 80)

Jensen's participation in these exhibitions is significant for several reasons. First, it demonstrates his continued interest in showing his work even as he entered his sixties. Second, the connection with Omar Ramsden (1873-1939) links him to an English designer who made important contributions to Arts and Crafts metalwork. And finally, his participation in this and other exhibitions suggest Jensen's ongoing desire to associate himself with the Arts and Crafts milieu that had so profoundly shaped his artistic vision. One can only surmise that Jensen kept abreast of the exhibits that showcased new talents of the period by these associations and through publications such as *The Studio* and *Pan* magazines and critical reviews of the art world.

THE IMPORTED LUXURIES EXHIBITION IN LONDON, 1932

In 1932, Georg Jensen Silversmiths participated in The Imported Luxuries Exhibition at Goldsmith's Hall in London.

George R. Hughes, former curator of Goldsmiths Hall at the time of the exhibition, later wrote regarding Jensen's exhibit, "..as I had collected most of the things myself, but looking back I am a little doubtful whether the trade at the time really thought it worthwhile. However, many friends were made for the [Jensen] Company through it." The exhibition is discussed further in the publication *The Worshipful Company of Goldsmiths as Patrons of their Craft 1919-53* by George Ravensworth Hughes, father of later Goldsmith's Hall Art Director Graham Hughes. After George R. Hughes retired in 1953 from Goldsmith's Hall, he compiled this publication to be a catalogue of all the exhibitions from 1919 to 1953, including the Danish silver from Georg Jensen and Just Andersen, and ceramics from the Royal Copenhagen Porcelain Company.

SPECIAL COMMISSIONS

Georg Jensen's output for the company included pieces made on commission to commemorate certain events and people. For example, his design of a ceremonial bell for the

parliament of Iceland was produced in 1930, and designs for the Copenhagen City Council's presidential hammer and block were produced in 1931. These pieces are well documented, but very little information is available about other designs he created during this period, regardless of whether they were executed in his home workshop or in the firm's smithy.

One interesting piece of hollowware, a pair of candlesticks, and bowl no.740 are suggestive of new directions in design Jensen was exploring during the thirties, but alone they do not provide sufficient evidence upon which to base characterizations of his design activity at the time.

Since Jensen was engaged by the firm as its artistic director, one may assume that he had significant influence upon such matters as which designers were engaged by the firm and which of their designs were selected for production. The designers he himself had brought into the company, principally Henry Pilstrup, Harald Nielsen, Gundorph Albertus, Johan Rohde, and Oscar Gundlach-Pedersen, continued to make major contributions to the company's output and their continuing work would seem to imply that his artistic authority remained substantial. Nevertheless, the firms' production of sleek new designs that reflected the rise of "functionalism" during the 1930s, notably the cool, minimally decorated hollowware and flatware of Sigvard Bernadotte, was such a marked departure from the firm's earlier designs that one wonders whether this was a direction that met with Georg Jensen's wholehearted approval.

A New Vision for Georg Jensen Silversmiths

In 1930, Sigvard Bernadotte joined Georg Jensen Silversmiths as a designer. His designs were a sharp departure for the firm which had established natural imagery in "the Jensen style." Bernadotte drew upon traditional Swedish design motifs of geometric, clean and functional symmetry. He introduced designs with distinctive, clear, and adroit lines, characterized as classical and formal, and spoke of elegance and dignity.

The Stockholm Exhibit of 1930 marks the beginning of Scandinavian functionalism design. Bernadotte brought a new direction and was a trailblazer of strong, geometric forms which influenced design in the 1950s and 1960s. The skillful craftsmanship of the smithy, together with brilliant forward-looking form, introduced industrial design into the firm's production.

Display from the Imported Luxuries Exhibition at Goldsmith's Hall in London, 1932. Courtesy of The Worshipful Company of Goldsmiths.

Designer Sigvard Bernadotte.

JENSEN QUALITY MAINTAINED

It appears that during his later years, Jensen also played a role in what we would today call "quality control." "Up to the time of his last illness every piece had to pass his exacting scrutiny before being stamped with his personal mark. In this way the world has been enriched by a far greater number of beautiful examples of silver work than one man alone could possibly have produced..." (Oscar Bensen, *The Studio*, obituary notice for Georg Jensen, January, 1936)

Georg Jensen died in Denmark on October 2, 1935. He was sixty nine years old. To say that he accomplished much during his life is an understatement. With a remarkable combination of artistic genius, hard work, and dedication to the highest standards of craftsmanship, he became the leading silversmith of his time, and certainly one of the most important of the twentieth century. His magisterial work in silver brought international acclaim not only to himself, but to the other decorative arts of Denmark, all of Scandianavia, and the world. His legacy is manifold: the extraordinary works of silver that he designed, the great work of the Jensen silversmiths who were inspired by his example, the tradition of excellence in design and craftsmanship that continues to be sustained by the company he founded, and the many designers who, figuratively speaking, stand on his shoulders.

Georg Jensen was described by the *New York Herald Tribune* as "the greatest craftsman in silver for the last 300 years"; and the *Times* in London concluded its obituary with a prediction that has become reality: "Jensen is one of those craftsmen whose pieces can safely be regarded as antiques of the future."

The Jensen store at 128 Rue Royale, Brussels. Georg Jensen Sølvsmedie, Gennem Fyrretyve Arr, 1904-1944.

Group of silver hollowware and serving pieces by Georg Jensen company, Copenhagen. Courtesy of Skinner's, Inc., Boston and Bolton.

Chapter 4
A New Market: Georg Jensen Silver in the United States

Between 1915 and 1980, Georg Jensen's work was included or featured in a number of exhibitions in the United States. In 1915, the Panama Pacific International Exposition in San Francisco marked the initial exhibition of Jensen silver in the United States. Between 1915 and 1927, Frederick Lunning established a commercial foothold for the Georg Jensen company in New York City. The Brooklyn Museum exhibit in 1927 simultaneously underscored Jensen's standing among the top decorative artists of Denmark, his solid international reputation, and the growing appreciation of his work in the United States.

The Panama Pacific Exposition in San Francisco, 1915

Jensen's first exhibition in the United States was at the 1915 Panama Pacific International Exposition in San Francisco, a cultural and commercial extravaganza comparable to previous world expositions. It opened on February 20, 1915 and closed on December 4, 1915. In addition to being a gargantuan display of the artistic, scientific and industrial achievements of many nations, this exposition was commemorative and symbolic as well. It commemorated the 400th anniversary of Balboa's discovery of the Pacific Ocean, as well as the opening of the Panama Canal; and it symbolized the phoenix-like rebirth of San Francisco after its devastation by earthquake and fire in 1906.

Arrayed along a large site overlooking the Golden Gate, the exposition consisted of many spectacular exhibition halls and other buildings designed and built especially for the event. One of the national pavilions was the Danish Pavilion designed by the Danish architect Anton Rosen, who built the Palace Hotel in Copenhagen in 1907. The pavilion was dominated by three towers, one of which was meant to represent the tower of the Castle of Kroneberg at Elsinore, made famous by Shakespeare as the home of Hamlet. The exterior of the pavilion was adorned with Nordic motifs and decorated with Danish sculpture. Interestingly, one of the sculptures was of King Gorm, the subject of one of Georg Jensen's boyhood attempts at sculpture. The pavilion's interior, designed to resemble a Danish home, was decorated with the finest Danish-made furnishings including furniture, porcelain, silver, glass, and other items. A number of paintings by Denmark's greatest masters decorated the walls. The pavilion was intended to showcase the high quality of Danish fine and decorative arts in a naturalistic setting. It was also meant to serve as a meeting place for Danes, many of whom had personally contributed money to the pavilion's construction.

More conventional displays of Danish-made goods were found elsewhere in the exposition, such as the Palace of Varied Industries, a large building devoted to a dizzying variety of manufactured products from around the world. Danish goods on display included bronzes, carpets, ceramics, clocks, embroideries, furniture, jewelry and other objects made of gold and silver. The official catalogue of exhibitors lists Georg Jensen's contributions as "silver jewelry" and "handwrought silver, original designs." Goods from Denmark included "wonderful work by the Danish gold and silversmiths, that of the sculptor George (sic) Jensen being especially good." (Frank Morton Todd, *The Story of the Exposition*, vol. 4.)

Panama-Pacific Exposition in San Francisco, 1915.

Tortoise shell comb designed by Georg Jensen and decorated with silver and cabochon garnet clusters. Private collection.

In this exhibit, the culture of the country was expressed through manufacturing and industrial products. Georg Jensen was one of a group of four silversmiths and goldsmiths displaying their wares in Group no. 46. He was also an exhibitor as a jeweler with the same group. Curiously, there is a group "Objects exhibited more for their ornamental design than for their utility, Group no. 49," where Jensen is listed as "Georg Jensen, Copenhagen: Handwrought silver, original designs."

The inclusion of Jensen silver in the Panama Pacific International Exposition was significant for several reasons. First, it confirmed his reputation as the preeminent Danish silversmith. Second, it presented his work alongside the work of the world's other eminent jewelers and silversmiths, thus confirming that he belonged in that select group. Third, it provided the first prolonged exposure to his work for large numbers of Americans. Fourth, it led to the sale of many of his pieces, virtually everything on display, to William Randolph Hearst, the wealthy American newspaper baron. Information about precisely which pieces Hearst acquired at the exposition, and their current location, has not yet come to light. It is difficult to assess the effect these points may have had on the fortunes of the Jensen company, yet it is reasonable to assume that each had some degree of impact on the opening of an American market. Hearst's purchase, aside from the income it generated, may have received publicity for the firm.

Frederik Lunning and the Georg Jensen Store in the United States, 1924

During the six years that followed the firm's involvement in the Panama Pacific International Exposition, the Georg Jensen company did not significantly break into the American market. Therefore, the firm made another attempt to reach American consumers in 1921, but now the objective was narrower in focus — to aggressively sell Jensen silver to American retailers. Frederik Lunning was chosen to spearhead this effort as the third important "emissary" in the firm's history.

Frederik Lunning was a young art and book dealer from Odense, Denmark, who admired and sold Jensen silver in his store. Lunning's keen business acumen was matched by a sharp eye for good art and an extraordinary ability and charm as a salesperson. Thorolf Møller was impressed with Lunning's knowledge of merchandising and his admiration for Georg Jensen silver. In 1918, Møller invited Lunning to be a salesman in the remodeled Jensen store at 21 Bredgade in Copenhagen. Lunning became the store manager in a short time.

Despite the fact that Georg Jensen had already won many prestigious international awards for his work, he was not at that time accorded the recognition or the sales one would expect in his home market. Accordingly, Lunning set out to capture more of the local market by staging an exhibition at Charlottenborg in 1920. This proved to be quite successful. Danish newspapers gave positive reviews and quoted art critics from other countries who heaped accolades on Jensen and remarked on Danish skillfulness in the decorative arts. In so doing, Jensen silver began to receive in Denmark the sort of recognition and praise it had already received elsewhere. Sales increased at home, but not enough to improve the company's financial situation.

The store in London unfortunately did not generate the amount of business that was hoped for. Since the relocation of the workshop to Ragnadage, a much larger facility, production had been increased, but an economic crisis in Denmark in 1921 was felt in the company's sales. Once again, as they had done in 1916, members of Georg Jensen's extended family, the Møllers, and friend P.A. Pedersen, both major stockholders, injected more capital into the firm in hopes of keeping it afloat. Realizing that this was probably a short-term solution to the firm's difficulties, some members of the firm saw expansion beyond the national boundaries as one possible long-term solution.

The success of Georg Jensen silver at the Panama Pacific Exhibition in San Francisco stirred Lunning's imagination. He proposed the idea to develope a new market in the United States. To him, the new territory appeared to be full of opportunity. The firm's executives, Møller and Pedersen, were initially skeptical of Lunning's proposal since the prevailing view in Copenhagen was that Americans wouldn't appreciate Danish silver. In the end, however, the great salesman convinced them it was worth a try, and they financed the venture to the United States. In 1922, Frederik Lunning boarded a ship bound for New York with trunks full of Georg Jensen silver.

Lunning tried first to interest upscale stores such as Tiffany & Co. and Black, Starr and Frost in handling Jensen silver. Their representatives, however, did not think American customers would buy Danish silver, and they considered the prices too high. Undaunted, Lunning struck out in another direction. Instead of continuing his attempts to sell to upscale department stores, he devised a novel means of dealing directly with well-heeled customers. In

Correspondence to Georg Jensen from Frederik Lunning when he was a book and art dealer in Odense, regarding the purchase of two combs. Dated December 1, 1912.

order to imbue Jensen silver with the aura of high-quality artistry and exclusivity he thought it deserved; Lunning adroitly staged small exhibitions in posh surroundings such as the Waldorf Astoria Hotel and small art galleries in New York. It is not clear precisely when the first of these exhibitions occurred, but the obituary for Georg Jensen, published in the October 3, 1935, issue of the *New York Times* suggests that it may have been in 1922: "An exhibition of Mr. Jensen's work was held in New York in 1922. The collection comprised of 400 specimens of his art and was shown at the Art Center, 65-67 East Fifty Sixth Street." The 400 pieces mentioned may well have been the contents of the trunks Lunning brought over from Copenhagen. The Art Center, a first-class institution founded by members of New York City's arts establishment for the elevation of fine and commercial art, would certainly have been the sort of venue Lunning sought for exhibitions of Jensen silver. Other issues of the *New York Times* document two later New York City exhibitions of Jensen silver, one in December of 1923 and another in November of 1924. Both were held at the Anderson Galleries at 489 Park Avenue, New York. It is unclear whether Lunning staged other exhibitions in New York during this period.

Lunning's strategy of marketing Jensen silver directly to wealthy, cosmopolitan taste-makers was successful, and he surprised his colleagues in Denmark by selling nearly all the pieces he had brought with him. Flush with this success, and further bolstered by the knowledge that he had only begun to awaken American's interest in Jensen silver, he returned to Copenhagen with a plan to open a store in New York where he would sell Georg Jensen silver.

Persuaded again by Lunning, their knight errant, Møller and Pedersen of Georg Jensen Sølvsmedie A/S agreed to grant Lunning the right to be the sole representative of Georg Jensen Silver in the United States for a period of 100 years. In the late 1920s, when this contract was agreed to, there was still great doubt whether Lunning would make a success of this venture. In reality, there was much skepticism in Copenhagen about this venture, but the possibilities of increasing sales seemed too good not to at least let Lunning try to establish a market in the United States.

In 1924, Frederik Lunning opened the first Georg Jensen store in New York City on West 57th Street, near Carnegie Hall. The store was small, and soon, when a larger, more impressive store became available across the street, at 169 West 57th Street, he moved to the larger space.

Advertisement for the Georg Jensen Handmade Silver store in New York from *International Studio*, April, 1931.

Known as "Georg Jensen Handmade Silver," the elegantly appointed store sold the finest silver, Georg Jensen, of course, and the finest china, notably porcelain by Royal Copenhagen. The customers came and bought, the experiment was successful. In 1935, Frederik Lunning moved the Georg Jensen store again, now to a three-story emporium at 667 Fifth Avenue, near 53rd street, a most prestigious address. The impressive location, with its ample size and elegant decor, made it one of the most upscale stores in New York. Before long, Lunning had established a substantial and loyal clientele, which itself came to be considered as stylish and unique as the store's merchandise. Eleanor Roosevelt, Bess Truman, Katherine Hepburn, Greta Garbo, Marilyn Monroe, and Thelma Ritt were among the store's many famous customers, as was related in personal interviews with members of the Lunning sales force. In addition to individuals who purchased Georg Jensen items for themselves, museums occasionally would purchase Jensen silver for their collections. The

Newark Museum, devoted to American Arts and Crafts, purchased Jensen jewelry and hollowware for their collection from the Georg Jensen Handmade Silver, Inc. store. According to Ulysses Dietz, the current curator of the Newark Museum's Decorative Arts Department, an original bill of sale indicates the following items were purchased in November of 1929: necklace no. 1 for $80.00, a pendant necklace with labradorites for $110.00, an ashtray for $75.00, and a Johan Rohde pitcher for $175.00. These prices included a 25% discount given to the museum.

Interior of shop.

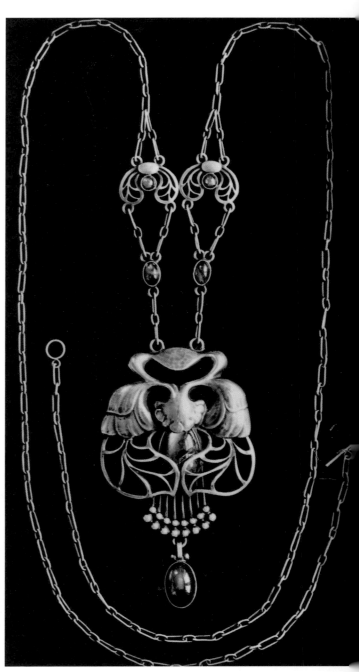

Georg Jensen Handmade Silver store at 667 Fifth Avenue, New York. Frederik Lunning, Managing Director.

Pendant necklace with silver and labradorite. Collection of The Newark Museum.

For tourists, the New York City Georg Jensen store became an important place to visit. Many returned home with jewelry or flatware as treasured mementos of the big city style. The store's refined salespeople enhanced its *savoir faire*; many were society women, others were natives of Denmark or other Nordic countries, and one was a Russian princess who served tea every afternoon at 4 p.m. on Blue Fluted Royal Copenhagen dishes, from a Georg Jensen silver tea pot, on a Georg Jensen silver tray. Former salespersons have related stories of their days at the Fifth Avenue store, such as that Swedish actress Greta Garbo only spoke when the Swedish salesperson addressed her. Most of the shoppers were women. The Georg Jensen store sold merchandise through their catalogue as well. Americans soon cultivated a taste for the unique Jensen style, and on their trips abroad they also purchased Jensen silver.

The success of Lunning's store proved to be a boon for the silversmithy in Copenhagen, which was kept busy with orders from New York. The American market had become the major marketplace for Jensen silver. Until 1940, Lunning was the best promoter of Danish silver and china in the United States.

The Brooklyn Museum's "Danish National Exhibition of Applied Art, Painting and Sculpture," 1927

A few years after Frederik Lunning secured a retail presence in New York, Jensen silver was included in an important exhibition that toured the United States and draw further American attention to Danish fine and decorative arts. The "Danish National Exhibition of Applied Art, Painting and Sculpture" was organized by the Brooklyn Museum, in Brooklyn, New York, and ran from November 15, 1927 through December 19, 1927. Prior to arriving in the United States, the chosen pieces were exhibited at the Kunst und Industrie Museum in Copenhagen.

Brooch no. 120 designed by Georg Jensen.

This exhibition was a watershed event in being the first major exhibition of Danish art to tour the United States. Its size and purview were impressive. Top Danish firms and dozens of stellar Danish artists were represented, and the display included paintings, bookbinding by Anker Kyster, furniture designed by Kaare Klint, sculpture, weaving, ceramics by Royal Copenhagen Porcelain Manufactory, and silver by Georg Jensen Sølvsmedie A/S. The integrated character of the exhibition was particularly striking, since it encompassed, and celebrated equally, folk art, fine art, and decorative or applied art. Departing from the more typical approach in exhibitions, whereby these categories are rigidly separated and evaluated from an elitist, or fine art, perspective, the exhibition's curators considered the many manifestations of Danish art in a refreshingly holistic way, one that would surely have gratified William Morris and his Arts and Crafts disciples.

Some observers of the arts comprehended this broad quality in its presentation, such as Elisabeth L. Cary, who reviewed the exhibition for the *New York Times*. She noted that the Danish tradition of using the talents of the nation's top artists to elevate the design of manufactured goods was a model worth emulating in the United States. "Most of the Danish crafts have been raised to a high technical plane and a full expression of national taste by the willingness of the artists trained in the field to cooperate with the leaders of the industries in producing distinguished design and by the readiness of the industrial leaders to turn to the artist for this cooperation." (*New York Times*)

The exhibition catalogue contains the following entry:

Georg Jensen's Silversmiths, Ragnagade 7, Copenhagen
159 West 57 Street, New York
Silverware after design by Georg Jensen, Gundorfph Albertus, Harald Nielsen, O.Gundlach Petersen, and Johan Rohde.

It heaped praise on Jensen and Rohde, in particular, for their roles in bringing international attention to Danish applied art. The catalog continued:

While the artists and craftsmen mentioned above have been important chiefly for the development of native art, the craftsmen of modern Danish silverware and porcelain have exerted an international influence. Georg Jensen has been the indisputable artistic leader of modern Danish silverware decoration and manufacture. Happily combining the personality and attainments of artist and craftsmen, he has executed a series of works, partly of his own designs, partly after the designs of eminent painter Johan Rohde, and the technique of his works, their simple forms and characteristic open work ornamentation, have spread his fame throughout Europe and America.

Brooch no. 181.

The American Federation of Arts Exhibition of Decorative Metalwork and Cotton Textiles, Third International Exhibition of Contemporary Industrial Art, 1930-1931

A major traveling exhibition of contemporary industrial arts was organized in 1930 to include displays from England, France, Germany, Holland, Sweden, Switzerland, Czechoslovakia, Denmark and the United States. This exhibit originated at The Museum of Fine Arts in Boston, Massachusetts and continued to The Metropolitan Museum of Art in New York; The Art Institute of Chicago in Chicago, Illinois; and The Cleveland Museum of Art in Cleveland, Ohio. As the third segment, it was the final event of a series which traveled throughout the United States and had the cooperation of several important organizations abroad. The catalogue introduction stated that the content:

> ...consists of a number of materials and techniques; silver, pewter, inlaid and patined brass and copper, iron, aluminum, lead, bronze, zinc, and a few examples of enamelling. Aesthetically, these specimens are of quite distinct categories. Contemporary design is to be found in all of them, but naturally in very different forms....Furthermore, no branch of applied art has so thoroughly failed to grasp the aesthetic qualities becoming to the machine product as commercial silver...the European craftsman has for the last thirty years been creating new and fresh forms in silver...

Foreign firms and many individuals were well represented in contrast to the degree of participation by American silver manufacturers. One goal of the exhibit was to encourage American manufacturers to gain insights from the foreign displays, and thereby further their silver manufacturing industry. Items from the following designers came from Denmark: Gundorph Albertus, Just Andersen, Kay Fisker, H.F.Gross, Gundlach-Pedersen, H. Hansen, Peter Hertz, Georg Jensen Handmade Silver, A. Michelsen, Evald Nielsen, Harald Nielsen, and Johan Rohde. Georg Jensen Handmade Silver exhibited the largest number of entries from Denmark, ten objects in silver: boxes, candlesticks, vases, bowls, cocktail shakers, cups and tea sets. Three entries were marked "Courtesy of Georg Jensen Handmade Silver, New York." In addition, each entry indicated the designer as well as the silversmith who executed the piece.

Not to be overlooked are items from impressive designers in other countries as well. For example, from England: Edward Spencer, Artificers' Guild, J. Paul Cooper, Goldsmiths and Silversmiths Company, Ltd., George G. Hart, Harold Stabler, Omar Ramsden of St. Dunstans, The Worshipful Company of Goldsmiths of London. From France: Edgar Brandt, Paul Brandt, Cartier, Inc., Jean Dunand, Orfèvrerie Christofle, Bouilhet and Company, Jean Puiforcat and others. From Germany as well other countries there were more items from distinguished designers, too many to mention here.

The inclusion of Georg Jensen silver in this very notable international venue placed the firm historically, and should have been a great source of pride during the last decade of Georg Jensen's life.

Silver caviar dish with glass liner inscribed with Georg Jensen's signature on the back. Horn and silver serving spoon in Cactus. Private collection.

A covered bowl and ornamental servers.

THE 1939 WORLD'S FAIR

On June 15, 1936, the Congress of the United States requested the President to invite the nations of the world to participate in the New York Worlds's Fair. Seventy foreign countries were invited to participate, including Denmark. In the Pavilion of Nations, Denmark's outstanding artists and craftsmen assembled an exhibit interepreting the social, industrial, and cultural aspects of their country. The noted Danish architect Tyge Hvass, who first won acclaim at the San Francisco Fair in 1915, directed the exhibit. A committee of art experts selected the outstanding creations of Danish art and industry, including Danish silversmiths, jewelers, wood carvers, potters, etc. As was stated in the official guidebook to the fair, under the description of Denmark, was the following, "Except for world famous porcelain, silverware and other Danish art craft, no commercial products are exhibited." In the Denmark House exhibit, the Georg Jensen store of New York and Royal Copenhagen company displayed porcelain, stoneware, handmade silver, crystal, wooden toys, and objects of pewter and bronze. The Georg Jensen display featured gold and silver jewelry and silverware. Record numbers of fair visitors therefore were exposed to Danish designs and Jensen silver.

THE NEW YORK STORE RESPONDS TO CHANGE

World War II created critical problems for both Frederick Lunning in New York and the smithy in Copenhagen. Silver was not readily available for the smithy to use, and therefore production of Jensen items was very limited. Shipping across the Atlantic Ocean became impossible due to submarine warfare. Lunning was confronted with the challenge of stocking the store with merchandise of the high standards he had established. When the deliveries from Denmark stopped, American handicrafts took the place of imported wares. The three-story building, with silver and porcelain on the main floor, glass and linen on the second floor, and furniture on the third floor, now included items representative of American pottery and ceramics, furniture, linen, ladies' handbags, and antique as well as contemporary jewelry. The store struggled to maintain its upscale image.

GEORG JENSEN, INC., U.S.A.

When the inventory of Jensen silver from Denmark was depleted Lunning could not replace the stock. He established a separate company, Georg Jensen, Inc., U.S.A. and arranged for American silver manufacturers to produce silver jewelry and hollowware that resembled Danish pieces. The American-made silver was marked "Georg Jensen, Inc. U.S.A." The American-made designs are often referred to as Georg Jensen "look-alikes;" they don't quite look like Jensen work, although often one responds to them with the question, "Is that Jensen?" This question is easily answered upon closer examination, and when the "U.S.A." mark is identified.

During the war years, Lunning filled his shelves with other luxury goods from the best Scandinavian and American designers he could obtain. Thus, the exclusive shop was transformed into an emporium selling a wide range of high-quality items, both at the store and through its catalogues.

Bottle of Flora Danica perfume marketed by Georg Jensen Inc. This is an example of one of the many various items that was sold by Frederik Lunning in the Jensen store in New York.

Two-page layout from a Georg Jensen Inc. catalogue of 1947 which shows the "Imported Silver" that was available in Lunning's New York City store.

Example of a silver brooch produced by an American silversmith and sold by Frederik Lunning in the New York Jensen store in the 1940s. Marked Georg Jensen Inc., U.S.A. Collection of Ed and Lisa Guari.

When Georg Jensen silver from Copenhagen again became available after the war, Lunning acquired Jensen silver but continued to market the broad range of luxury goods as well. In the catalogue for 1947, there are 71 pages of goods, but the first two pages only contain designs and hollowware by Georg Jensen, Johan Rohde, Sigvard Bernadotte and others, and they are labelled "Imported Silver." In the catalogue's jewelry section, text accompanying the items refers to "old favorites... and the introduction of the work of several talented young newcomers whose craftsmanship so obviously and definitely expresses the feeling in jewelry we are constantly seeking...some of the new names are: Bjarne Meyer, Maria Regnier, Anna Halasi, A. LaPaglia, M. Cusick and others." These are names of American designers, specifically contracted to produce jewelry with similar motifs to Georg Jensen jewelry and hollowware.

These "new names" have not left their mark on jewelry or hollowware design in America or elsewhere. More than any of the others named, Alphonse LaPaglia's jewelry designs, marked "L.P." or "A.L.P.," is familiar today, and appears at auction houses and in the inventories of antique dealers. The jewelry of LaPaglia incorporated the arts and crafts naturalistic style of images such as leaves in designs. Silver hollowware pieces by William DeMatteo look naturalistic as well, and are reminiscent of original Georg Jensen silver designs. Some pieces even appear to be "replicas" of Jensen designs, an obvious source of confusion for budding collectors of Jensen silver.

The Georg Jensen Handwrought Silver store, or Georg Jensen, Inc., acted as other retail stores selling a variety of items. Items marked "Georg Jensen, Inc., U.S.A." or "Handwrought Georg Jensen, Inc., U.S.A." are American-made silver, not to be confused with silver made by the Georg Jensen silversmiths in Denmark. The jewelry and other silver produced by the Georg Jensen smithy in Denmark during the war years was marked "Georg Jensen & Wendel A/S, Denmark." This mark was clearly used to identify pieces produced in Denmark and sold between 1945 and 1951 in the United States. Around 1950, an agreement was reached between Lunning and the Georg Jensen company in Denmark that ended production and sales of silver marked "Georg Jensen, Inc., U.S.A."

CELEbRATiNG SCANdiNAViAN DEsiGN --
THE LUNNiNG PRiZE, 1951-1970

To draw attention to the New York Jensen store and to encourage the development of Scandinavian design, Frederick Lunning established the Lunning Prize in 1951.

The prize, in the form of a travelling scholarship, stipulated two winners each year, but in any one year, the awards were not to go to two artists of the same nationality. It generated exhibitions around the world that established the concept of Scandinavian design and prompted cooperation between Nordic designers and industry in the 1950s. The Georg Jensen store in New York held exhibitions of the work of the Lunning Prize winners, including several designers for Georg Jensen, Denmark. For example, Tias Eckhoff, Henning Koppel, Nanna and Jørgen Ditzel, Torun Bülow-Hübe, Bent Gabrielsen, and Kim Naver were among the recipients of the Lunning Prize. The collaboration of the leaders of the national institutions for design in Norway, Finland, Sweden, and Denmark, along with the prominent committee members who were designers, art critics and leaders in these countries, helped the prize winners to achieve worldwide recognition. The Lunning Prize ended in 1971.

Necklace hanger no. 169 and pendant no. 135 with rock crystal designed by Torun Bülow-Hübe.

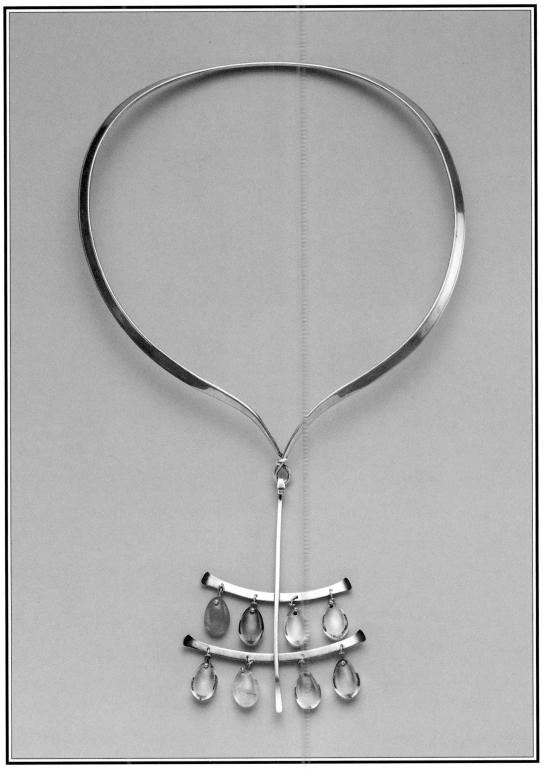

THE CONTINUATION OF GEORGE JENSEN, INC.

When Frederick Lunning died on September I, 1952, at 70 years of age, his son, Just Lunning, assumed leadership of the New York store. Just Lunning had joined his father at the George Jensen, Inc. Fifth Avenue store in 1947. Subsequently, three branch stores were established in Scarsdale, New York; Manhasset, Long Island, New York; and Millburn, New Jersey. In addition to their retail establishments, Georg Jensen, Inc. included a division to import and distribute other Scandinavian products. Lunning also marketed Georg Jensen silver to leading upscale stores elsewhere in the country, including Gump's in San Francisco, Marshall Fields in Chicago, and Nieman Marcus in Dallas. Thus, due in large measure to the entrepreneurial drive of Frederik Lunning, Americans could find Georg Jensen silver in exclusive stores throughout the United States.

When Just Lunning died in August of 1965, at the age of 55, Georg Jensen, Inc. was without leadership. Through management changes, the company experienced financial problems as well, and was sold several times.

THE METROPOLITAN MUSEUM OF ART'S EXHIBITION "THE ARTS OF DENMARK: VIKING TO MODERN," 1960-1961

Jensen silver was among the items featured in a major exhibition that opened at New York's Metropolitan Museum of Art in 1960. Titled "The Arts of Denmark: Viking to Modern," the exhibition presented a broad view of Denmark's artistry and was arranged by the Danish Society of Arts and Crafts and Industrial Design and the Danish Government. Honorary patrons were His Majesty King Frederik IX and The Hon. Dwight D. Eisenhower, President of the United States of America. Historic examples were shown from the National Museum of Denmark. Georg Jensen Sølvsmedie A/S was represented with examples of jewelry, flatware and hollowware by the following designers: Sigvard Bernadotte, Nanna and Jørgen Ditzel, Erik Herlow, Georg Jensen, Søren Georg Jensen, Henning Koppel, Arno Malinowski, Harald Nielsen, Johan Rohde, Magnus Stephensen, and Olaf Staehr-Nielsen. The chairman of the working committee in Denmark was A. Hostrup Pedersen, who was president of the Danish Society of Arts and Crafts and Industrial Design. Just Lunning, president of Georg Jensen, Inc., was chairman of the working committee in the United States.

Candelabrum no. 383, designed by Georg Jensen in 1920. Collection of The Newark Museum, Gift of Mr.and Mrs.Robert Solomon, 1991, in memory of her parents, Rita and Nathan Goldberg. Photograph by Sarah Wells.

With the international reputation of the Metropolitan Museum behind it, this exhibition attracted thousands of visitors and firmly established Danish designs as influential to modern styles. As the most well-known Danish designer to the American public, Georg Jensen's place in history was secured.

The Renwick Gallery's Exhibition "Georg Jensen Silversmith: 77 Artists, 75 Years," 1980

The most recent major exhibition focusing only on Jensen silver was held in Washington, D. C., at the Smithsonian Institution's Renwick Gallery in 1980. Titled "Georg Jensen Silversmith: 77 Artists, 75 Years," the exhibition presented 147 examples of the work of some of the firm's most accomplished designers. In addition to illuminating the artistic excellence of Jensen silver over the course of the silversmithy's 75-year history, and identifying some of the individuals most responsible for this continuity, a central goal of the exhibition was calling attention to the influence of Georg Jensen designs on independent silversmiths and firms in the United States. The exhibition's excellent and profusely illustrated catalogue is one of the most important contributions to the literature on Jensen in recent years. Similar to the centennial exhibit of 1966 held in Goldsmith's Hall, London, this exhibit had the backing of one of the world's preeminent museum groups, and reached out to thousands of visitors, both American and foreign. Although he never set foot in America, Georg Jensen's reputation and influence there was duly credited.

Clock no. 333, designed by Johan Rohde in 1919. Courtesy of Georg Jensen/Royal Copenhagen.

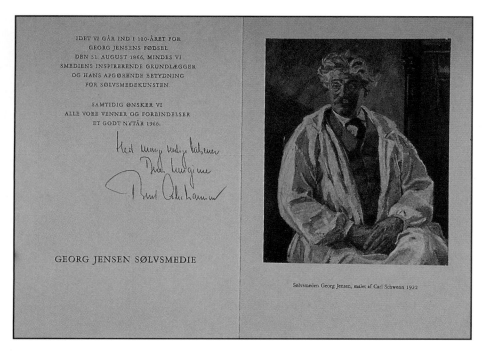

IDET VI GÅR IND I 100-ÅRET FOR
GEORG JENSENS FØDSEL
DEN 31. AUGUST 1866, MINDES VI
SMEDIENS INSPIRERENDE GRUNDLÆGGER
OG HANS AFGØRENDE BETYDNING
FOR SØLVSMEDEKUNSTEN.

SAMTIDIG ØNSKER VI
ALLE VORE VENNER OG FORBINDELSER
ET GODT NYTÅR 1966.

GEORG JENSEN SØLVSMEDIE

Sølvsmeden Georg Jensen, malet af Carl Schwenn 1922

New Year's card sent by the Jensen company. Translation, "As we enter the 100 years of Georg Jensen's birth, 1866, we remember the smithy's inspiration for silver, his meaning and contributions to the art of the silversmith. At the same time, we wish all our friends and customers a Happy New Year of 1966." Private collection.

Brooch no. 78 with amber and chrysophrase and brooch no. 152 with carnelian and green agate.

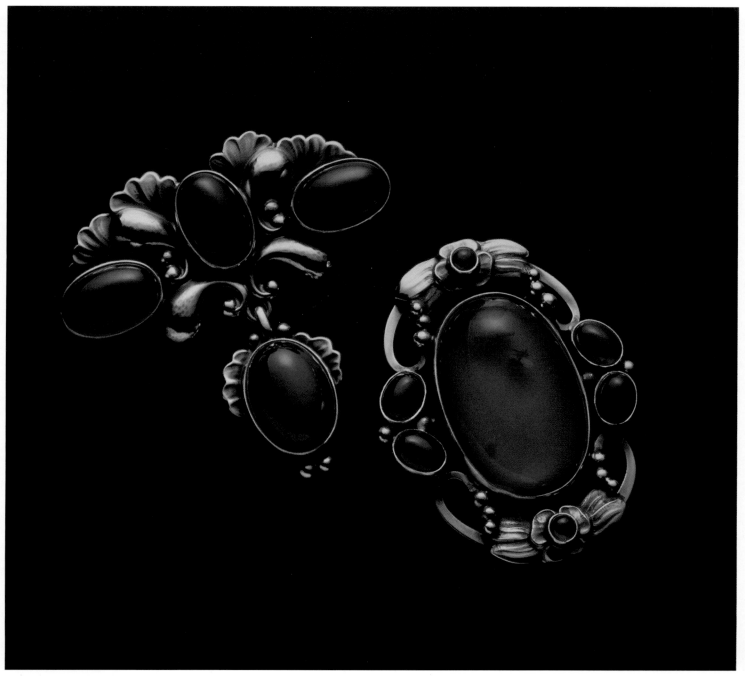

CHAPTER 5

THE GEORG JENSEN COMPANY AFTER 1935

Upon Georg Jensen's death, Harald Nielsen became the artistic director of the company and remained with the firm for the remainder of this life. Along with Johan Rohde, he had been with Jensen through the beginning years when the Georg Jensen style was established. It was Harald Nielsen's responsibility to continue this tradition. His flatware designs Pyramid and Old Danish remain Jensen favorites.

After Georg Jensen died in 1935, the company drew upon the skills of Gundorph Albertus (1887-1970), who had joined the firm in 1911. Trained as a sculptor and a graduate of the Academy of Fine Art in Copenhagen, he showed an unusual aptitude in understanding the qualities of silver. He began as a chaser and, because of his skill, became the company's assistant director in 1926 and remained in this position until 1954. His standards for maintaining the highest quality of silver craftsmanship earned him a reputation as a perfectionist. He received a gold medal at the Paris World Exhibition in 1925 and the Diplôme d'Honneur at L'Exposition Internationale in Paris in 1937.

Original drawing of circular plate with acorns by Gundorph Albertus. Courtesy of Ole Pedersen.

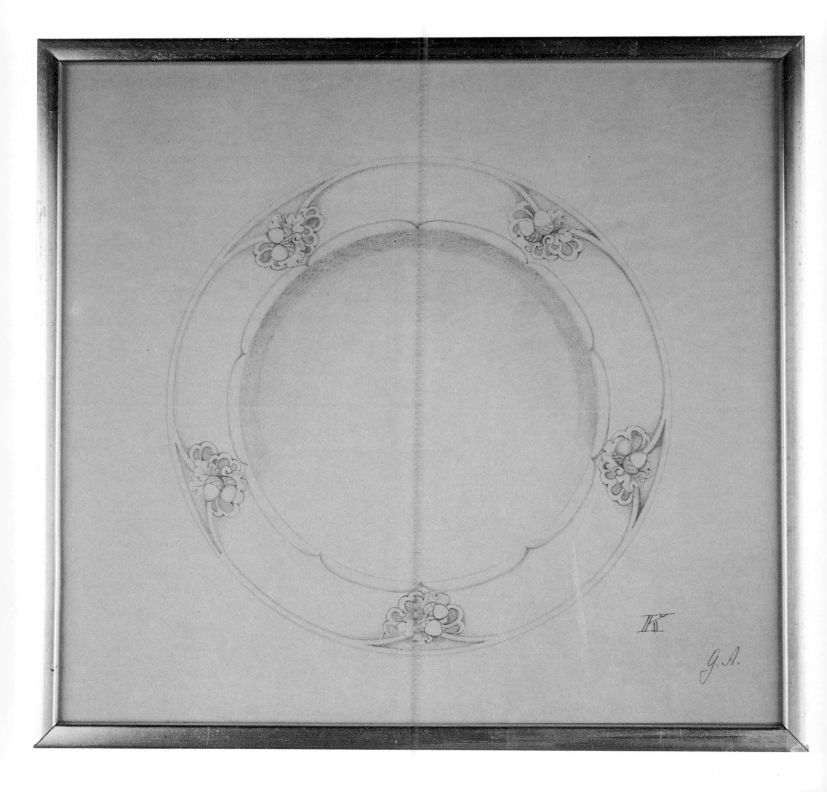

Four pairs of Pyramid salts and peppers, designed by Harald Nielsen. Private collection.

Jern/Sølv items, 1944.

The first commitment for Nielsen in 1935 was to search for new designers who exemplified the creativity and vision that he had helped to establish. Nielsen looked for young talent that was capable of continuing the tradition of fine craftsmanship and renewing it with contemporary designs.

Arno Malinowski (1899-1976) belongs to the middle generation of Jensen artists. Malinowski trained as a sculptor and engraver and worked for the Georg Jensen firm from 1936 to 1965. He was the creator of the Jensen line of "Jorn/Sølv" (Iron and Silver) jewelry and objects.

An economic depression and the onset of World War II marked the climate when the scarcity of sterling silver slowed the production of luxury items.

Ashtray and cigarette cup, cigarette box, and pendant designed by Sigvard Bernadotte, circa 1944. Courtesy of Georg Jensen/Royal Copenhagen.

Mirror and jewelry in iron and silver (Jern/Sølv) designed by Arno Malinowski, 1944. Courtesy of Georg Jensen/Royal Copenhagen.

Crown Princess Ingrid viewing the Jensen exhibit at Charlottenborg in 1938 with Thorolf Moller, Director of Georg Jensen. Georg Jensen Sølvsmedie, Gennem Fyrretyve Arr, 1904-1944.

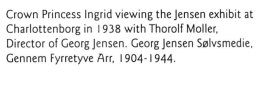

Director A. Hostrup Pedersen and Sigvard Bernadotte showing the Crown Princess the silver work of Gundorph Albertus at Charlottenborg in 1938. Georg Jensen Sølvsmedie, Gennem Fyrretyve Arr, 1904-1944.

Silver designs by Sigvard Bernadotte, 1938. Courtesy of Georg Jensen/Royal Copenhagen.

Three enamel brooches: from top to bottom, no. 306, no. 314, and no. 307 designed by Henning Koppel.

The most successful of Harald Nielsen's recruits was Henning Koppel (1918-1982), who began his work with Georg Jensen in 1945. Koppel was educated as a sculptor and designer at the Royal Danish Academy of Fine Art and won many awards for himself and the Georg Jensen Company, including The Lunning Prize in 1953, gold medals at the Milan Triennial in 1952, 1954 and 1957, and many others. Although Koppel and Jensen never met, Koppel's versatile approach and passion about design in silver matched Jensen's spirit.

Koppel departs from the ornamental naturalistic Jensen form to amorphic shapes more modern and contemporary to his time. Koppel introduced his flowing forms of pitchers and bowls to smaller versions of amoebae and biomorphic jewels. Koppel's name soon became synonymous with the term "Scandinavian Modern." His amoebae shapes, floating abstract geometric shapes, clean asymmetrical forms, and shiny treatment of the silver surface brought the Jensen firm once again to the forefront of the design world. American designers Nelson, Noguchi, and others echoed these forms. Today, Koppel's work is represented in museums throughout the world. An outstanding event, that perhaps brought the Georg Jensen firm into a new arena, was Henning Koppel's participation in 1966 in the New York Diamonds International competition where Koppel jewelry designs won three of twenty-one awards. The Jensen firm has a history of encouraging their designers to work in other materials besides silver, and Koppel, the versatile designer, worked in a broad spectrum of materials including textiles and furniture. Just as Georg Jensen had created his own personal interpretation in silver fifty years before, Koppel struck a personal idiom in his sweeping abstract shapes of free forms in silver. His grand forms, graceful and with a contour line of the art of the 1950s, helped to place the Jensen firm in contemporary art. Scandinavian design of the 1950s was epitomized by Koppel's designs in silver. He was given a one man show in 1966 at the Fifth Avenue, New York, Jensen store, and he participated in the Jensen Centenary Exhibition at Goldsmith's Hall in London in 1966.

Bracelet no. 89 designed by Henning Koppel. Courtesy of Georg Jensen/Royal Copenhagen.

Other designers continued to join the firm. Nanna and Jørgen Ditzel were a husband and wife team who began to work in the Georg Jensen firm in 1954. Both were trained as industrial designers Ditzel designed rings, necklaces, and bracelets. Her designs have a clarity and eternal harmony and represent a syntheses of material and form, the best of Danish 1950s and 1960s designs, and appear contemporary forty years later.

The company continued to evolve under Harald Nielsen's artistic direction through the 1940s and 1950s. The American market grew under Frederick Lunning's care and provided orders to keep the Copenhagen smithy active. Details about the American market's development can be found in chapter four.

International Exhibition of Modern Jewelry, 1890-1961

In 1961, in conjunction with the Victoria and Albert Museum, the International Exhibition of Modern Jewellry 1890-1961 was held at Goldsmiths' Hall in London. This very impressive collection offered a survey of the best jewelry designs at the institution that is dedicated to the preservation of the creative art of the silversmith. It included jewelry by Georg Jensen and many of the designers for Georg Jensen Silversmiths including Nanna Ditzel, Søren Georg Jensen, Erik Herlow, Henning Koppel, Arno Malinowski, Christian Mohl-Hansen, Oscar Gundlach-Pedersen, and Johan Rohde. The inclusion of so many designers affiliated with the Jensen company and Georg Jensen's own work attests to the continuation of the standard of artistic excellence that Jensen had established at the beginning of the century.

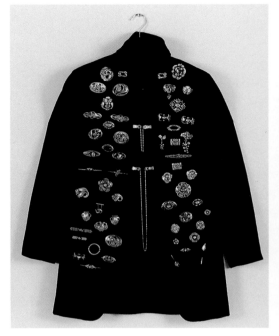

Jensen brooches and bib clips as worn on an enthusiastic collector's jacket. Private collection.

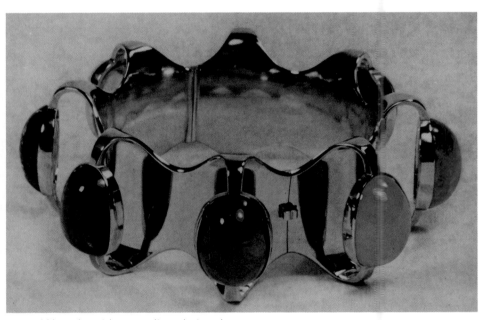

18K gold bracelet with tourmalines designed by Nanna Ditzel, 1962. Courtesy of Georg Jensen/Royal Copenhagen.

Bracelet and fruit bowl designed by O. Gundlach-Pedersen, circa 1927-1929. Georg Jensen Sølvsmedie, Gennem Fyrretyve Arr, 1904-1944.

Modern necklace designed by Søren Georg Jensen. Courtesy of Georg Jensen/Royal Copenhagen.

Brooch no. 167.

Pendant necklace designed by Arno
Malinowski. Collection of Anne Shannon.

GEORG JENSEN, 1866-1966, A CENTENARY EXHIBITION

Graham Hughes, Art Director of the Worshipful Company of Goldsmiths in London and chairman of the Crafts Centre of Great Britain, continued with his father's work to recognize the art of Georg Jensen. In 1966, on the centenary of Georg Jensen's birth, the man, Georg Jensen, as well as his company were featured in an exhibition at Goldsmiths Hall. It is noteworthy that in England, with it's many revered historic silversmiths, a singular exhibition to the Danish silversmith was staged.

The Georg Jensen Centenary Exhibition, 1966.
Courtesy of The Worshipful Company of
Goldsmiths.

Jensen had been deceased for over thirty years when this exhibition took place. A special issue of *Mobilia*, the independent Scandinavian monthy for applied art, is the catalogue for the show. A message in the catalogue from Sir Frederick Hoare, Bart., Prime Warden of the Worshipful Company of Goldsmiths, reads in part:

> ...We are now delighted to pay our tribute to the man Jensen who re-established silversmithing where it belongs, as one of the creative arts. We welcome not only his original ideas, but also the flow of new Jensen designs which continued after his death in 1935 and which still continues today. At Goldsmiths' Hall we encourage modern craftsmanship in many different ways. It is no exaggeration to say that Jensens are partners in this challenging enterprise, and I wish them every success.

The Georg Jensen Centenary Exhibition, 1966. Courtesy of The Worshipful Company of Goldsmiths.

The Company Today

During 1985-1987, Georg Jensen Silversmiths merged with Royal Copenhagen Porcelain, Bing & Groendahl Porcelain, and the Holmegaard Glassworks into the Royal Copenhagen Group, Scandinavia's largest decorative arts company.

The international exposure that began with Georg Jensen's first store abroad, in Germany in 1909, continues to this day with 66 Georg Jensen Company stores worldwide in Japan, Canada, Sweden, Norway, Australia, the United Kingdom, France, Germany, Italy, Taipei, Hong Kong, Singapore, and the United States. In the United States, there are three Georg Jensen stores: New York, Chicago, and Costa Mesa, California.

The little workshop that began in 1904 at 36 Bredgade, with Georg Jensen, one apprentice, and a helper, has grown to become a distinguished international firm.

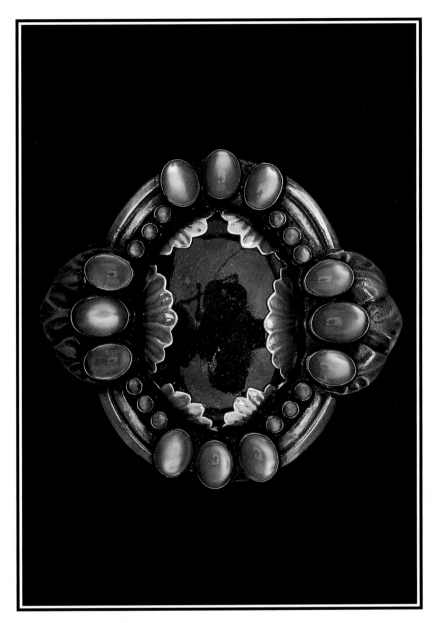

Brooch no. 1 with labradorite and moonstones
designed by Georg Jensen. Collection of Janet
and Scott Lehr.

Chapter 6
Jewelry

The First Fifteen Years

Of all the work Georg Jensen produced, his jewelry is perhaps the most numerous, varied, fascinating and unique. Today, it may also be the best known and most avidly collected of his creations. Jewelry was always a central focus of his work, and it first attracted the attention of Danish art critics. In the tiny workroom at 36 Bredgade, the little works of art elicited an observer's response that Jensen's love and gentle spirit is imbued in every piece.

Through his jewelry, Jensen successfully advanced his goal of producing beautiful art that could be acquired and enjoyed by a broad public. Almost immediately, the high quality, affordability, and artistic appeal of Jensen's jewelry was noticed, and sales and publicity began to come his way. Even before Jensen opened his workshop in 1904, Pietro Krohn, who was then director of the Museum of Applied Art in Copenhagen, bought some of the silver jewelry Jensen made while he was working at the Mogens Ballin workshop.

Jewelry drawing and top of handle for a salad serving set, possibly no. 159. Two of the drawings look like the inspiration for brooches no. 100 and no. 4. The no. 4 brooch was featured in the orignal 1912 Georg Jensen catalog. Courtesy of Georg Jensen Museum Copenhagen

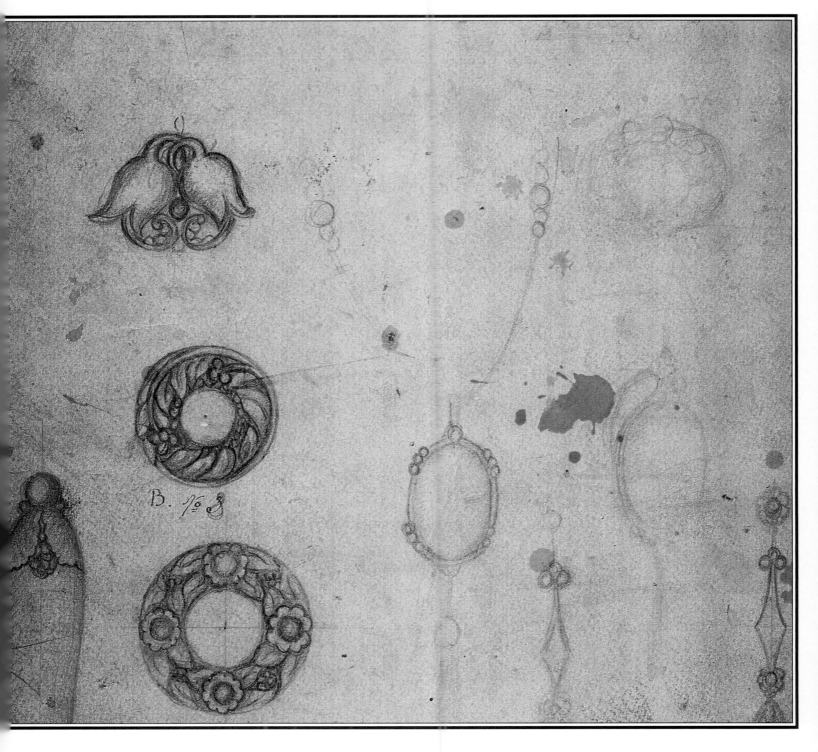

Necklace no. 8 with opals and labradorite. Collection of Sophie Hallstrom.

Back of necklace no. 8.

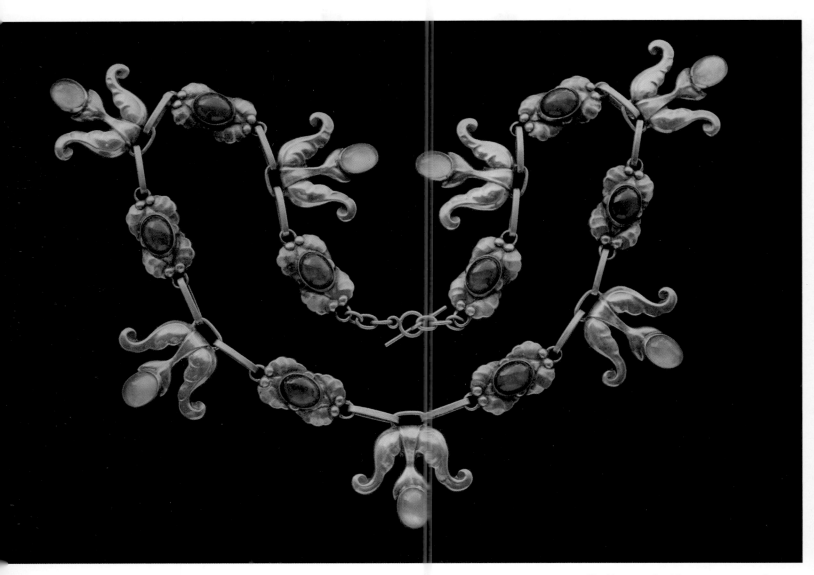

Necklace no. 9 with moonstones and labradorite. Collection of Louisa Hallstrom.

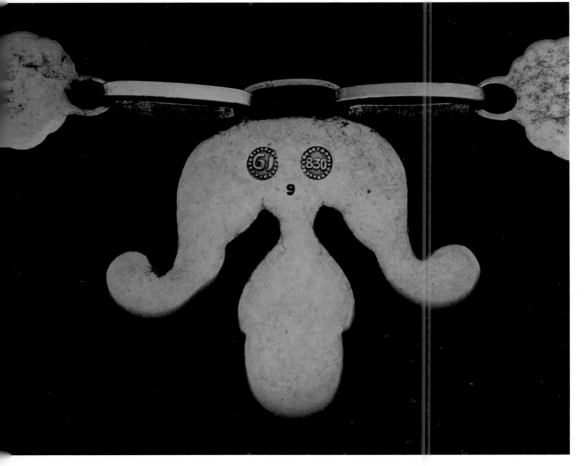

Back of necklace no. 9.

Forty pair of Georg Jensen sterling silver cufflinks. When the number
appears twice, this indicates either different production marks,
different size, or different backs on the cuff link.

Top row: no. 35, no. 189, no. 209, no. 32, no. 43, no. 62B
2nd row: no. 44, no. 25, no. 2, no. 309, no. 53, no. 9
3rd row: no. 14, no. 57, no. 25, no. 78A, no. 44, no. 9
4th row: no. 70, no. 46, no. 25, no. 78B, no. 44B, no. 61B
5th row: no. 50, no. 5, no. 17, no. 2X, no. 66
6th row: no. 64, no. 91, no. 96, no. 109, no. 80, no. 61A
7th row: no. 64, no. 42, no. 67, no. 27, no. 114
Collection of Dr. Barry Goozner.

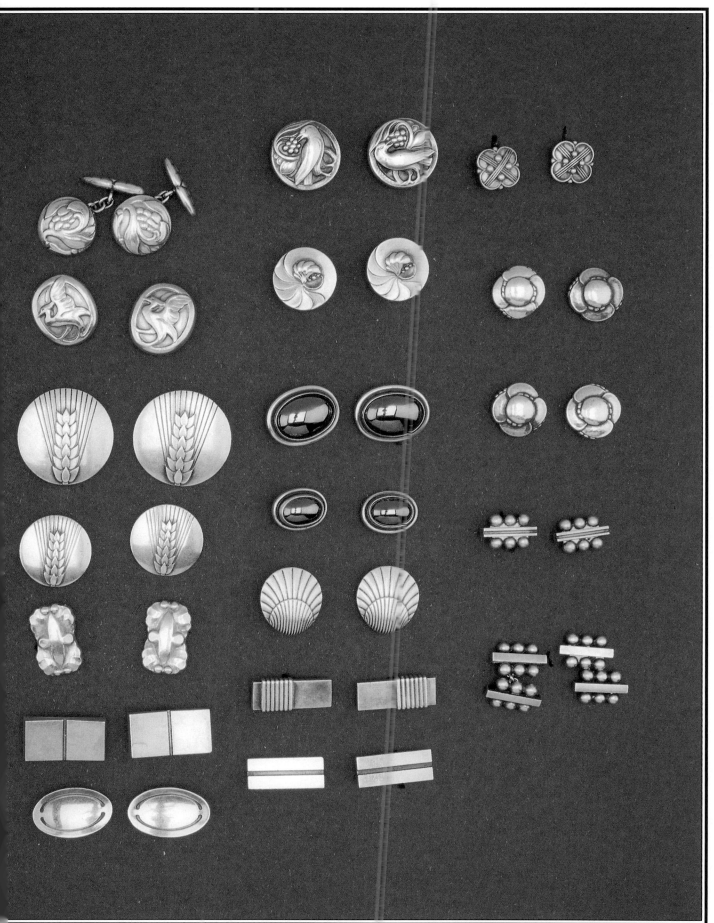

In 1907, Emil Hannover (1864-1923), the director of the Danish Museum of Decorative Arts, purchased two pieces of Jensen's jewelry for the museum's collection: a large silver brooch set with amber and decorated with a leaf motif, and a pendant decorated with silver grapes. Both pieces were pictured in the museum's annual report, bringing honor to Jensen as well as public attention. In Jensen's autobiographical essay in *Samlerer*, he relates a story with apparent pleasure about Emil Hannover attending a meeting of museum curators and showing off his shirt sleeves adorned with Jensen cuff links. As Hannover pre-

pared to tell of the wonderful silversmith he had discovered, all the other curators waved their shirt sleeves as well. It seems obvious now that Jensen's genius was recognized very quickly. As early as 1906, Hannover cited Jensen "the very master of the jeweller's art in this country." (Ivan Munk Olsen, *Sølvsmeden Georg Jensen*.) Jensen's growing success with silver jewelry buoyed his spirits and helped convince him that his decision to return to silversmithing—the trade in which he had received his first training—was a correct one.

Stylistic Influences

The myriad jewelry designs Jensen conceived and expertly fashioned at 36 Bredgade exhibit a mature, masterful style that is unmistakably Jensen's alone. His style did not simply burst forth, but was developed over many years. The first piece of jewelry we know about is the Adam and Eve belt clasp Jensen made in 1899. It seems to reflect his searching for a personal style in that it is quite unlike his later work: the design is rather stiff and unsophisticated, human figures are depicted, the subject matter is biblical, and the workmanship seems less finished.

As far as can be determined, Jensen recorded nothing in print about his stylistic influences. Nevertheless, it is possible to gather some inferences from his early work and his exposure to the work of other jewelry makers. It is highly likely that he took note of the work of English jeweler Charles R. Ashbee when Ashbee's work was exhibited at the Danish Museum of Decorative Art in 1899. Ashbee's jewelry, fashioned from oxidized silver and decorated with colored cabochon stones, made a major impression on Danish silversmiths. (Thage) A brooch by Ashbee and a brooch by Jensen, no. 154, exhibit some similarities in the wire scroll work, the oval cabochon, and the image of a naturalistic flower.

A brooch by C. R. Ashbee that was exhibited in Copenhagen in 1899.

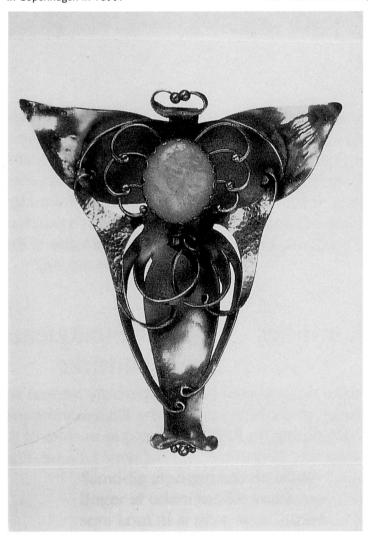

Brooch no. 46 with amber designed by Georg Jensen, marked 826S. Collection of Anne Shannon.

Brooch no. 154 designed by Georg Jensen which can be compared with Ashbee's piece that was exhibited in 1899 in Copenhagen.

Brooch no. 55 designed by Gudmund Hentze, 1910. Courtesy of Georg Jensen/Royal Copenhagen.

Pendant no. 80 and earrings with amber designed by Georg Jensen. Collection of the author.

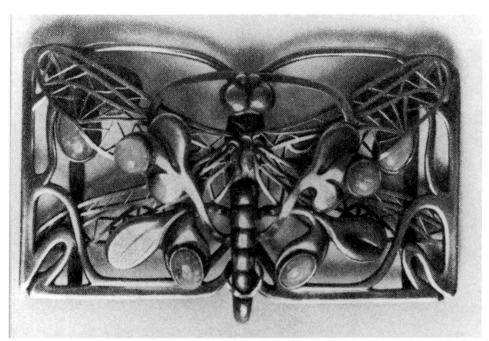

Dragonfly belt buckle set with opals designed by Georg Jensen, 1903.

Brooch no. 95 designed by Georg Jensen.

The work of the celebrated French jeweler René Lalique appears also to have inspired Jensen. The dragonfly silver belt clasp Jensen designed in 1903 that features a highly realistic dragonfly amid floriforms adorned with opals is evocative of Lalique's style, and of French Art Nouveau generally. Certainly, Laliques's work could not have escaped Jensen's attention since it was often featured in the leading decorative arts magazines of the day, and examples were purchased and exhibited by the Danish Museum of Decorative Arts. Moreover, when Jensen attended the epochal 1900 Paris World Exposition, it is highly likely that he took note of the supremacy of Lalique and other French jewelers.

Lalique's influence can also be seen in the work of the accomplished Danish jeweler Erik Magnussen (1884-1960) one of Jensen's contemporaries, especially in a brooch (Grasshopper on Mistletoe) done in 1907 depicting a realistic grasshopper clinging to a mistletoe branch in silver, amber and emeralds. Magnussen continued to use animal motifs in other pieces of jewelry, however Jensen's dragonfly belt clasp appears to be a transitional piece since, as far as is known, he produced no other pieces that so closely mirror Laliques's work.

One other piece of jewelry which is reminiscent of Lalique's work is the silver necklace no.15, which hung on a silk cord similar to Lalique's glass pendants.

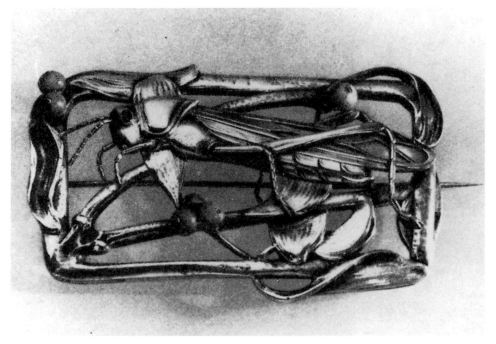

Dragonfly brooch designed by Erik Magnussen.
Dansk Kunsthaandvaerk, vol. 25, 1952.

Brooch designed by the sculptor Siegfried
Wagner.

In his comments on the the evolution of Jensen design, Graham Hughes wrote, "It is in
Denmark, in the Jensen factory, that pre-war and post-war designs merge. Jensen, Rohde
and Magnussen all used an art nouveau inspiration based on high-relief hand-chasing, on
craftsmanship, rather than on paperwork; and this conception continued into their neat
machine-embossed lotus and fish scales of the 1920s and 1930s." (Hughes)

Georg Jensen's early years of work as a journeyman in the workshop of Mogens Ballin in
1901 and 1902 were inspirational as well. Perhaps the flower forms and hammered surfaces
of Mogens Ballin and Sigfried Wagner left their impressions with Jensen. Although their
designs are not immediately apparent in Jensen's work, it is probable that the work of prominent Danish artist/designers with whom he is known to have associated also shaped his
thinking. In Jacob Thage's book *Danish Jewelry*, reference is made to Danish artists who
"regularly visited the workshop and were able to make their contributions." The artists mentioned are Bindesbøll, Joakim Skovgaard, Anton Rosen, N.V. Dorph, and Harald Slott-Møller,
some of the most accomplished artist/designers working in the skønvirke style.

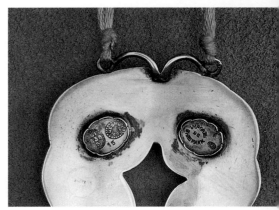

Pendant no. 15 designed by Georg Jensen and
hung on a silk cord in the style of René
Lalique, marked "Import de Denmark." Private
collection.

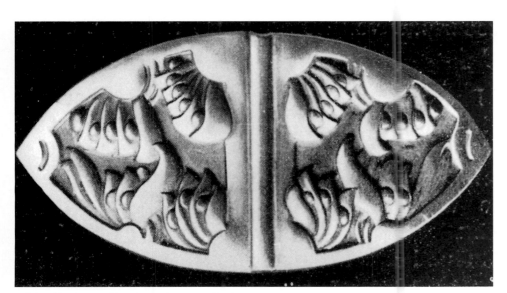

Belt buckle designed by the sculptor Siegfried Wagner.

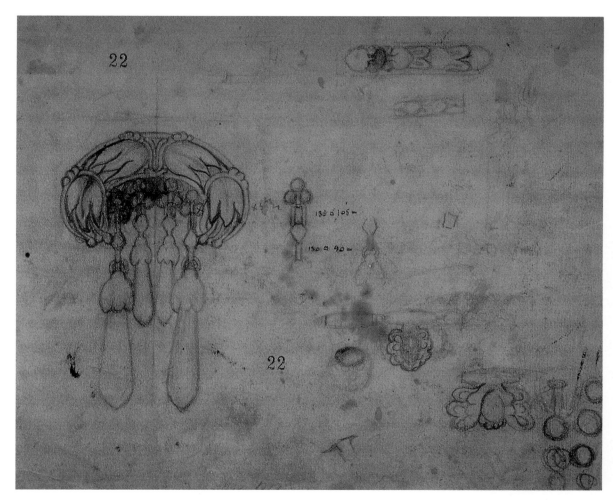

Drawing for brooch no. 22 by Georg Jensen. Courtesy of Georg Jensen/ Royal Copenhagen.

Brooch no. 22 with labradorite. Marked 830S and Copenhagen. Collection of Gail Roeshman Selig.

Reverse of brooch no.22.

Analyzing the mysteries of circumstances and artistic influences that lead to the formulation of an artist's own style is seldom easy, and Georg Jensen is a case in point. Apparently, preferring that his work speak for itself, he revealed only one artistic inspiration—Raadvad. In the article he wrote for *Samleren*, when he was 60 years old, he chose to emphasize the profound way Raadvad's natural landscape influenced him when he was a small boy, stayed with him throughout his life, and manifested itself in the multitude of naturalistic forms he employed in his jewelry, hollowware and flatware.

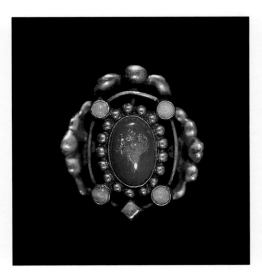

Stickpin no. 17 with large black opals surrounded by smaller opals designed by Georg Jensen. Collection of Anne Shannon.

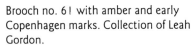

Brooch no. 148 with amber and malachite, marked GEORG JENSEN, COPENHAGEN and GI 830S. Collection of Leah Gordon.

Brooch no. 61 with amber and early Copenhagen marks. Collection of Leah Gordon.

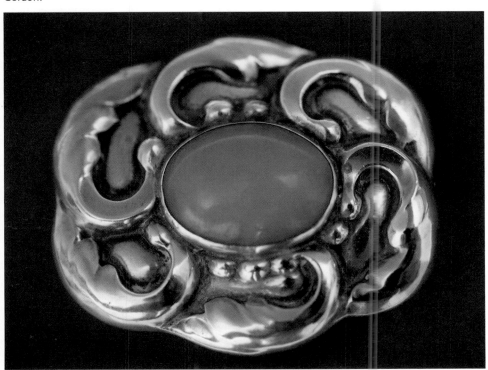

Belt buckle with opals designed by Georg
Jensen. Collection of Robert Fredieu and
Rosemary Schulze.

No. 1

No. 59

No. 71

Three lockets, no 1, no. 59, and no. 71.
Courtesy of Georg Jensen Museum
Copenhagen.

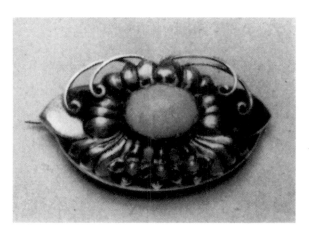

Brooch with opal designed by Georg Jensen, circa 1904.

Necklace no. 33 with three lapis teardrops and five cabochon lapis stones. Collection of Anne and David Bromer.

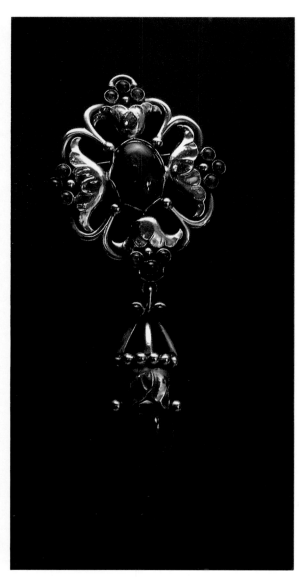

Brooch no. 40 with labradorite teardrop marked 830S Denmark. Collection of Linda Morgan.

Brooch no. 146 with sodalite, marked Gi in a beaded circle and 830S.

Pendant necklace no. 21 with coral, green agate and amber designed by Georg Jensen. Marked 830S and COPENHAGEN. Collection of Anne Shannon.

CHARACTERISTICS OF THE JENSEN STYLE

By 1904, Georg Jensen's artistic vision seems to have crystalized into a unique style. While it continued to evolve in subtle ways throughout the rest of his life, his style exhibited a number of characteristic features, most of which consistently appear in his jewelry. An especially prominent feature is the use of vines, leaves, flowers, buds, and berries. Jensen's interpretation of the vitality and motion of Art Nouveau is shown, not through the "whiplash" line favored by French artists, but through his own lyrical winding vines and leaves. One could find the sweeping vines that enclose Jensen's lush flowers analogous to the flowing hair of the sensuous ladies that appear in Laliques's jewelry. In regard to the use of the human body as subject matter, apart from the Adam and Eve buckle, Jensen did not use it, a preference shared by most English Arts and Crafts jewelers, but definitely not by most French jewelers. In fact, the female form did not impact on the design vocabulary of Danish jewelry. Jensen imbues the graceful lines and silhouettes of fruit-like forms with his sculptural technique and silversmith's loving care for detail.

Jensen's leaves, vines, flowers, seed pods, acorns, grape clusters and berries do not depict actual fruit or flora, yet his artistry is such that one is left with the impression that his precise, unexaggerated versions could well represent real plants. Jensen acknowledged the perfection of nature's creation and that supported his concept not to copy it, but to create his own ideas based on that inspiration; Jensen created his own world in silver. Jewelry historian Graham Hughes has noted: "If not for Georg Jensen, silversmiths today might still be making copies not creations." (*Modern Jewelry*.)

With respect to composition, Jensen's jewelry is characterized by a superb integration of all design elements—lines, shapes, proportion, color and texture—translated into Jensen's motifs and ornaments that result in a harmonious whole, a consumate whole. Each detail, whether it is the swell of a leaf or the small silver ball, is important to the perfect jewel. There is not a detail that could be added and there is nothing to be taken away to make each piece more perfect.

Pendant necklace no. 14 with labradorite and opals on paper clip chain, designed by Georg Jensen. Collection of Janet Morrison Clarke.

Pendant necklace no. 13 with labradorite, marked with oval Georg Jensen and 830. Collection of Janet Laws and Steve Mey.

Jensen's style is also characterized by the use of a large number of motifs, some that are interpretations of natural forms and others that appear to be decorative. The diversity of ways a motif is used and in a medley of combinations is another Jensen characteristic. For example, a small floral arrangement in rings no. I and IA is repeated in brooch no. 93. There are also a number of varieties of stone combinations used as well as a rendering all in silver. The five bead cluster, sometimes all in silver and at other times in colored stones, appears in different brooches. The cluster motif may escape recognition because it was transformed when integrated into different designs. For examples, the cluster motif appears in brooches no. 4, 59, 64, and 67, and in the belt buckle no. 2. One of the most well-recognized motifs in Jensen jewelry, generally referred to as "the Jensen bird," is found in many different forms of jewelry: brooches, bracelets, necklaces, and earrings.

Another distinguishing feature of Jensen's jewelry is its highly sculptural quality, attributable, of course, to Jensen's training as a sculptor. He was able to transform the silver from a hard substance into a soft, pliable-looking material that begs to be touched. Jensen's use of low relief, which is quite extraordinary for jewelry, provides depth that simultaneously imparts realism and attracts attention. The depth of the pieces, which often produces interesting life-like shadows, is accentuated by planned oxidization, especially in grooves and depressions, to creat a powerful chiaroscuro effect. Adding further to the unique quality of the jewelry is Jensen's treatment of the silver surface by hexagonal hammering which reflects light and conveys the silversmith's blows with a hammer. Also, the mellow patina looks soft; that cannot be achieved with a shiny silver surface. The color and texture of the silver are important features of his style.

Brooch no. 95 with labradorite teardrops designed by Georg Jensen. Collection of Wiener Interieur.

Belt buckle no. 2 with five clusters of five cabachon garnets, made in two sections. Marked with 830S and oval GI Denmark. Collection of Leah Gordon.

Brooch no. 105 with silver pearls.

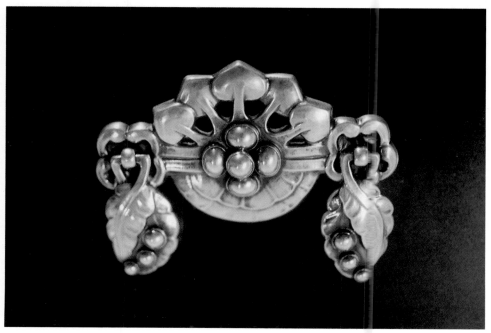

Brooch no. 9 designed by Georg Jensen. Collection of Robert Fredieu and Rosemary Schulze.

Brooch no. 67 with colored stones. Courtesy of
Georg Jensen/Royal Copenhagen.

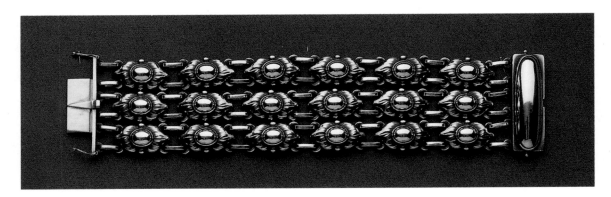

Clockwise from top, triple bracelet no. 15 with
silver pearls, brooch no. 125 with green agate,
and brooch no. 152 with silver pearls.
Courtesy of Georg Jensen Museum
Copenhagen.

From left, pendant no. 16 with silver pearl and pendant no. 42 with green agate.

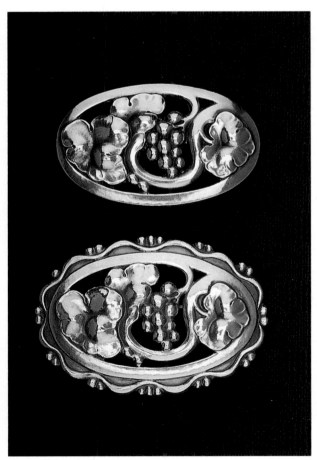

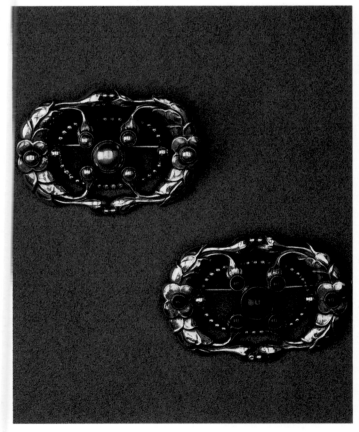

Brooch no. 177B without a border design and, below, brooch no. 177A with a border design. Collection of Dr. Barry Goozner.

Two brooches no. 76, top with sterling silver pearls, and, below, with carnelian.

Brooch no. 98 with labradorite and opal and earrings no. 23 with silver bead. Courtesy of Georg Jensen Museum Copenhagen.

Four bird brooches, no. 111, no.144, no. 136, and no. 165 with green agate and coral. Courtesy of Georg Jensen Museum Copenhagen.

Brooches, no. 12 with opal and no. 12 with coral, and belt buckle no. 15 with green agate. Courtesy of Georg Jensen Museum Copenhagen.

The Materials in Jensen Jewelry

Jensen chose his stones, some opaque and some transparent, to represent a varied and exciting palette of colors. Most frequently he used onyx, carnelian, labradorite, amber, opal, coral, and moonstone. Although these stones were not precious and costly, their mounting—a silver bezel, beading, and sometimes leaves that couched the stone—was done with superb craftsmanship. A ring may have delicate tracery of silver placed over the stone as filagree work. The combinations of stones clearly made vastly different appearances. Opal used together with moonstone continued the light effect achieved by the hammered surface. Synthetic sapphire was sometimes used together with moonstone and it emphasized the blue of the moonstone. From each variety of his palette emerged a distinctive and new image in the jewelry.

Cape clip no. 47 with labradorite designed by Georg Jensen.
Collection of the author.

Back of cape clip no. 47.

Gentlemen's watch fob with green agate designed by Georg Jensen.

Pendant with opals, turquoise and enamel designed by Georg Jensen, 1914. Courtesy of The National Swedish Art Museums, Stockholm.

Brooch no. 47.

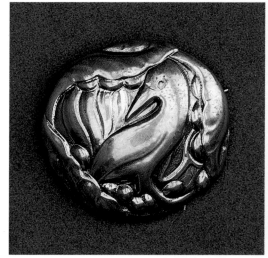

Brooch no. 95 with amber, pendant no. 39 with green agate, and pendant no. 2 with green agate. Courtesy of Georg Jensen Museum Copenhagen.

Necklace no. 1 with lapis designed by Georg Jensen.

Below, left to right, brooch no. 14 with gilt leaves and carnelian, and brooch no. 14 with malachite and matching earrings. Courtesy of Georg Jensen Museum Copenhagen.

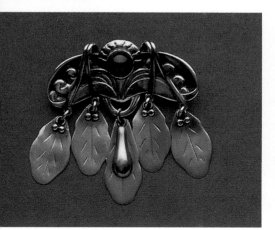

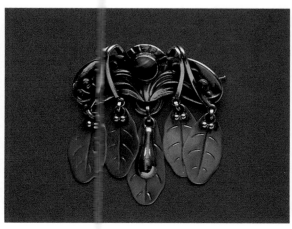

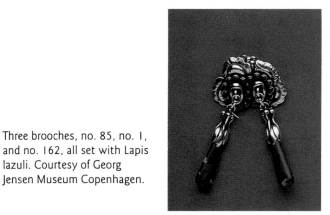

Three brooches, no. 85, no. 1, and no. 162, all set with Lapis lazuli. Courtesy of Georg Jensen Museum Copenhagen.

no. 85

no. 1

no. 162

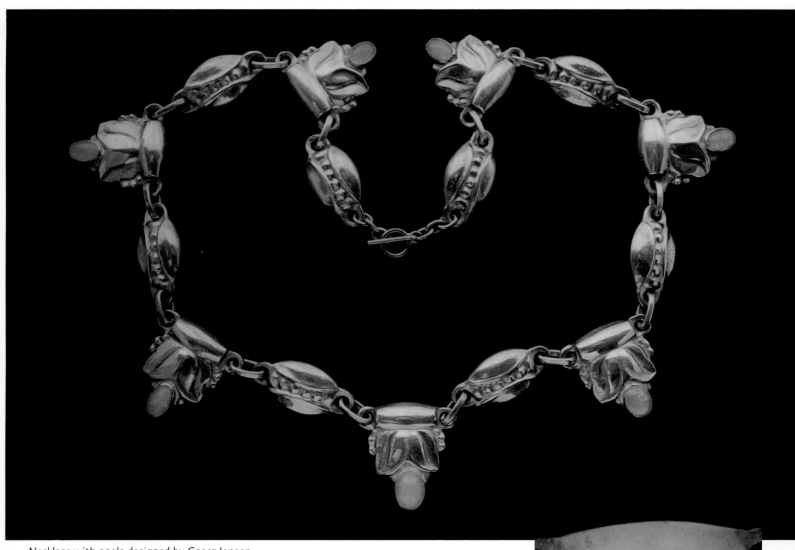

Necklace with opals designed by Georg Jensen. Collection of Lolo Hallstrom.

Back of necklace with opals.

Jensen used cabochon-cut stones for a smooth and rounded shape that intensifies their colors. He avoided competition with the textured surface of the silver by not choosing faceted stones. In addition to the various colored stones, he used silver beads, sometimes called "silver pearls," of round or oval shape and in different sizes, in combination with colored stones and by themselves. The "silver pearls" were set in the same manner as the colored cabochon stones: with a bezel, couched by leaves, or sometimes surrounded by simple and elegant beading. The variety of shapes and colored stones always were in perfect harmony.

Items of Jewelry

A wide array of jewelry was produced, including earrings, brooches, necklaces, pendants and rings that are common today and other items that are more scarce such as belt buckles, buttons, hair combs, hat pins, cape and dress clips, pocketbook frames, stick pins, and watch fobs. Of course, clothing worn by men and women in the beginning of the century was quite different than that which is worn today. Jensen responded to the needs of people of his day when he created clasps to close the necks of large capes and cloaks and one- or two-part buckles for belts worn with oversized jackets and with long, flowing skirts. The elaborately decorated tortoise shell and silver combs were used by women to keep their long hair piled high atop their heads. Jensen also made special pieces of jewelry for custom orders, such as a ring designed in 1906 by painter/sculptor J.F. Willumsen (1863-1958) for the poet Holger Drachmann's 60th birthday.

Drachmann's ring designed by the poet J.F. Willumsen and executed by Georg Jensen. Georg Jensen Sølvsmedie, Gennem Fyrretyve Arr, 1904-1944.

Selection of fifteen pairs of earrings.

Tortoise shell hair comb designed by Georg Jensen.

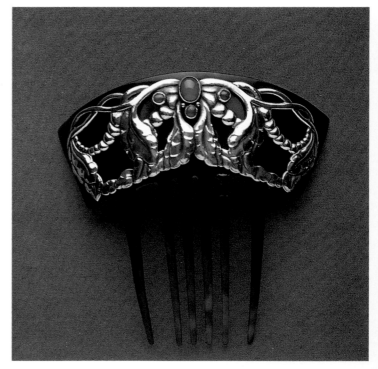

Tortoise shell hair comb no. 5 with amber and green agate. Courtesy of Georg Jensen Museum Copenhagen.

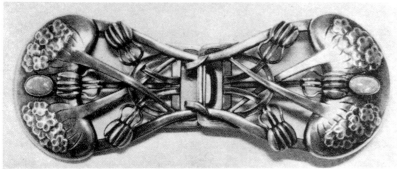

Belt buckle with opals designed by Georg Jensen in 1904. Georg Jensen Sølvsmedie, Gennem Fyrretyve Arr, 1904-1944.

Brooch no. 5 with green onyx and amber designed by Georg Jensen, circa 1905-1910. Georg Jensen Sølvsmedie, Gennem Fyrretyve Arr, 1904-1944.

Tortoise shell hair barrette no. 20, brooch no. 122, and belt buckle no. 6. Courtesy of Georg Jensen Museum Copenhagen.

Descriptions of Selected Items

Given the tremendous number and variety of Jensen's jewelry designs, it would be impractical to describe them all. However, select pieces will be described here to illustrate the characteristics of Jensen's style.

Jensen's early brooches tend to be large and their designs reminescent of the girandole style with an ovoid form accompanied by a single or multiple drops. Examples of such pieces are pendants no. 13 and 96, both designed prior to 1915.

Brooch no. 259 with silver balls designed by Georg Jensen. Measuring 2 inches in height and 3 inches in width, this brooch is larger than most and has two bar pin closures to bear the weight.

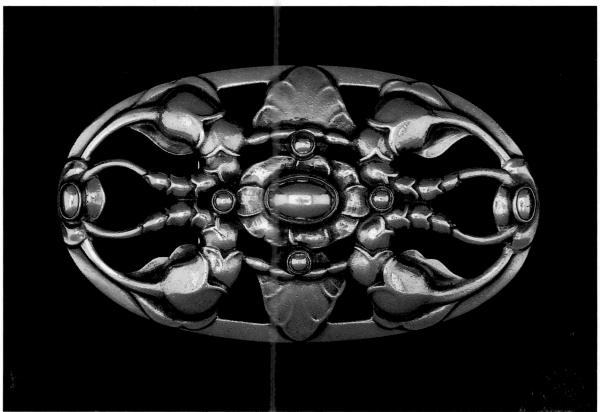

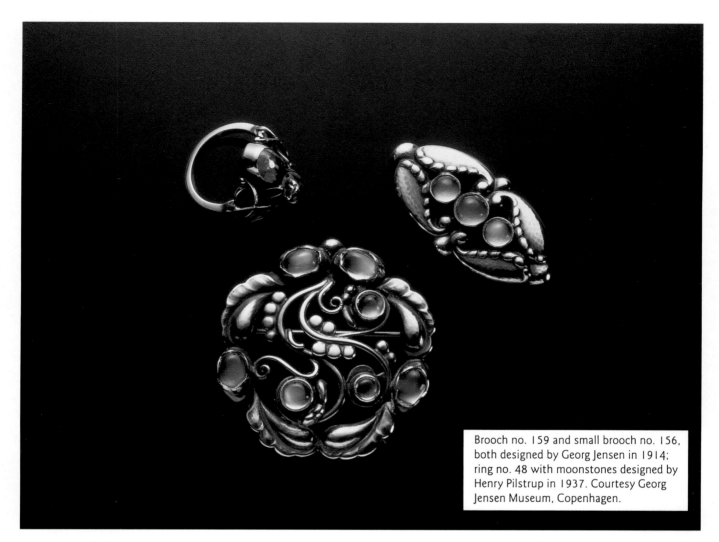

Brooch no. 159 and small brooch no. 156, both designed by Georg Jensen in 1914; ring no. 48 with moonstones designed by Henry Pilstrup in 1937. Courtesy Georg Jensen Museum, Copenhagen.

Brooch no. 159 designed by Georg Jensen in 1914.

Brooch no. 162 with moonstones and green agate teardrops designed by Georg Jensen, marked GI and 830. Collection of Anne Shannon.

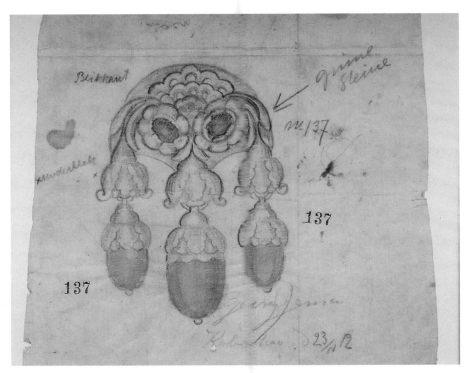

Drawing for brooch no. 137 by Georg Jensen.
Courtesy of Georg Jensen/Royal Copenhagen.

Brooch no. 14 marked 826S. Collection of
Yvette Scobie.

Brooch no. 74 with three amber teardrops.
Collection of Linda Morgan.

A remarkable number of Jensen's jewelry designs have remained popular through the years since they were introduced and some are in production today Examples are brooches no. l0, 20, and l59 which are perennial favorites designed by Georg Jensen during the first fifteen years of his workshop. Brooches no. l0 and 20 have earrings that match. Brooch no. l59 is replete with leaves, flowers, buds and vines. Although the composition does not resemble real flora it is Jensen's interpretation of flora with a certain playfulness. Brooch l59 exhibits energy produced by the careful integration of elements in a variety of shapes artfully placed. Not to be overlooked is his careful attention to the couching of each stone with silver scallops that pretend to hold the bud in place. The totality of the composition creates a miniature work of art.

Small details that would escape the attention of a novice, such as surface patina and clasp design, are important criteria in evaluating the quality of each piece. Knowledge about the origin and history of a particular design are also important. For example, bracelet no. 3 was designed as early as l905 by Georg Jensen, and it is available from the company today. Many pieces of jewelry could be ordered originally in all-silver or with different decorative stones.

Brooch no. l2 with green agate and necklace no. 2, both designed by Georg Jensen. Collection of Barbara and Steve Herman.

Brooch no.l57 and bracelet no. 25B, both with carnelian. Collection of Robert Fredieu and Rosemary Schulze.

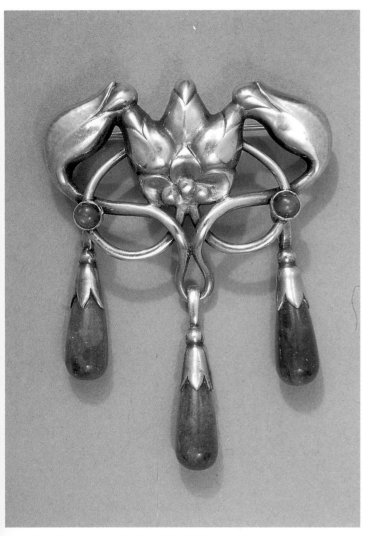

Brooch no. 151 with three labradorite teardrops, marked GI and 830S. Collection of Janet Laws and Steve Mey.

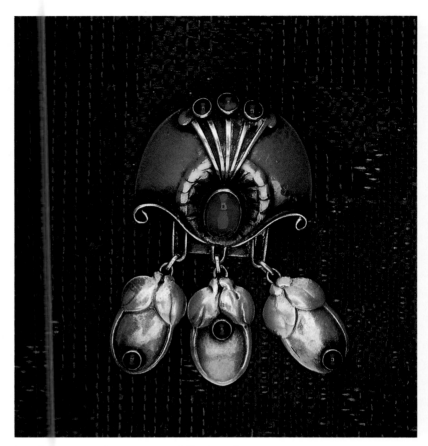

Brooch no. 153 with green onyx. Collection of Ed and Lisa Guari.

Brooch no. 160 with synthetic sapphire surrounded by moonstones, and bracelet no. 19 with synthetic sapphires. Collection of JoAnn Schrier.

Brooch number 132 is less common and is no longer in production. Its upper half consists of a girondole form and the lower half consists of three slender, free-swinging drops made of hematit or lapis topped with silver bell-shaped caps that resemble a motif in Wiener Werkstätte graphics. There is a hint of the Jugendstil style in the overall design as well.

Brooch no. 96, designed in 1905, is referred to as a "master brooch." It is illustrated in two variations: with labradorite and in a combination of amber and chrysoprase. The designation "master brooch" is made because it is larger than most other brooches and probably took more time to complete. The image of ripe fruit, robust acorns of amber or labradorite are capped with silver and hang from a symmetrical cluster of color-studded leaves and vines with another acorn at the bottom. The impact of the naturalistic interpretation remains strong in both of the choices of stones. Close examination reveals that each hand-made piece differs: the size of a leaf that embraces one of the stones is varied, and one has a tiny silver ball which is absent on the other. The markings on their backs indicate these were made at different times.

Brooch no. 132 with hematite.

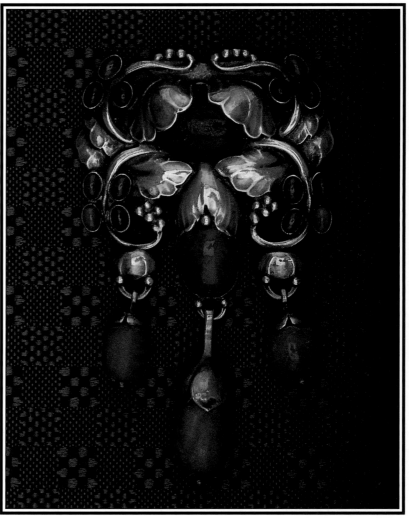

Master brooch no. 96 with amber teardrops and green agate, designed by Georg Jensen, circa 1905. Collection of the author.

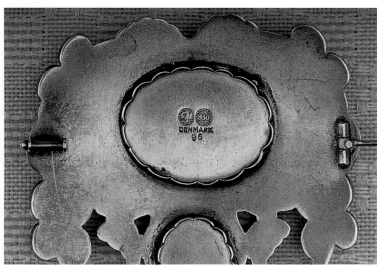

Back of master brooch no. 96 with plunger clasp, marked 830 alongside Ci in a beaded oval.

Master brooch no. 96 with labradorite designed by Georg Jensen. Collection of the author.

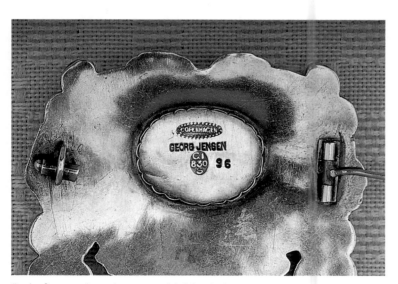

Back of master brooch no. 96 with labradorite marked 830S, COPENHAGEN and GEORG JENSEN.

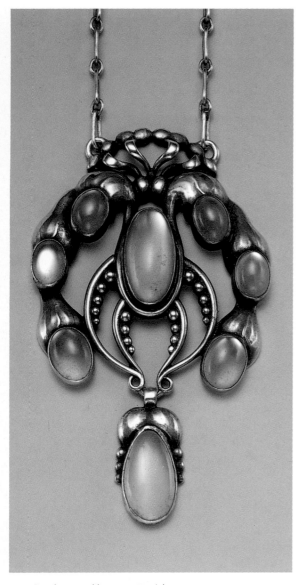

Pendant necklace no. 7 with moonstones. Marked 826S, Georg Jensen and COPENHAGEN with Gi and GJ superimposed.

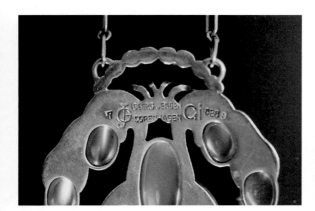

Back of pendant necklace no. 7.

From left, bar pins no. 221, no. 288 and no. 248. Collections of Ed & Lisa Guari and Dr. Barry Goozner.

Bar brooch no. 112 has sweeping lines that spring from a center oval. The lines would appear limitless if it were not for the lovely, small clusters that act as a terminus. The piece has carefully defined layers and scallops surrounding the stone which are repeated in an outer ring that adds a sense of depth. The many layers and small details coalesce to create a grand, flowing gesture.

Pendant necklace no. 7 is mounted with a large oval moonstone surrounded by smaller, cascading stones that appear to be dripping from the silver caps around each stone. The linear design of the silver reveals a slight Jugendstil tone. The last teardrop is topped with leaves that enclose the shape perfectly. In this necklace, Jensen achieved a ripple effect in the silver which is effective as the light reflects from the varied surfaces of silver and blue-grey moonstones. The chain is of paper-clip style, or tracery pattern, and the closure is a "t-bar," which was commonly used in Jensen's work.

Brooch no. 160, cabochon labradorite encircled by cabochon moonstones, marked Gi and 925. Collection of Janet Laws and Steve Mey.

From top, bar pin no. 99 with silver pearls and bar pin no. 112 with green onyx. Private collection.

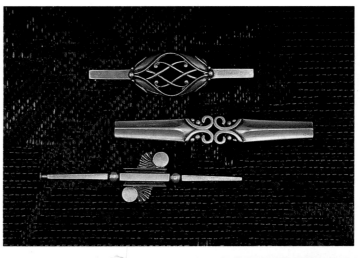

THE "PARIS MODELS"

Only one "Paris necklace and bracelet" probably was made of this design, in Paris, in 1925, for a special customer. There is no production number, only Jensen and Paris markings appear. The silver on each oval labradorite is finished in the same way on the back and the front. The connecting link which holds the two labradorites together is sculptured with applied silver scrollwork, not unlike silver overlay on glass decanters. The silver streaks in the labradorite appear to move as the light glances the surface. The labradorites are graduated in size, as a string of pearls, and the amount of silver overlay on each is adjusted to correspond with the size of each stone. When the catch closure is secured, the repeated pattern is complete. The stones are gently shaped so that the necklace rests comfortably on the wearer's neck.

Bracelet no. 30 is also considered a "Paris model," according to Museum curator Michael von Essen, since it was designed during Jensen's stay in Paris in 1925-26.

Necklace and bracelet with labradorite, designed by Georg Jensen with Paris touchmarks. Private Collection.

Bracelet no. 30 with amber, designed by Georg Jensen. This bracelet was designed by Jensen while he was in Paris from 1925-26 and is called "a Paris design."

Necklace no. 2 with labradorite designed by
Georg Jensen.

Back of necklace no. 2.

Gold brooch designed by Johan Rohde, 1913.
Georg Jensen Sølvsmedie, Gennem Fyrretyve
Arr, 1904-1944.

DESIGNERS IN JEWELRY

Johan Rohde is well known for his designs of flatware and hollowware; the few designs he made for jewelry are in current production: cufflinks no. 60B and tiebar 77. Both are simple in design and classical in style.

Henry Pilstrup created necklace no. 4 in Georg Jensen's workshop in 1909. It was exhibited at and bought by the Art and Industry Museum in Copenhagen. Pilstrup was honored with a grant for the most beautiful piece in the exhibit. While Pilstrup was foreman of the jewelry workshop in 1937, he designed cufflinks no. 64 and shirt studs to accompany them. They were produced in gold and silver and remain in production.

Barrel link necklace and bracelet no. 40 also were designed by Pilstrup and remain in production. An early version of this necklace with corals is illustrated.

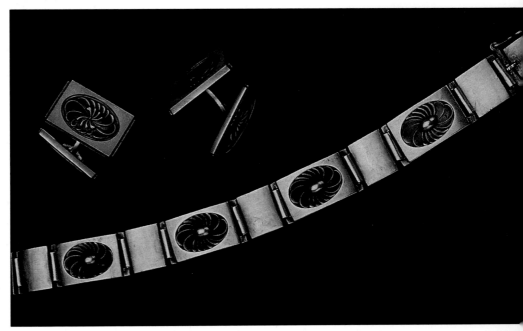

Bracelet no. 56 and cuff links no. 59A designed
by Henry Pilstrup. Collection of Ed & Lisa
Guari.

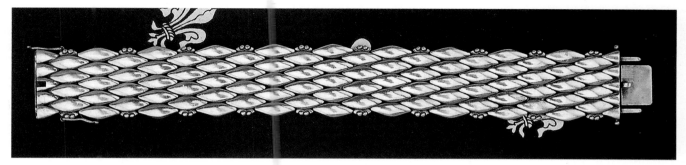

Bracelet no. 86 designed by Harald Nielsen, 1945.

Earring no. 40 designed by Harald Nielsen.

Group of three charms: from left, elephant charm no. 3, bird in a heart charm no. 17, and frog charm no. 5, all designed by Harald Nielsen.

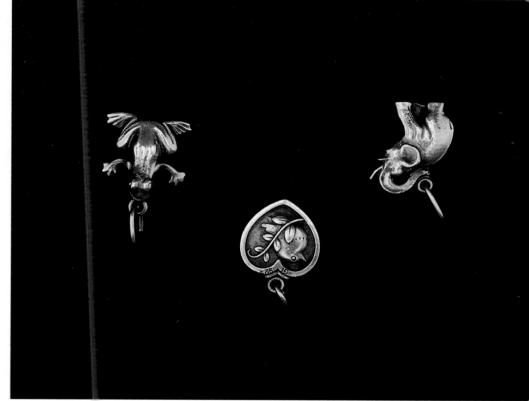

Grape Brooch no. 217B designed by Harald Nielsen.

Harald Nielsen designed numerous jewelry pieces, and many continue in production. The no. 96 leaf and bud necklace and bracelet are as wearable today as when Nielsen designed them. His very familiar no. 55 bangle bracelet or armring are Nordic inspired designs. The most well recognized of Nielsen's designs is the grape brooch no. 217B. In combination with the no. 96 leaf necklace, the grape brooch no. 217B worn as a percant is luxurious. During the 1920s, the designs of Harald Nielsen made a transition in style from the naturalistic organic forms of Georg Jensen to a more streamlined image.

Brooch no. 274 designed by Gundorph Albertus.

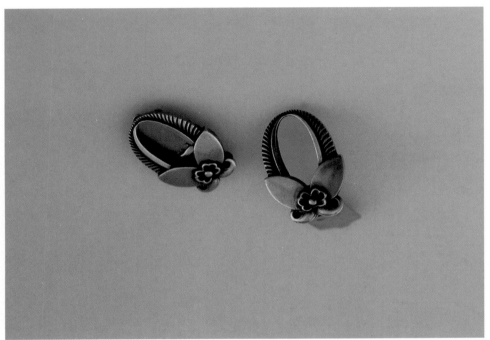

A pair of dress clips no. 227 designed by Gundorph Albertus.

Brooch no. 296 designed by Vilhelm Albertus, circa 1942. Courtesy of Georg Jensen/Royal Copenhagen A/S.

Then, Sigvard Bernadotte, in 1930, introduced the moderne, clean, sophisticated lines that would greatly influence a new direction in style for the Jensen firm. Bernadotte's signature style was linear, unadorned, clean and precise, more industrial in look and a clear departure from the images created by Georg Jensen. Functionalism is often used to describe the mathematical, geometric character of Bernadotte's forms. The clarity of Bernadotte's design is evident in cuff links no. 67, produced in both silver and gold, which are in demand today. Brooch no. 30I, a simple wreath-like design, is also in production.

Gundorph Albertus was trained as a sculptor in the Royal Academy of Art. He joined Georg Jensen in 1911. His grasp of the potential in the malleability of silver contributed to sustaining the continued high quality of production at the smithy. His designs for flatware were adapted to a number of jewelry items, i.e. bracelet no. 94B, earring no. 113, earring no. 110, and brooch no. 227.

Bracelet no. 73 designed by Sigvard Bernadotte.

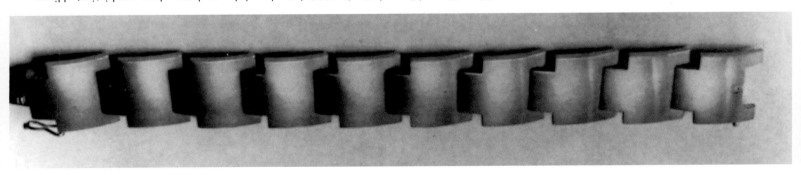

Iron and sterling brooch and cuff links
designed by Arno Malinowski.

Group of iron and silver (Jern/Sølv) objects
designed by Arno Malinowski, circa 1933.
Georg Jensen Sølvsmedie, Gennem Fyrretyve
Arr, 1904-1944.

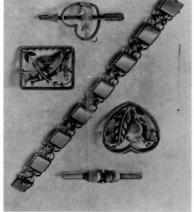

Collection of Arno Malinowski
designs, 1943. Georg Jensen
Sølvsmedie, Gennem Fyrretyve Arr,
1904-1944.

Heart and bird bar pin designed by
Arno Malinowski, circa 1942. Georg
Jensen Sølvsmedie, Gennem Fyrretyve
Arr, 1904-1944.

The "Jorn/Sølv" (Iron and Silver) line of jewelry and objects was devised for the Jensen company by designer Arno Malinowski. This combination of materials, a departure from the traditional materials used in making jewelry, was inspired by the Japanese method of mixing metals. These pieces of jewelry, done for a brief period, are rare. Examples of dresser items made in this style are illustrated in the hollowware section, chapter seven.

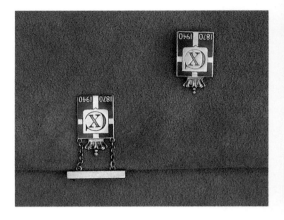

Enamel brooch and tie bar commemorating the 70th birthday of King Christian X, designed in 1940 by Arno Malinowski.

Brooch no. 256 with green enamel designed by Arno Malinowski

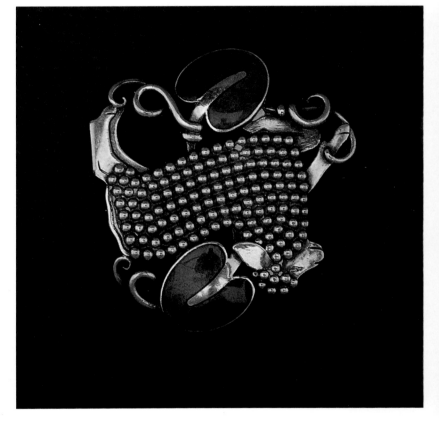

Malinowski became well known for his design of the royal emblem Kongemaeket, which was designed for His Majesty King Christian the X, King of Denmark, and issued by the Georg Jensen firm to celebrate the king's 70th birthday on September 26, 1940. This commemorative design was made into various pieces, such as brooches, cuff links, letter openers, and matchbox holders. On the occasion of His Majesty Christian X's 75th birthday, in 1945, the design was reissued and the year was changed to read 1945.

The Jensen firm sold 1.3 million pieces of this commemorative jewelry. For a small country of five million people, this number is extraordinary. In those days, it was a common sight to walk the streets in Denmark and see many people wearing the Christian X pin. The wearing of the emblem was a symbolic gesture of resistance to the German occupation, as well as a sign of respect and affection for the king.

In addition to this particular design, Malinowski designed other brooches such as a kneeling deer no. 318, two butterflies no. 283, and a dolphin no. 251. These very popular brooches appear to be theme oriented, and are in current production.

Iron and steel jewelry designed by Arno Malinowski, 1942. Courtesy of Georg Jensen, Copenhagen.

Necklace no. 110 designed by Arno Malinowski.

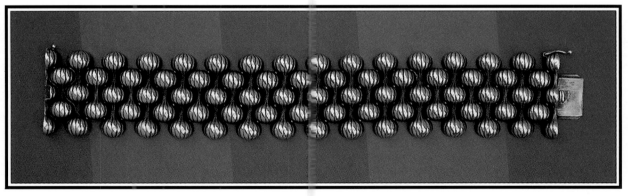

Bracelet no. 110B designed by Arno Malinowski.

The sculptural jewelry of Henning Koppel was at once startling and beautiful. His abstract forms like the work of artist Jean Arp reflected a sculptor's hand rather than a jeweler's. Koppel, like Jensen, treated the silver surface with concern for how it would interact with light. The rounded edges of the free-form jewelry, with spaces instead of jewels, was the best of modern design of its time. Koppel used enamels in place of jewels. His designs almost reach out for the hand to hold and stroke.

Nana Ditzel's forms in both silver and gold are almost streamlined, clean, and undecorated. Bracelet no. 111, designed in 1955, is a simple sculptural bangle of spatial geometric design which was inspired by an Iron Age ornament. Nanna Ditzel continued to work for the Jensen firm after her husband's death in 1961.

Vivianna Torun Bülow-Hübe began work with the Georg Jensen Silversmithy in 1967 and created jewelry using sculptural, simple spiral forms. She is well known for necklaces that wind around the neck and body and use rock crystals and rutilated quartz as jewels. Bülow-Hübe noted that jewelry must marry with the contours of a woman's body, and many of her award-winning designs conjure images of the beach. Bülow-Hübe, the designer who in 1962 was called "the girl who makes silver sensuous," continues creating designs for the Georg Jensen firm.

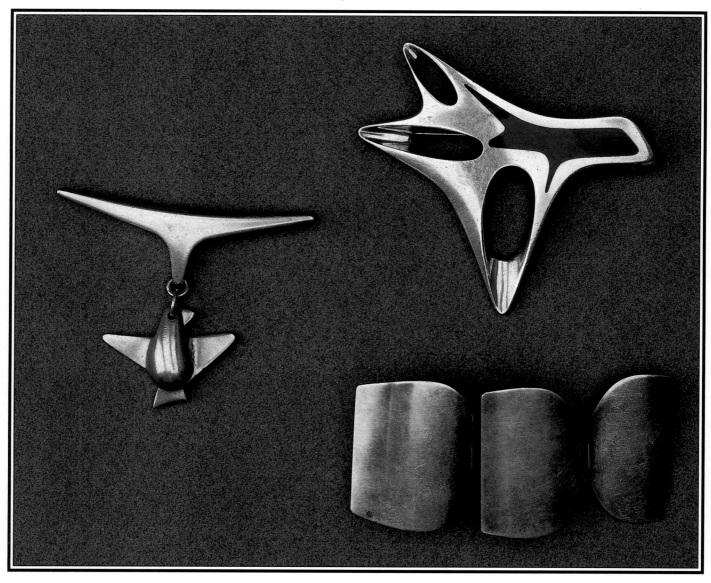

Three brooches designed by Henning Koppel:
left, brooch no. 334; upper right, brooch no.
323 with enamel; lower right, brooch no.
338A.

Brooch no. 370 with blue enamel designed by Henning Koppel.

Bracelet no. 130B with green agate designed by Henning Koppel.

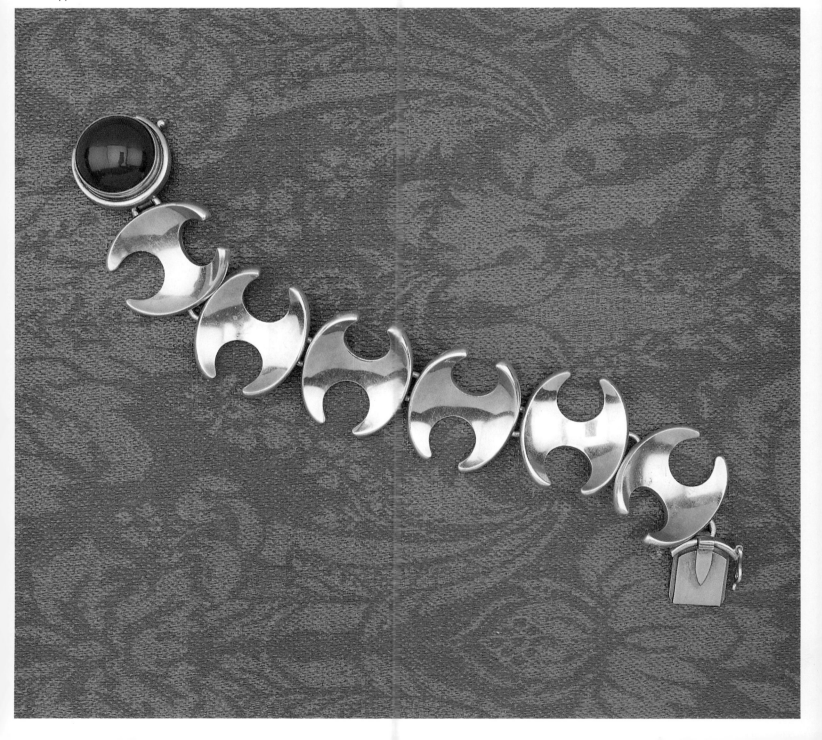

Sterling silver brooch no. 343 designed by Henning Koppel. Courtesy of Skinner's Inc., Boston and Bolton.

From left to right, bracelet no. 121, corkscrew no. 135, and ring no. 91 designed by Nanna Ditzel. Courtesy of Georg Jensen/Royal Copenhagen .

Bracelet and earrings designed by Nanna Ditzel. Courtesy of Georg Jensen/Royal Copenhagen.

Bracelet no. 111 in silver and no. 1111 in gold designed by Nanna Ditzel, 1956. Courtesy of Georg Jensen/Royal Copenhagen.

Bracelet no. 203B with rock crystal designed by Torun Bülow-Hübe.

From top to bottom: two watches designed by
Torun Bülow-Hübe, ring designed by Nanna
Ditzel, bracelet designed by Erik Herlow, and
necklace pendant designed by Bent Gabrielsen.
Courtesy of Tadema Gallery, London.

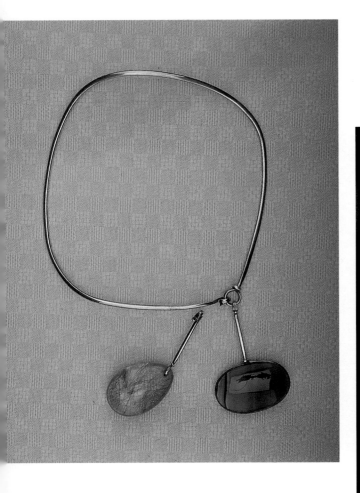

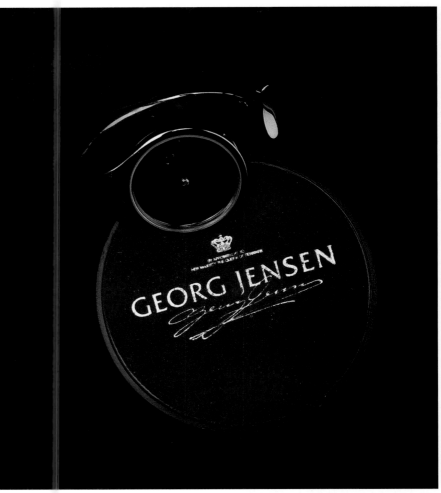

Neckring no. 173 with two pendant drops, rutilated quartz no. 131 and agate no. 129, designed by Torun Bülow-Hübe; below shown in original Georg Jensen box.

Watch no. 326 designed by Torun Bülow-Hübe.

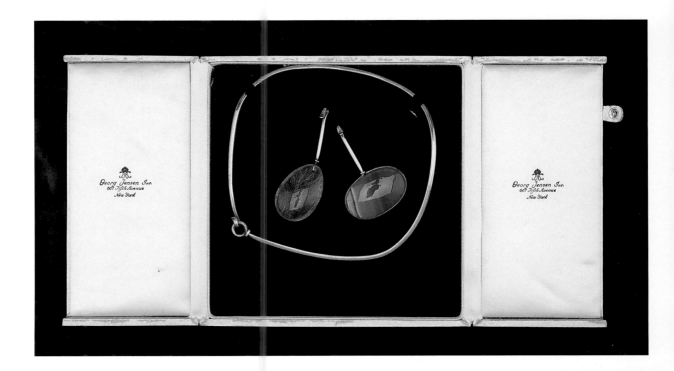

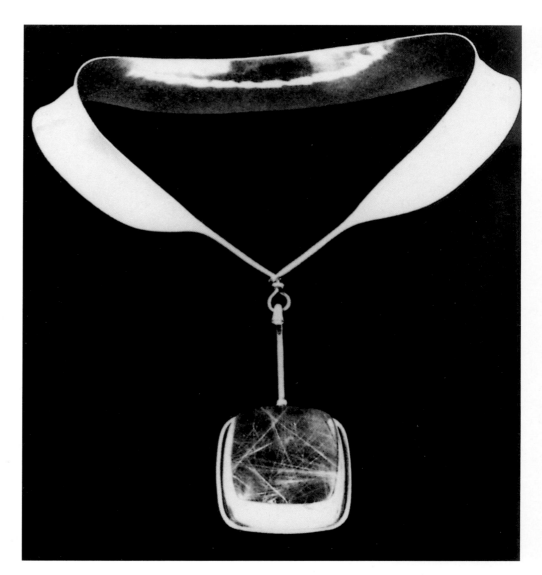

Silver neckring with removable rutilated quartz pendant designed by Torun Bülow-Hübe. Courtesy of Georg Jensens Royal Copenhagen.

Brooch no. 373 with moonstone designed by Torun Bülow-Hübe.

Jensen Jewelry Designs

Bird bracelet no. 24, bird brooch no. 70, and bird earrings no. 66 with labradorite. Collection of Robert and Barbara Paul.

Necklace and bracelet no. 108.

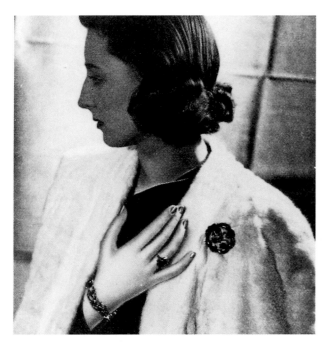

Jensen advertisement for jewelry, circa 1940.
Courtesy of Georg Jensen, Copenhagen.

Jensen advertisement for women's jewelry, circa 1940. Georg Jensen
Solvsmedie, Gennem Fyrretyve Arr, 1904-1944.

Pendant with green agate on a paper clip chain
and bracelet no. 53 with green agate. Collection of Kitty and Martin Jacobs.

Brooch no. 30 with moon-
stones and pendant no. 5
with opal. Courtesy of Georg
Jensen Museum Copenhagen.

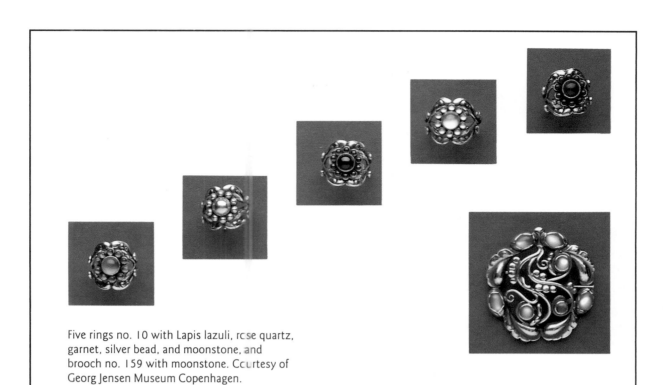

Five rings no. 10 with Lapis lazuli, rose quartz, garnet, silver bead, and moonstone, and brooch no. 159 with moonstone. Courtesy of Georg Jensen Museum Copenhagen.

Bracelet no. 9 with green agate and brooch no. 189 with coral. Collection of Robert and Barbara Paul.

Necklace no. 29B with silver oval graduated links spaced with coral beads, marked Gi and KOPENHAGEN. Also from left, tulip pin no. 100A, tulip pin no. 100A with coral, and bar pin no. 103 with two corals marked 828 and script GJ. Collection of the author.

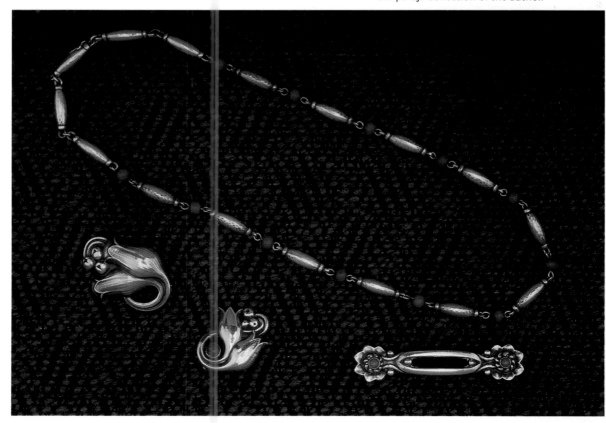

Barrettes

Hair barrette. Collection of Debra and David
Rosensaft.

Bracelets

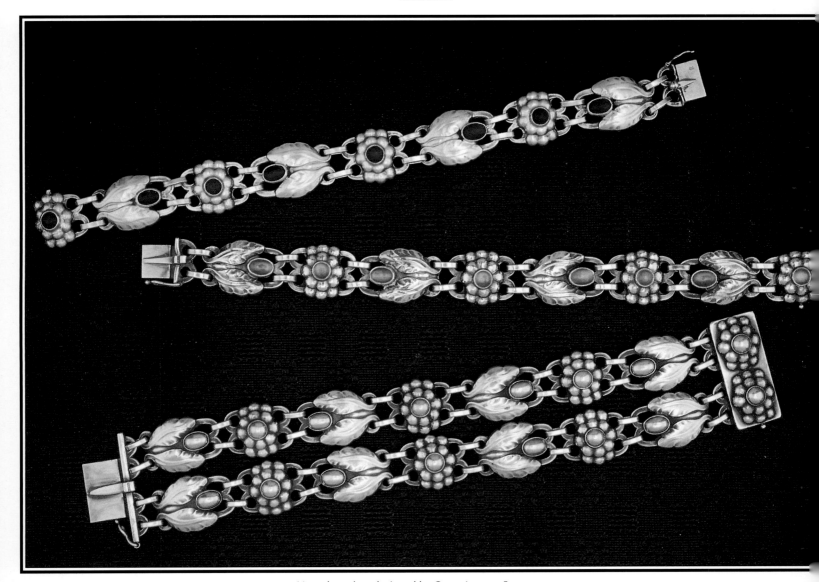

No. 3 bracelets designed by Georg Jensen. From
top, bracelet no. 3 with lapis, bracelet no. 3
with moonstones and double bracelet no. 3
with silver pearls.

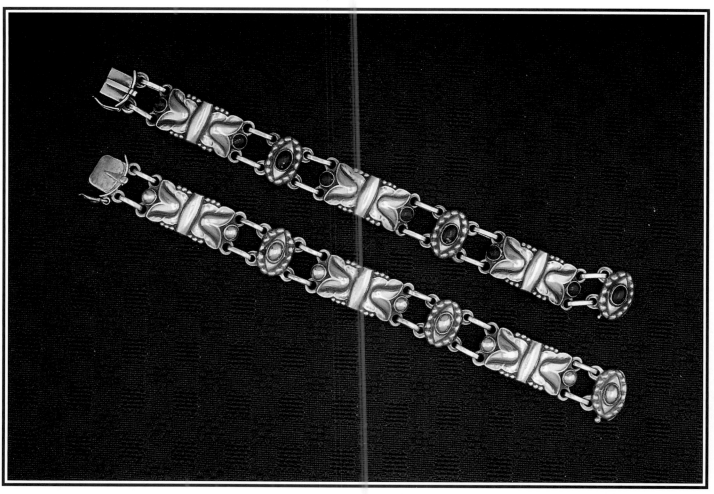

Above: Two bracelets no. 7, one with lapis and the other with silver pearls.

Below: Two bracelets no. 4 designed by Georg Jensen, one with moonstones and one with lapis.

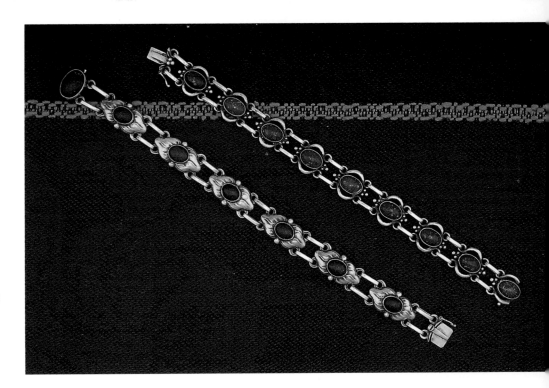

From top, bracelet no. 10 with lapis and bracelet no. 15 with lapis. Collection Janet Morrison Clarke.

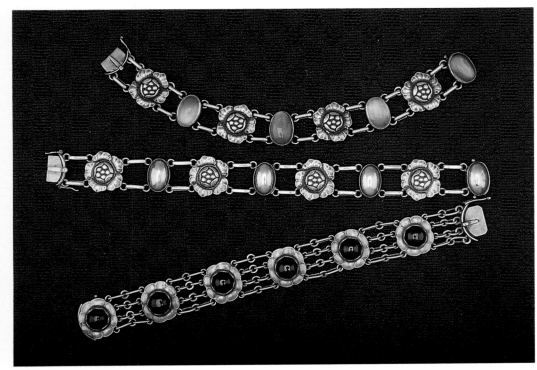

From bottom, bracelet no. 3l with cabochon garnets, bracelet no. 12 with silver pearls, and bracelet no. 12 with moonstones.

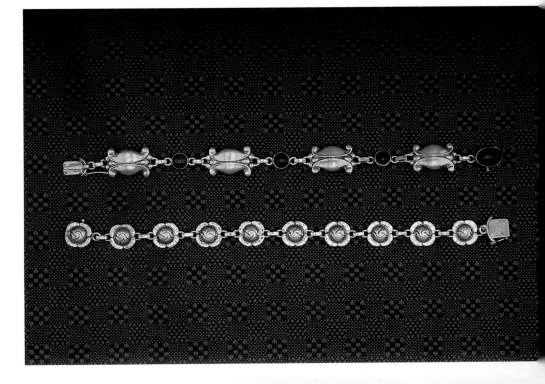

From top, bracelet no. 15 with green agate and bracelet no. 44, both designed by Georg Jensen.

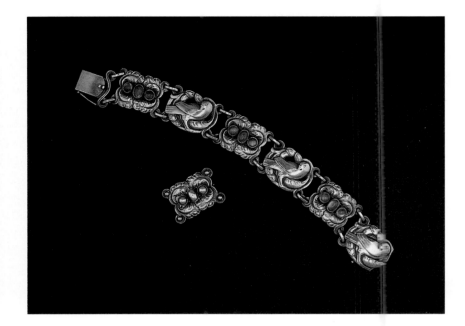

Bracelet no. 14 with moonstones and brooch no. 15 with silver pearls, both designed by Georg Jensen. Private collection.

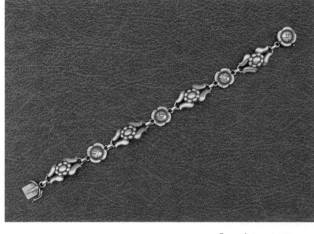

Bracelet no. 18.

Link bracelet no. 22. Collection of Kitty & Martin Jacobs.

Two no. 29 bracelets. From top, one with green amazonite and one with synthetic sapphires and moonstones.

Bracelet no. 32 with bird motif.

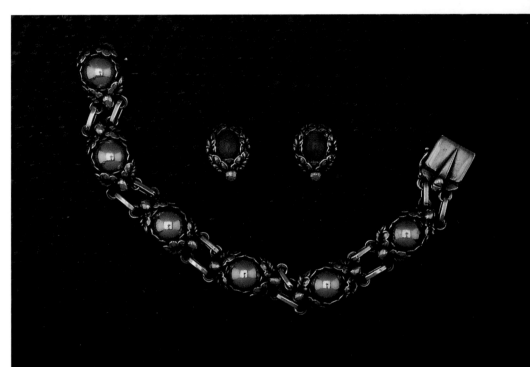

Bracelet no. 57 and coordinating earrings no. 34A with coral.

Bracelet no. 61 designed by Georg Jensen.

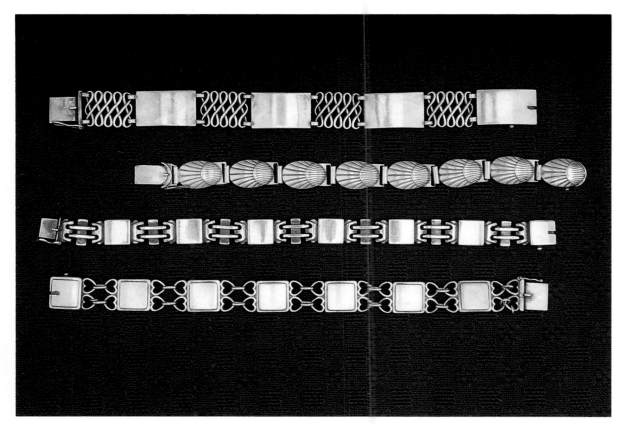

From top, bracelet no. 62, bracelet no. 77,
bracelet no. 48, and
Bracelet no. 70.

Bracelet no. 63 with green agate. Collection of
Janet Morrison Clarke.

Bracelet no. 63A with lapis. Collection of
JoAnn Schrier.

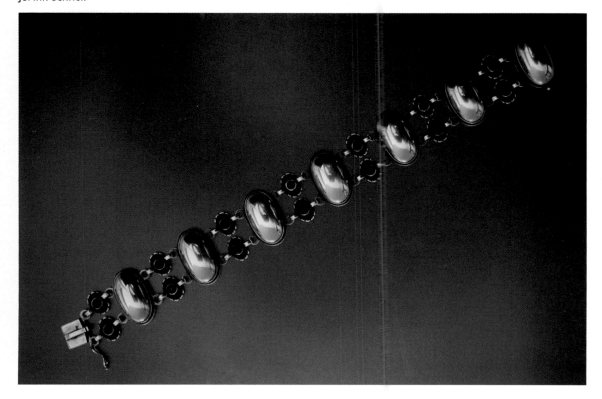

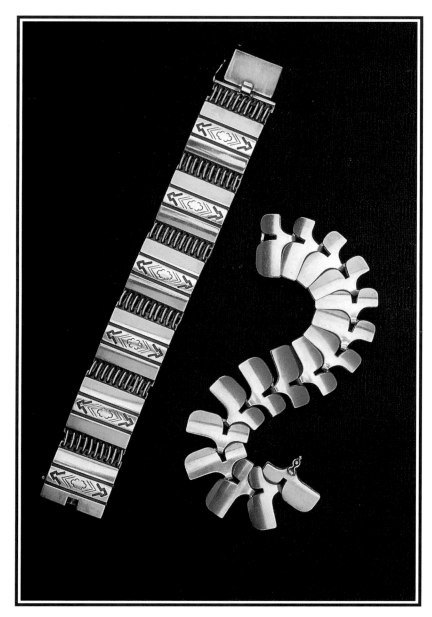

From left, bracelet no. 65B marked GJ script, and bracelet no. 149B designed by Ibe Dalquist.

Bracelet no. 83. Private collection.

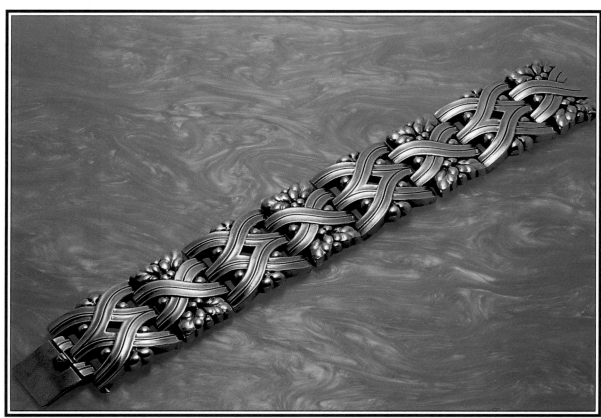

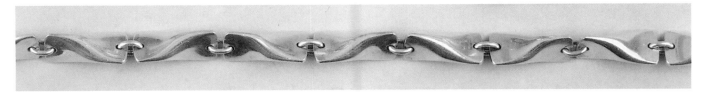

Sterling silver link bracelet no. 104B. Courtesy of Skinner's Inc., Boston and Bolton.

Sterling bracelet no. 105 and gold bracelet no. 1105. Collection of Debra and David Rosensaft.

Reverse of bracelets no. 105 and no.1105.

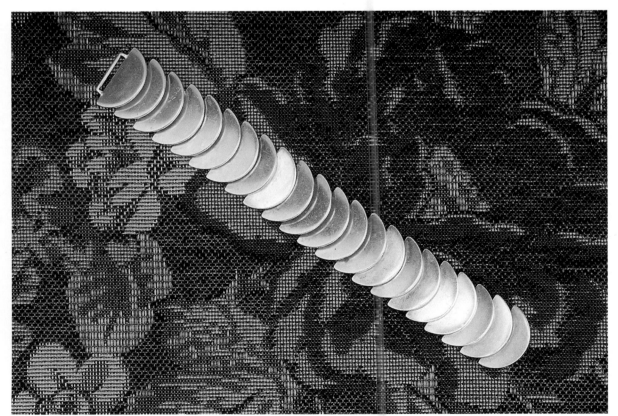

Bracelet no. 169 designed by Astrid Fog.

Bangle bracelet no. 117 with assorted charms and anniversary pendants. Private Collection.

Bracelet with assorted charms, each piece with the company mark.

Arm ring no. 235 designed by Astrid Fog, 1971. Courtesy of Georg Jensen/Royal Copenhagen.

Bracelet no. 307. Collection of Ed and Lisa Guari.

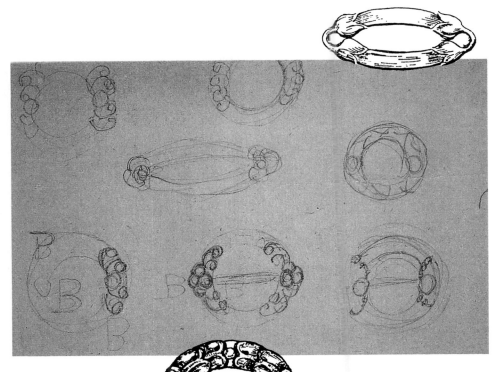

Brooches

A small drawing of design ideas on a scrap of paper. Second row, first drawing looks like the inspiration for brooch no. 141 (above). Bottom row of drawings could be the inspiration for brooch no. 49 (below). Both brooches are in the original Georg Jensen catalog of 1912. Courtesy of Georg Jensen Museum Copenhagen.

Two brooches. Collection of Robert Fredieu and Rosemary Schulze.

Three brooches with early Georg Jensen marks. Collection of Robert Fredieu and Rosemary Schulze.

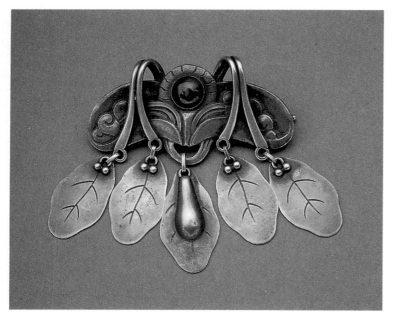

Early brooch. Collection of Robert Fredieu and
Rosemary Schulze.

Back of early brooch.

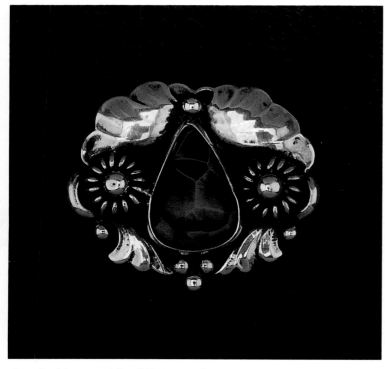

Brooch with unusual "turtle" stone and no
production number.

Two brooches no. 8, one with amber and green
agate, the other with labradorite. Designed by
Georg Jensen, 1904-1905.

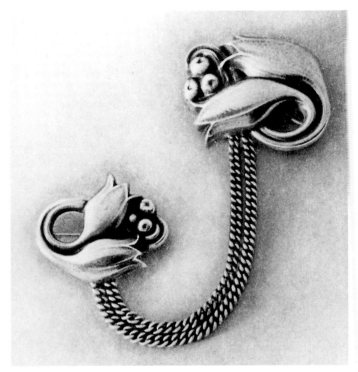

Pair of no. 100c brooches with silver chain swag.

Advertisement for Jensen jewelry, 1943. Courtesy of Georg Jensen, Copenhagen.

Five brooches: left side, no. 110; below left, no. 121 with silver bead; right side, no. 75 with silver bead; no. 73 with amethyst; no. 72 with synthetic sapphire. Courtesy of Georg Jensen Museum, Copenhagen.

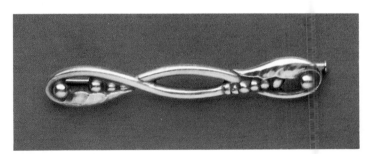

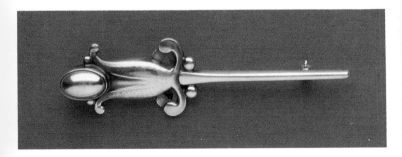

Brooch no. 3 designed by Georg Jensen.

Snail brooch no. 279 designed by Georg Jensen.

From top, brooch no. 157 with green agate, brooch no. 4 with silver pearls designed by Georg Jensen, brooch no. 91 with carnelian designed by Georg Jensen, and brooch no. 169 with green agate and silver pearls designed by Georg Jensen.

Brooch no. 16 designed by Georg Jensen.

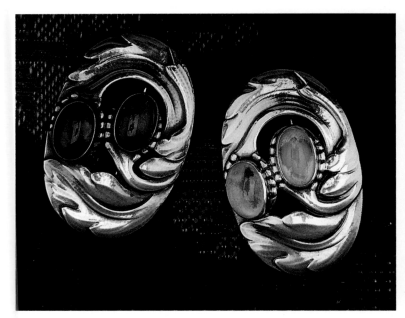

Two brooches no. 7, one with labradorites and one with moonstones. Collection of Dr. Barry Goozner.

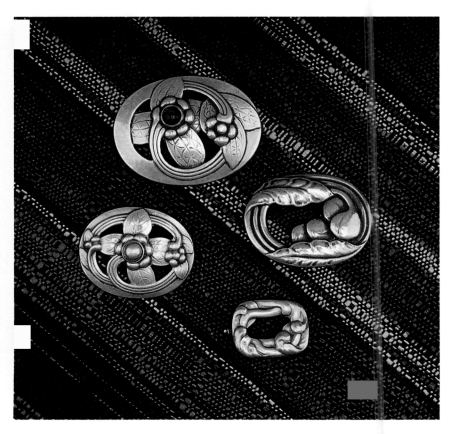

Clockwise from top, brooch no. 18 with lapis, brooch no. 13 with silver cherries in lower right corner, brooch no. 31, and brooch no. 138 with silver pearls, all designed by Georg Jensen.

Three no. 28 brooches with silver pearls, lapis and amber. Collection of Dr. Barry Goozner and Collection of Janet Morrison Clarke.

Brooch no. 21 with silver pearls designed by Georg Jensen.

From top, brooch no. 34 with labradorite and brooch no. 66 with moonstones, both designed by Georg Jensen.

Brooch no. 42 with garnet designed by Georg Jensen. Collection of Leah Gordon.

Sterling silver brooch no. 46. Courtesy of Skinner's Inc., Boston and Bolton.

Two no. 47 brooches, one with lapis and one with sterling silver pearls.

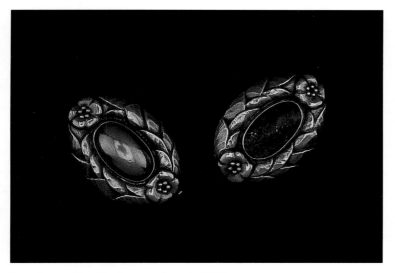

Brooch no. 51B with silver pearl, marked 925, and brooch no. 51A with lapis, marked 830S. Private collection.

Brooch no. 59 with onyx and moonstones designed by Georg Jensen.

Brooch no. 60 with oval cabochon labradorite, marked Gi, 830S and Importe de Danemark. Collection of Janet Laws and Steve Mey.

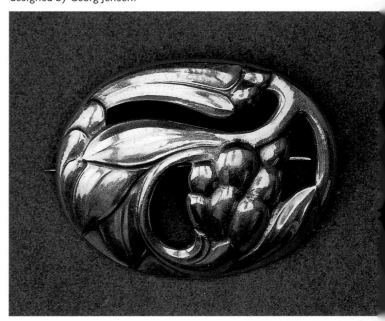

Brooch no. 65.

Pair of dress clips no. 68 designed by Georg Jensen.

Brooch no. 75. Private collection.

Brooch no. 81.

Brooch no. 75 with cabochon labradorite and four smaller cabochon moonstones, marked 925. Collection of Janet Laws and Steve Mey.

All silver brooch no. 72 marked Gi and 925, and brooch no. 104 with moonstone, both designed by Georg Jensen. Collection of Anne Shannon.

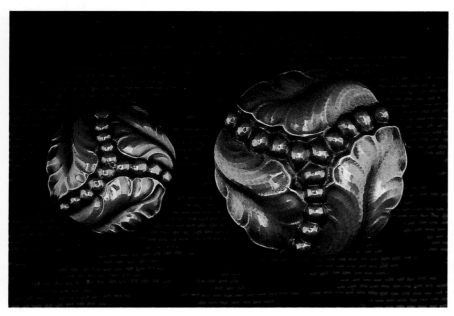

Brooch no. 82 in two different sizes.

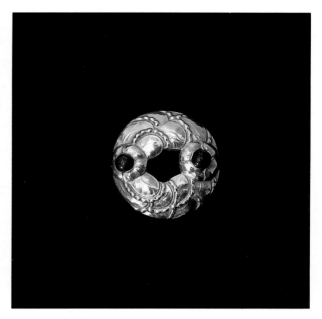

Brooch with lapis.

Brooch no. 90 with large lapis teardrop, marked 830S, designed by Georg Jensen. Private collection.

Brooch no. 92 with moonstones, designed by Georg Jensen.

Brooch no. 89 with lapis designed by Georg Jensen.

Brooch no. 92 with teardrop of moonstone, designed by Georg Jensen. Collection of Brenda Mixson and Thomas Thornton.

Brooch no. 92 with labradorite and moonstones designed by Georg Jensen. Collection of Anne Shannon.

From left, brooch no. 93 with large oval amber and four small clusters of leaves, unnumbered round brooch with large cluster of amber marked 830S and COPENHAGEN, and brooch no. 138 with amber pearl. All three designed by Georg Jensen.

Brooch no. 93 with oval amber and four green agate cabochons.

Brooch no. 112 with lapis, designed by Georg Jensen.

Brooch no. 125 with lapis. Collection of
Geraldine Wolf.

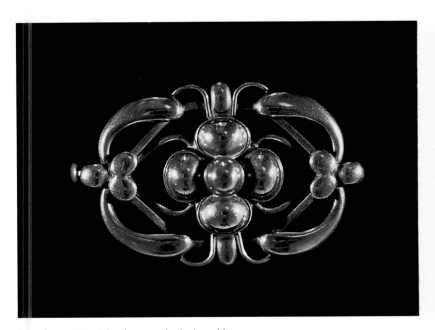

Brooch no 161 with silver pearls designed by
Georg Jensen. Collection of LeeEllen Friedland.

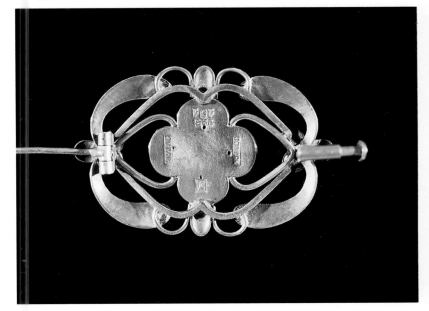

Back of brooch no. 161.

Clockwise from top, brooch no. 164 with
green agate, brooch no. 236B with green
agate designed by Georg Jensen, brooch no.
60 with green agate designed by Georg
Jensen, and brooch no 78 with amber and
green agate designed by Georg Jensen.

Brooch no. 173 with amber designed by Georg Jensen.

Brooch no. 189 with lapis, designed by Georg Jensen.

Brooch designed by Georg Jensen.

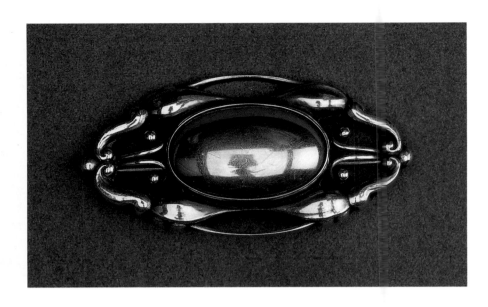

Brooch no. 197. Collection of JoAnn Schrier.

Bird pin no. 204 with green agate.

Bird pin no. 204 with silver pearls.

Sterling silver brooch no. 236. Courtesy of Skinner's Inc., Boston and Bolton.

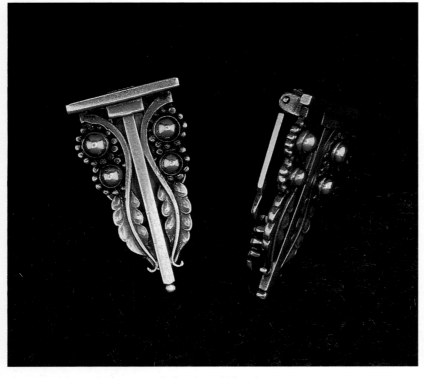

Pair of dress clips no. 231. Collection of Ed and Lisa Guari.

Clockwise from top left, round bird brooch no. 297, round duck brooch no. 299, and square bird brooch no. 300, all designed by Hugo Liisberg.

Sterling silver brooch no. 295. Courtesy of Skinner's Inc., Boston and Bolton.

Large brooch no. 312 and small brooch no. 242A. Collection of Ed and Lisa Guari.

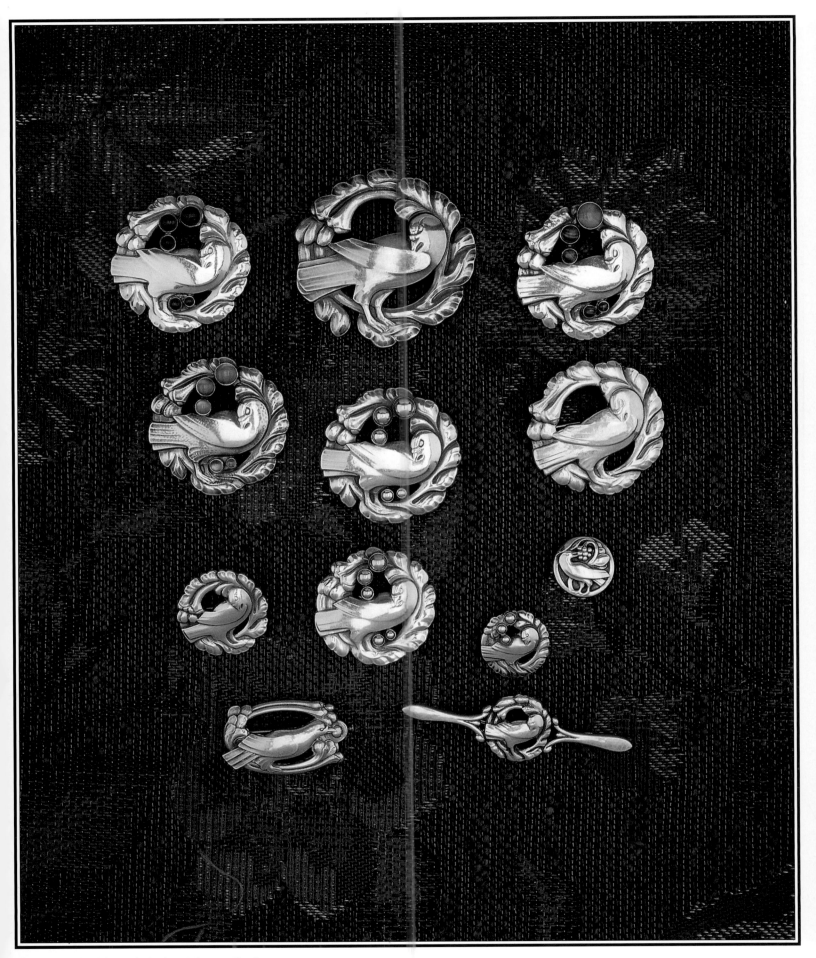

Twelve bird design brooches. Private collection.

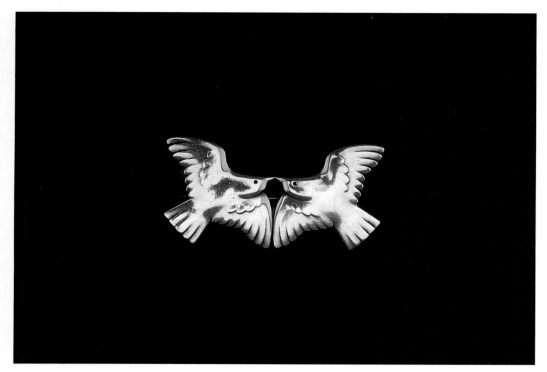

Double bird brooch no. 316.

Bird brooch no. 320 with coordinating earrings.
Collection of Robert and Barbara Paul.

Brooch designed as the silhouette of a horse's
head, no number.

Buckles

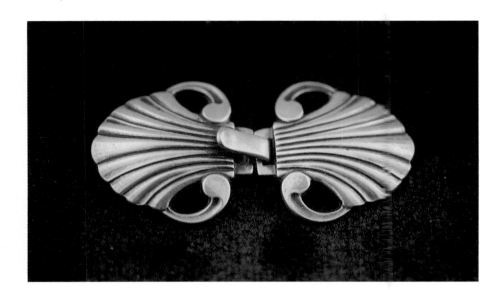

Belt buckle by Georg Jensen.

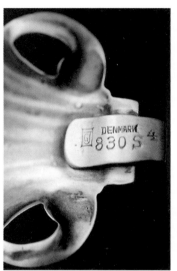

Reverse of belt buckle.

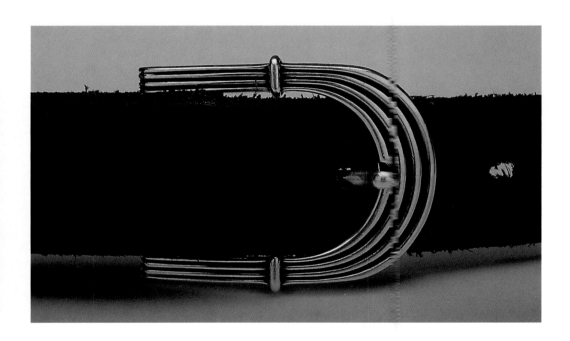

Belt buckle no. 112.

Buttons

Four buttons by Georg Jensen.

Cuff Links

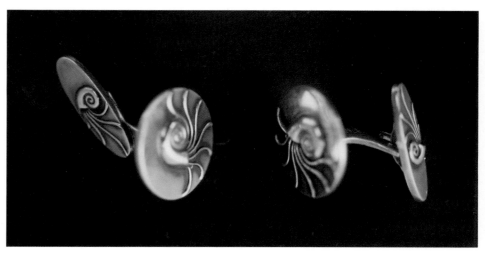

Silver and gold nautilus cuff links no. 52.
Collection of Robert and Barbara Paul.

Cufflinks no. 76 with panther design. Collection of Daniel Birnbaum.

Cuff links in star design.

Cufflinks no. 115 designed by B. Holse
Petersen. Courtesy of Georg Jensen Royal
Copengagen.

EARRINGS

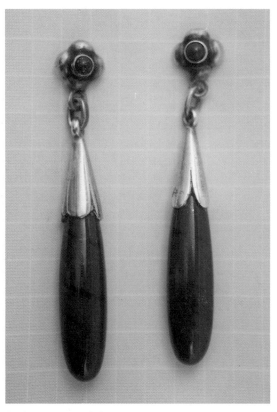

Earrings no. 6 with lapis tear drop. Collection of Debra and David Rosensaft.

Earrings no. 4 with Acorns.

Earrings no. 8 with silver ball and beading.

Earrings no. 11, early date, designed by Georg Jensen. Private collection.

Earrings no. 12 with carnelian teardrop designed by Georg Jensen.

Earrings no. 28 designed by Georg Jensen.
Private collection.

Sterling silver earrings no. 50.

Earrings no. 102 with small leaf.

Sterling silver earrings no. 116B. Courtesy of
Skinner's Inc. Boston and Bolton.

Earclips designed by Jorgen Jensen, 1938.
Georg Jensen Sølvsmedie, Gennem Fyrretyve
Arr, 1904-1944.

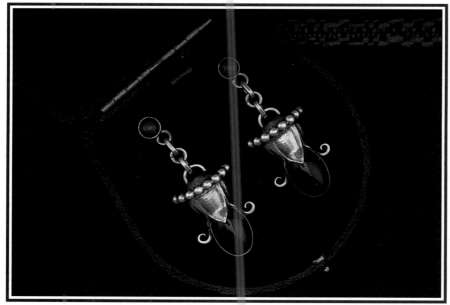

Earrings no. 435 with green agate. Collection
of Ed and Lisa Guari.

HAT PINS

Hatpin designed by Georg Jensen.

Necklaces

Necklace no. 1 with carnelian. Collection of
Kitty and Martin Jacobs.

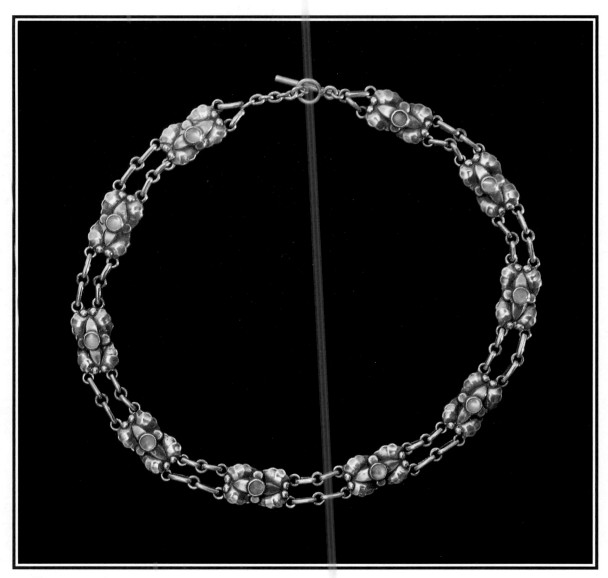

Necklace no. 2 with moonstones, designed by
Georg Jensen. Collection of Barbara and Steve
Herman.

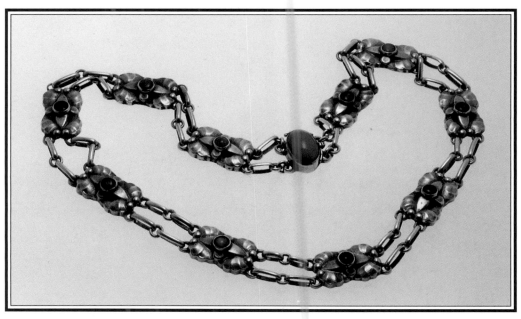

Necklace no. 2 with amber and an early
830 silver mark, designed by Georg
Jensen. Private collection.

Necklace no. 5 with green agate and pendant center, designed by Georg Jensen and marked Copenhagen. Collection of Janet Morrison Clarke.

Necklace no. 5 with lapis. Collection of Rhonda Rosenbaum Drucker.

Back of necklace no. 5.

Back of necklace no. 7.

Necklace no. 7 with labradorite.

Necklace with green agate designed by Georg Jensen.

Necklace no. 17 and three brooches, from left to right, no. 18, no. 177, and no. 60 with labradorite. Collection of Kitty and Martin Jacobs.

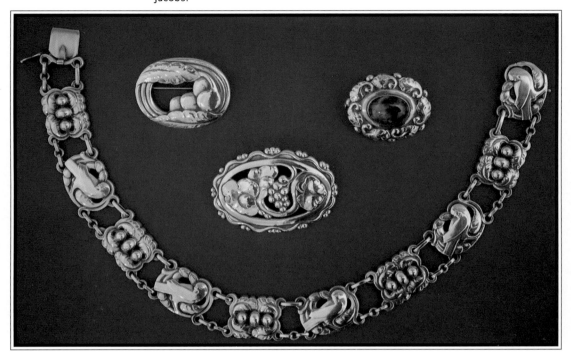

Necklace no. 18B with green agate, designed by Georg Jensen.

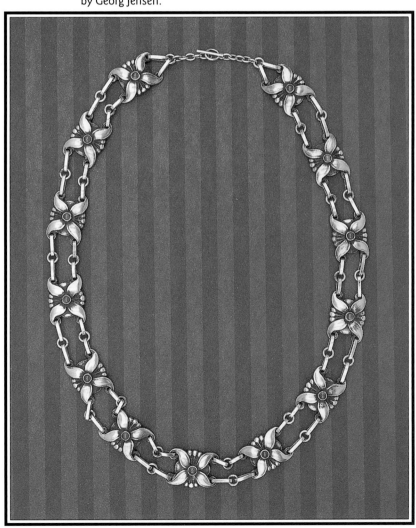

Necklace no. 21B. Private collection.

From top, necklace no. 25 with lapis and bracelet no. 6 with lapis, both designed by Georg Jensen.

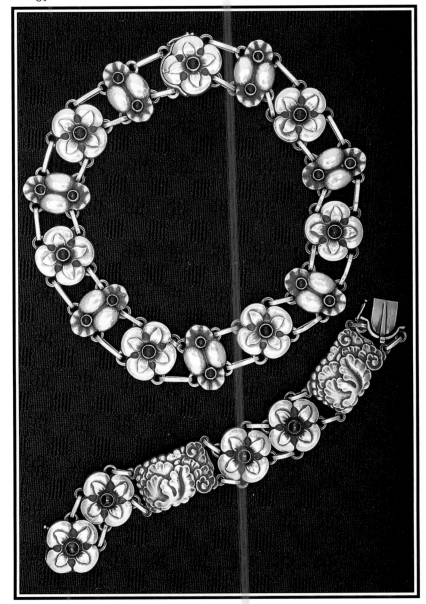

Necklace no. 51 with silver pearls and bracelet no. 57 with labradorite. Collection of Kitty & Martin Jacobs.

Necklace no. 53 with swans and matching bracelet no. 42.

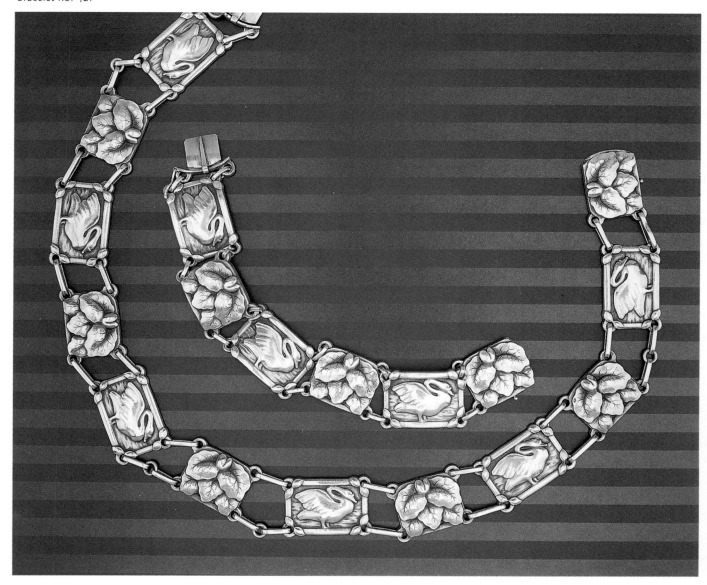

Necklace no. 66 and bracelet no. 93.

Necklace no. 66

Necklace 88B designed by Henning Koppel in 1947.

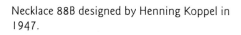

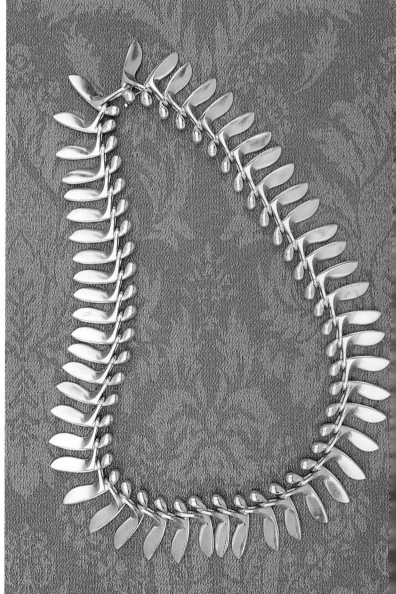

Necklace no. 89 and matching bracelet no. 89 designed by Henning Koppel.

Necklace no. 115 designed by Bent Gabrielsen.

Abstract modern double row necklace.
Courtesy of Georg Jensen/Royal Copenhagen.

Necklace no.136 designed by Arno
Malinowski.

Advertisement for Jensen jewelry, circa 1960.

Pendant Necklaces

Pendant necklace no. 5 with amber and green onyx. Private collection.

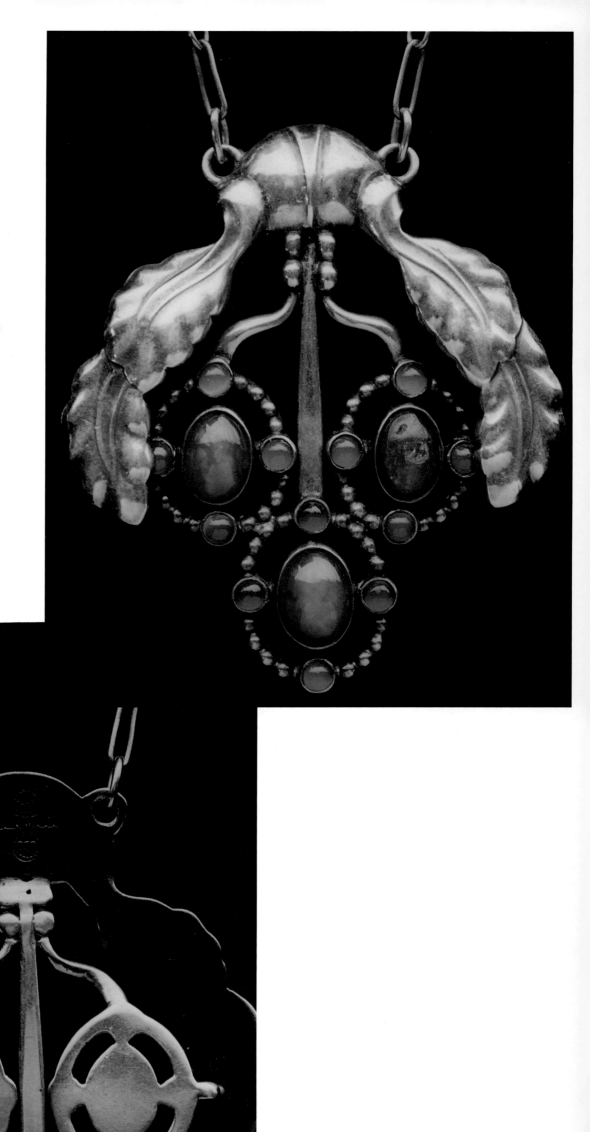

Pendant necklace no. 15 with silver pearl, designed by Georg Jensen.

Pendant necklace no. 19 with amber. Private collection.

Pendant no. 22 with labradorite and opals on paper clip chain. Collection of Janet Morrison Clarke.

Clockwise from bottom left, pendant necklace no. 19 with sterling oval cabochon, pendant necklace no. 171 with one large and four small green agate cabochons, pendant necklace no. 158 with one large and four small carnelian cabochons, pendant necklace no. 158 with silver pearls, and pendant necklace no. 40 with malachite marked GJ Ltd. and English export marks.

Back of pendant no. 22.

Green agate pendant no. 36. Private collection.

Pendant necklace no. 38. Collection of Janet Laws and Steve Mey.

Pendant necklace no. 43 with carnelian. Collection of Ed and Lisa Guari.

Three vintage pendants: one with green agate, one with moonstone, one with labradorite and opals. Collection of Debra and David Rosensaft.

Reverse of the three vintage pendants.

Reverse of pendant no. 45.

Pendant with amber no. 45.
Collection of Kitty & Martin
Jacobs.

Pendant no. 54 with labradorite marked
830S. Collection of Ed and Lisa Guari.

Pendant no. 64 with lapis on a paper clip
chain.

Rose quartz pendant no. 56 with paper clip
chain. Collection of LeeEllen Friedland.

Pendant necklace no. 74 marked 830S designed by Georg Jensen. Collection of LeeEllen Friedland.

Pendant necklace no. 153 designed by Ibe Dahlquist. Collection of Leah Gordon.

Pendant necklace with green agate designed by Georg Jensen.

Pendant necklace with coral and mother of pearl. Designed by Georg Jensen. Collection of Anne Shannon.

Pendant necklace of silver.

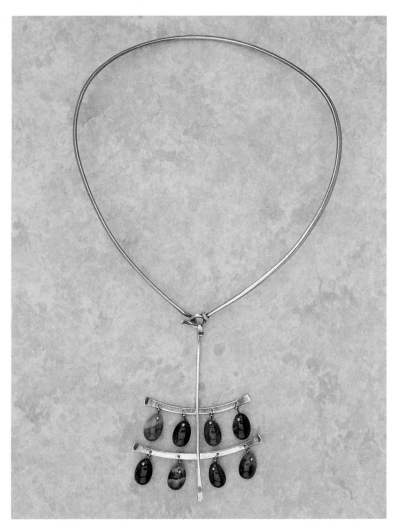

Torque necklace no 135 with amethyst drops, designed by Torun Bülow Hübe.

Sterling silver pendant no. 143, circa 1950. Courtesy of Skinner's Inc.

VINTAGE JENSEN IN CONTEMPORARY PENDANTS

Jensen Anniversary Pendants, made each year since 1988, are recent adaptations of early company designs. Accordingly, for students of Jensen's work, it is highly interesting to observe the ways in which the firm has recombined old motifs, stones and elements to create new, but seemingly old, designs. Even in these new combinations, Jensen's design vocabulary remains constant in harmony and beauty. Each of the limited-edition pendants is impressed with the year it was released and the Georg Jensen company mark.

1988 Anniversary Pendant. Courtesy of Georg Jensen/Royal Copenhagen.

1990 Anniversary Pendant. Courtesy of Georg Jensen/Royal Copenhagen.

1989 Anniversary Pendant. Courtesy of Georg Jensen/Royal Copenhagen.

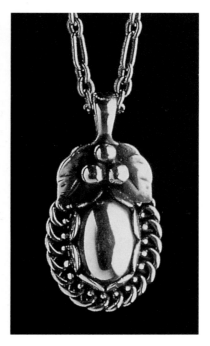

1992 Anniversary Pendant. Courtesy of Georg Jensen/Royal Copenhagen.

1991 Anniversary Pendant. Courtesy of Georg Jensen/Royal Copenhagen.

1993 Anniversary Pendant with amethyst and one with silver pearls. Courtesy of Georg Jensen/Royal Copenhagen.

1994 Anniversary Pendant and matching earrings, one set with silver pearls and one set with carnelian. Courtesy of Georg Jensen/Royal Copenhagen.

1995 Anniversary Pendant. Courtesy of Georg Jensen/Royal Copenhagen.

1996 Anniversary Pendant. Courtesy of Georg Jensen/Royal Copenhagen.

Rings

Three coral rings: from left, no. 45A with three stones, no. 13 with large oval stone, and no. 3 with scrolled silver work.

Ring no. 10 designed by Georg Jensen.

Ring no. 58 with lapis designed by Georg Jensen.

Sterling silver ring no. 75. Courtesy of Skinner's Inc., Boston and Bolton.

Blossom ring no. 61. Collection of Janet Laws and Steve Mey.

Sterling silver ring. Courtesy of Skinner's Inc., Boston and Bolton.

Ring no. 166 designed by Astrid Fog, circa 1971.

Franklin Mint ring. Collection of Amanda Herman.

Watch Fob

Slide for a chain with fob no. 12 with green agate and onynx, designed by Georg Jensen. Private collection.

Scarf ring with red and clear Lucite, no number, company mark.

Excerpt from a catalogue with 40 Ostergade, Copenhagen address showing jewelry designs and production number, as well as a variety of stones with which each design can be executed, 1940s.

	No. 12	No. 11	No. 54	No. 56
Amazonian	45.—	34.—	65.—	27.—
Amethyst	60.—	50.—	x	60.—
Carnelian	40.—	30.—	60.—	24.—
Green Onyx	40.—	30.—	60.—	24.—
Lapis lazuli	55.—	40.—	110.—	35.—
Malakite	45.—	32.—	65.—	27.—
Moon-stone	75.—	60.—	x	x
Turquise-Matrix	75.—	60.—	x	x
All-silver	35.—	25.—	38.—	16.—

	Pendant No. 23	Pendant No. 45	Brooch No. 134	Prooch No. 10
Amazonian	38.—	26.—	16.—	14.—
Amber, old dark	48.—	25.—	15.—	14.—
Carnelian	38.—	22.—	14.—	12.—
Garnet	100.—	x	18.—	20.—
Green Onyx	40.—	22.—	14.—	12.—
Lapis lazuli	55.—	32.—	18.—	16.—
All-silver	27.—	18.—	11.—	11.—

	Brooch No. 100	Brooch No. 189	Brooch No. 71	Brooch No. 159	Brooch No. 51
Amazonian	13.—	10.—	16.—	85.—	26.—
Carnelian	12.—	9.50	14.—	80.—	20.—
Coral	13.—	10.—	27.—	85.—	50.—
Green Onyx	12	9.50	14.—	80.—	20 —
Lapis lazuli	13.—	11.—	19.—	85.—	34.—
Synth. Sapphire	24.—	11.—	35.—	120.—	x
Turquise	22.—	11.—	30.—	120.—	x
All-silver	19.—	7.50	12.—	65.—	12.—

	Brooch No. 155	Brooch No. 132	Brooch No. 30	Brooch No. 93
Amazonian	24.—	75.—	32.—	45.—
Carnelian	20.—	60.—	26.—	42.—
Green Onyx	20.—	55.—	26.—	42.—
Lapis lazuli	26.—	x	34.—	50.—
All-silver	15.—	36.—	21.—	26.—

Brooch No. 101, all Silver	16.—	
,, ,, 212, ,, ,,	5.50	
Ring ,, 23, ,, ,,	12.—	
,, ,, 12, ,, ,,	11.—	
Bracelet 46, ,, ,,	65.—	Choker to match..
,, ,, 42, ,, ,,	65.—	Choker to match..

Hans Andersen: „The ugly duckling"

	Brooch No. 165	Bracelet No. 18
Amazonian	22.—	48.—
Carnelian	18.—	45.—
Garnet	27.—	55.—
Green Onyx	18.—	45.—
Lapis lazuli	24.—	55.—
All-silver	13.—	35.—

	Bracelet No. 3	Bracelet No. 12	Bracelet No. 34	Brac No.
Amazonian	75.—	75.—	150.—	150
Amber and Onyx	70.—	o	o	
Carnelian	70.—	60.—	x	135
Coral	80.—	x	225.—	x
Green Onyx	70.—	60.—	130.—	135
Lapis lazuli	85.—	95.—	x	
Lapis, Chile-	85.—	65.—	125.—	x
Labradorite	75.—	70.—	145.—	150
All-silver	65.—	50.—	o	

Chokers 16¹/₂ inch

Choker no. 5 is made with one link and a little stone between the flowers.

	No. 1 to match Bracelet No. 3	No. 5 to match Bracelet No. 12	No. 17 to match Bracelet No. 14	No. to m Bra No.
Amazonian	95.—	75.—	175.—	70
Amber and Onyx	95.—	75.—	175.—	
Carnelian	90.—	70.—	160.—	70
Coral	110.—	80.—	200.—	75
Green Onyx	90.—	70.—	180.—	70
Lapis lazuli	110.—	80.—	195.—	75
Lapis, Chile-	110.—	80.—	175.—	75
Labradorite	95.—	75.—	175.—	70
All-silver	85.—	60.—	150.—	55

The Numbering System

There is a general order to the numbering system in Jensen jewelry, although there are many exceptions. The pieces are numbered chronologically, yet occasionally a number was skipped, and some numbers were reassigned at a later date. It is logical to assume that the design of brooch no. 80 precedes the design of brooch no. 110. It is not clear as to why some necklaces have matching bracelets with different numbers, and some necklaces have the identical number as the matching bracelet. A selected list of matching necklaces and bracelets follows.

		Earrings No. 24
Earrings No. 40, all silver	27.—	
Pin ,, 110, ,, ,,	9.—	
Cufflinks ,, 9, ,, ,, (2 studs)	11.—	All-Silver, Carnelian and Onyx .... Kr. 48.—
Cufflinks ,, 9, ,, ,, (4 studs)	15.—	Moon-stone, Synth. Sapphire and Turquise.. Kr. 55.—
Cufflinks ,, 30, ,, ,,	12.—	All other stones .... Kr. 52.—
Brooch ,, 178, ,, ,,	12.—	
,, ,, 31, ,, ,,	8.—	
,, ,, 34, ,, ,,	8.—	
Pin ,, 36, ,, ,,	11.—	

	Ring No. 46	Ring No. 11 oval	Ring No. 18	Ring No. 11 A large	Ring No. 11 B small	Ring No. 1
Amazonian	30.—	30.—	60.—	18.—	13.—	24.—
Carnelian	25.—	25.—	60.—	15.—	12.—	20.—
Coral	50.—	60.—	x	35.—	25.—	50.—
Green Onyx	25.—	25.—	60.—	15.—	12.—	20.—
Lapis lazuli	40.—	32.—	x	23.—	15.—	34.—
Synth. Sapphire	85.—	60.—	x	50.—	38.—	x
All-silver	18.—	20.—	o	12.—	10.—	16.—

	Ring No. 1 oval	Ring No. 21	Cufflinks No. 14	Cufflinks No. 45	Pin No. 117
Amazonian	19.—	18.—	16.—	60.—	22.—
Carnelian	18.—	15.—	16.—	48.—	17.—
Garnet	35.—	26.—	17.—	x	x
Green Onyx	18.—	15.—	16.—	48.—	17.—
Lapis lazuli	22.—	24.—	17.—	70.—	28.—
Synth. Sapphire	40.—	38.—	17.—	x	65.—
All-silver	15.—	12.—	13.—	30.—	14.—

	Earrings No. 11	Earrings No. 23	Brooch No. 22	Buckle No. 45
Amazonian	60.—	55.—	x	35.—
Amber and Onyx or Malakite	60.—	o	225.—	o
Carnelian	52.—	50.—	x	35.—
Green Onyx	55.—	50.—	x	35.—
All-silver	40.—	42.—	o	30.—

x = *Prices furnished upon request.* o = *Cannot be recommended.*
All Prices are given in Danish Kroner. Prices subject to change without notice.

Matching Necklaces and Bracelets

Necklace No.	Bracelet No.
1	3
10	18
15	11
18B	37
19	19
20	29
21	49
22	15
23	2 and 35
24	4
25	27 and 26
27	22
29A, 29B	40
32	5
33	30
34	28 and 25
39	39
42B	44
43B	45
44	33
45	54
46	46
47	72
49	8
51	57
54	68
55	50
59	53
61	79
62	70
63	75
64	63B
66	93
77	77
87	87
88	88
89	89
94	94
94A	94A
94B	94B
97	10
99	48
100A	100A
100B	100B
102	101
104	104
105	105
106	106
108	108
109A	109A
109B	109B
112	112
114	114
115	115

Advertisement for Jensen jewelry from the 1930s.

Necklace no. 1 and bracelet no. 3 with green agate, designed by Georg Jensen.

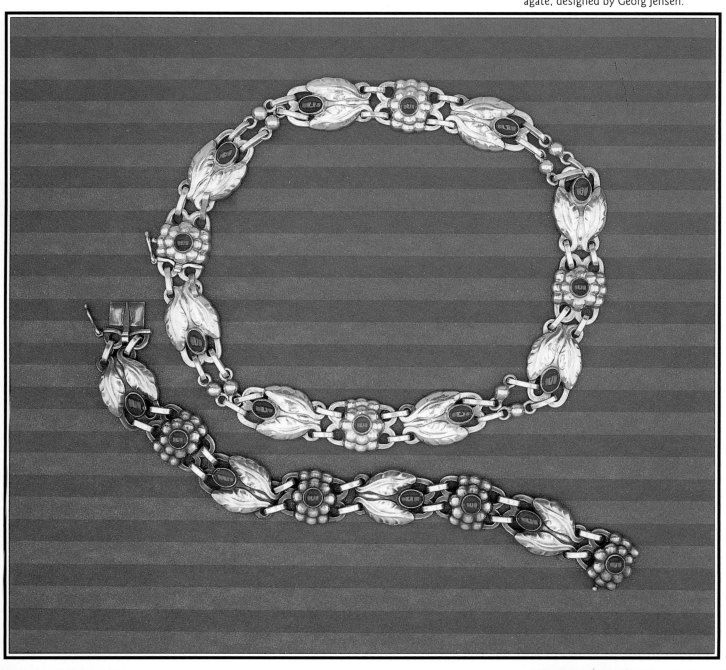

Necklace no. 1 and coordinating bracelet no. 3 with lapis, both designed by Georg Jensen.

Necklace no. 1 and ccordinating bracelet no. 3 with moonstones, both designed by Georg Jensen.

Advertisement for matching necklace, bracelet and barrette from the 1930s.

Bracelet no. 53 with moonstones and
coordinating necklace no. 59 with silver pearls.

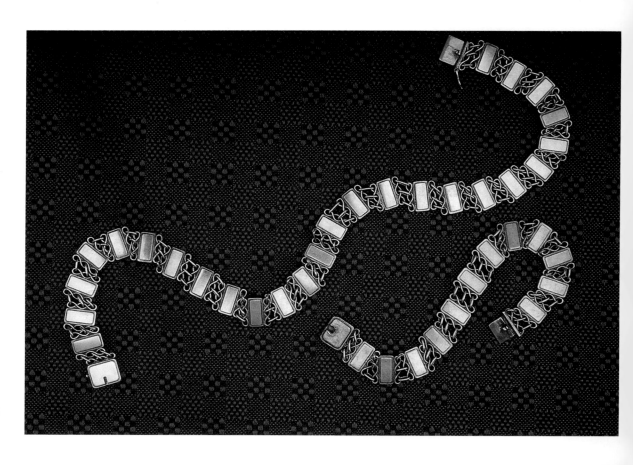

Necklace no. 63 and matching
bracelet no. 75.

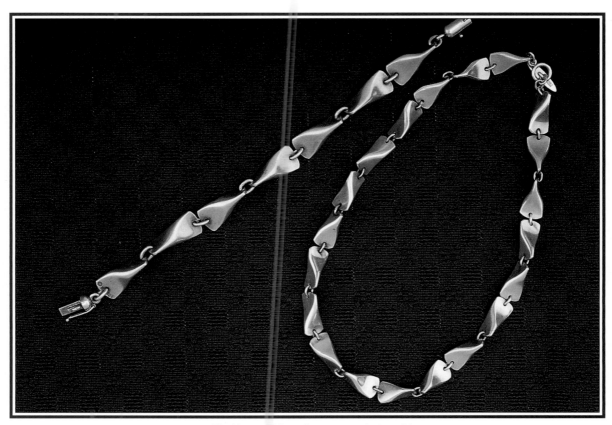

Necklace no. 94 and bracelet no. 94. Collection of Debra and David Rosensaft.

Necklace and bracelet no. 104 designed by Edvard Kindt-Larsen.

Necklace no. 127 and matching bracelet no. 220.

Necklace no. 137 and matching bracelet no. 218.

Necklace and bracelet no. 181, both designed
by Ibe Dahlquist.

Gold Jewelry

Without a doubt, Jensen is best known for jewelry produced in silver, but the firm also made limited quantities of gold jewelry, quite early, in the workshop. According to Michael von Essen, the curator of the Georg Jensen Museum in Copenhagen, records indicate that certain designs were executed in gold during the first 15 years of Jensen's workshop, and that in a catalogue issued prior to 1920 there were at least 300 designs for gold jewelry. A design in gold could cost up to ten times as much as the same design produced in sterling silver.

Rings and bracelets in 18K gold appear more frequently than brooches. Neatly chased rings, often with a single pearl or other cabochon stone centered on a shank and decorated with shell or leaf forms, remain classical in design. The firm also produced gold versions of more modern designs, such as those of Koppel, Ditzel and Torun; selected designs are produced in gold as well as silver.

Jensen gold jewelry is marked 765, representing the 18 1/2 Karat gold standard that was required to import merchandise to France and Sweden prior to 1930. In 1918, when the Jensen store was opened in Paris, the company had to comply with the established requirements for importing goods from Denmark. The current gold standards require 18 Karat, which is indicated by the mark 750, or 14 Karat, which is indicated by the mark 585. All Jensen gold jewelry is marked with a production number as well as the company name, and a standard gold mark.

Gold pendant no. 65 with sapphire designed by Georg Jensen.

Gold pendant with diamonds and sapphires designed by Georg Jensen, 1913. Georg Jensen Sølvsmedie, Gennem Fyrretyve Arr, 1904-1944.

18K gold bracelet no. 306 and earrings made from two links.

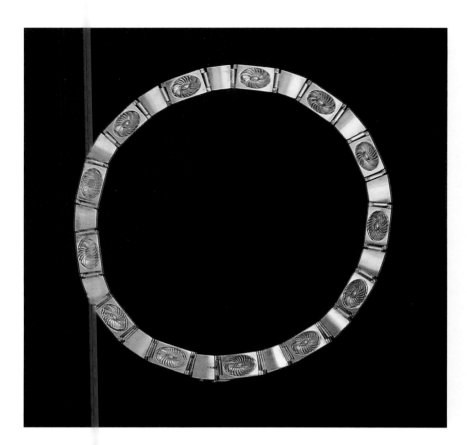

Sterling silver and 18K gold necklace no. 68.

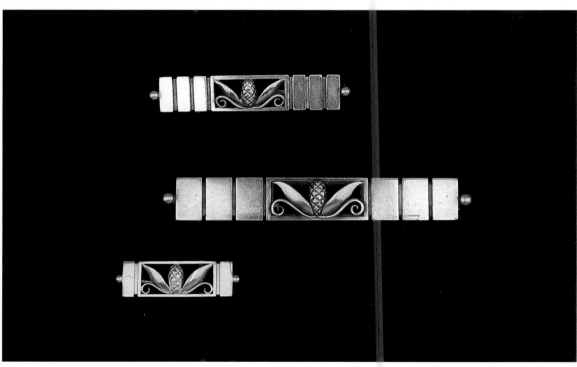

Brooch no. 276 in three sizes: -two in silver and small brooch in 18K gold. Collections of Ed & Lisa Guari and Dr. Barry Goozner.

18K gold cuff links no. 91 designed by Søren Georg Jensen.

18K gold cufflinks designed by Georg Jensen in their original box.

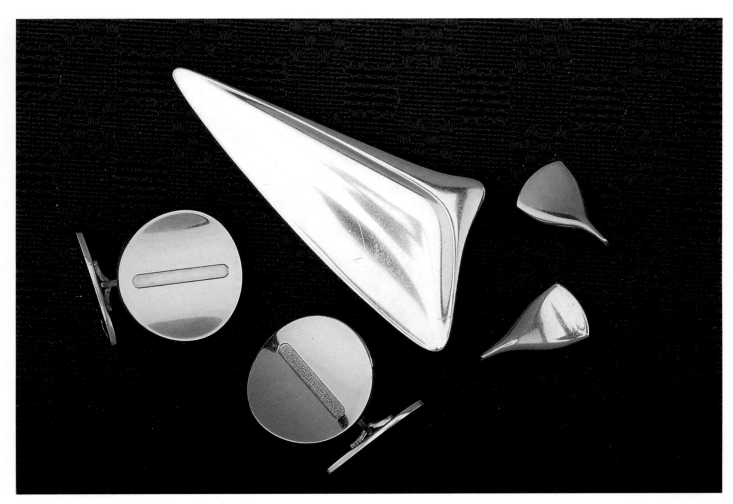

From left, 18K gold cuff links no. 1105 designed by Nanna Ditzel, 18K gold brooch no. 394 designed by Henning Koppel, and 18K gold earrings no. 1116 designed by Edvard Kindt-Larsen.

18K gold ring with rock crystal designed by Bent Gabrielsen Pedersen.

18K gold ring with pearl designed by Georg Jensen, 18K gold bangle bracelet and 18K gold ring, both designed by Torun Bülow-Hübe.

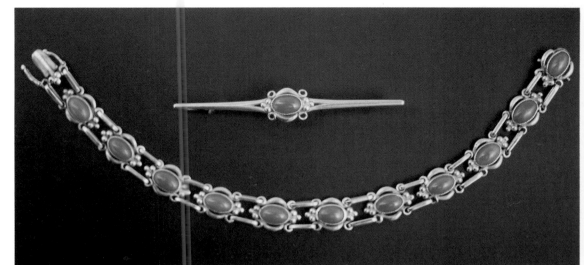

18 K gold bar brooch and 18 K gold bracelet with coral. Collection of Debra and David Rosensaft.

14K gold bar pin no. 272 with blue stone and 18K gold and sapphire ring. Courtesy of Skinner's Inc., Boston and Bolton.

From top, 18 K gold bracelet, 18K gold necklace, and small 18K gold brooch with pearl.

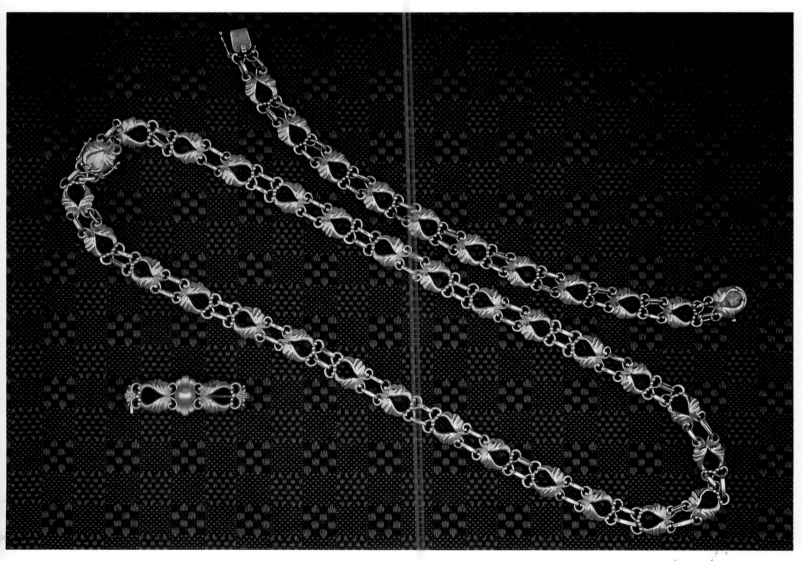

Collection of gold jewelry, 1943. Courtesy of Georg Jensen/Royal Copenhagen.

18K gold bracelet no. 1126 designed by Harald Nielsen. Private collection.

From top, gold earrings no. 170 with pearls, 18K gold bracelet no. 248 with pearls, and gold bracelet no. 172 with pearls, all designed by Georg Jensen.

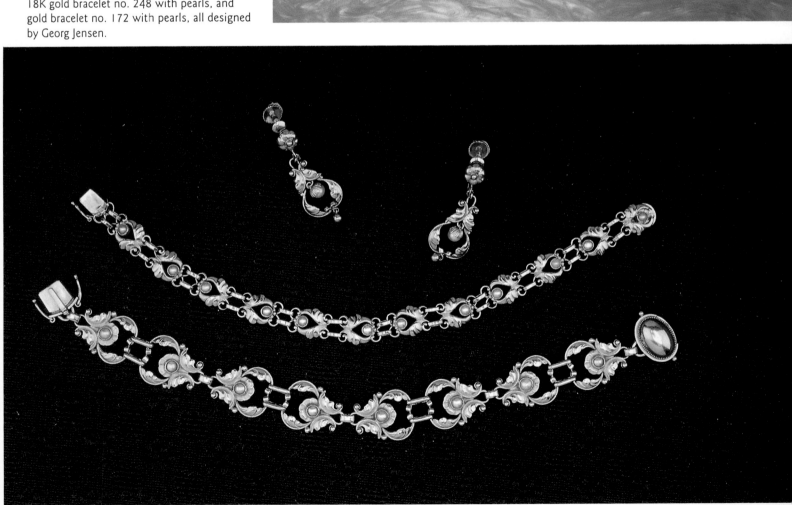

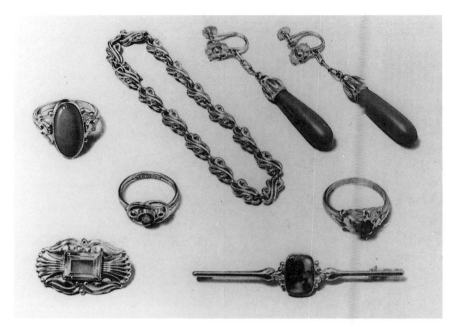

Group of gold jewelry. Courtesy of Georg Jensen/Royal Copenhagen.

Gold necklace designed by Jørgen Jensen, 1939. Georg Jensen Sølvsmedie, Gennem Fyrretyve Arr, 1904-1944.

Group of gold jewelry. Courtesy of Georg Jensen/ Royal Copenhagen.

18K gold pendant with tourquoise. Private collection.

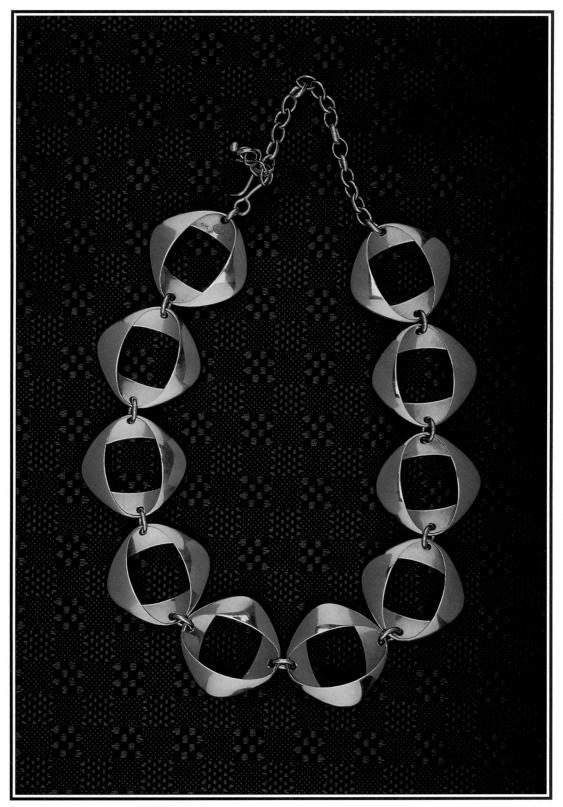

18K gold necklace no. 1190 designed by Henning Koppel. Collection of Janet Morrison Clarke.

Bracelet no. 190 in 18K gold designed by Henning Koppel.

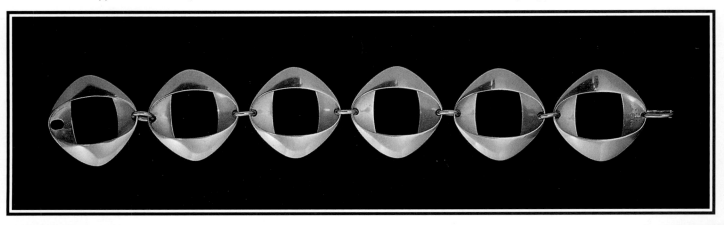

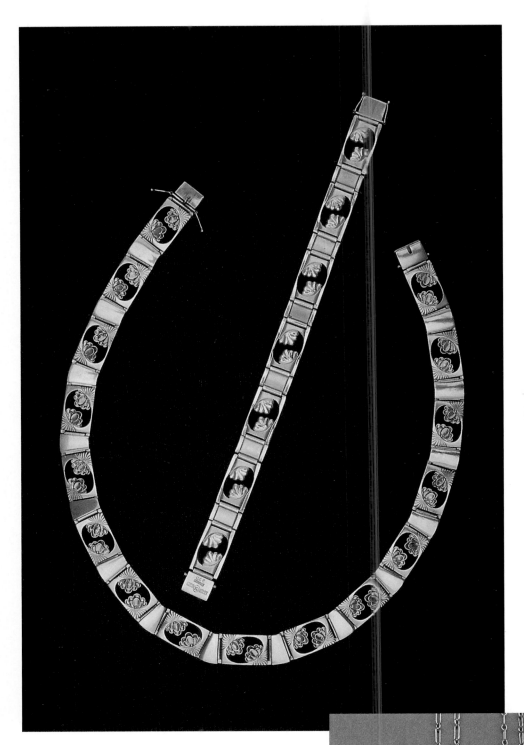

18K gold necklace and bracelet, both no. 275. Private collection.

18K gold pendant with sapphire, 18K gold pendant with pearl, and 18K gold brooch with citrines. Collection of Robert Fredieu and Rosemary Schulze.

18K floral earrings. Private collection.

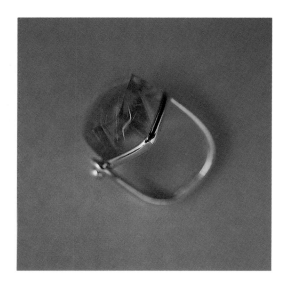

14K gold ring with rock crystal designed by
Torun Bülow-Hübe.

18K ring with two moonstones designed by
Henning Koppel, circa 1960. Courtesy of
Tadema Gallery, London.

18K gold and turquoise bracelet. Private
collection.

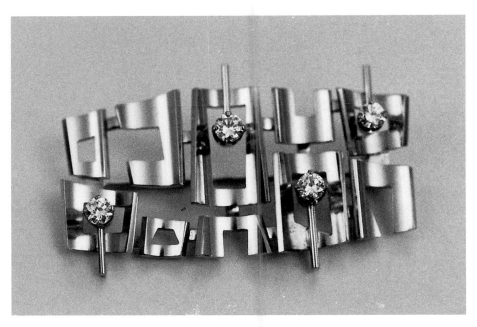

18K gold brooch no. 835 with diamonds,
designed by O. Zhaler, circa 1961. Courtesy of
Georg Jensen/Royal Copenhagen.

Blossom tray with teapot, creamer and sugar.
Collection of Ed and Lisa Guari.

CHAPTER 7
Hollowware

The hollowware that Georg Jensen produced earned him international recognition during his lifetime. By prevailing artistic standards, a silversmith's elevation to the highest ranks within the profession could be determined by the quality of his hollowware, generally considered one of the zenith's of the silversmith's art. Therefore, all serious silversmiths made hollowware, one of the most prestigious endeavors they could undertake. Since more labor and material went into each piece and since each creation was so costly, hollowware was a monumental task for the silversmith. It took great skill to execute, but, since holloware items were generally so costly, commercial demand was not as great as for jewelry and flatware.

Hollowware tends to be a term that is not well understood by laymen. Hollowware refers to man-made objects that have depth or hollowness, objects such as bowls, teapots, vases, jugs, candle sticks, salts, sugar casters, cigarette cases, pill boxes, and more. Within the trade, the term also refers to a number of objects that are not particularly characterized by the presence of hollowness, objects such as trays, letter openers, corkscrews, mirrors, brushes, combs, etc. Therefore, perhaps the simplest way to remember what constitutes hollowware is to bear in mind that anything that isn't clearly jewelry or flatware is probably considered hollowware.

Georg Jensen's commitment to hollowware is evidenced by the large number of hollowware pieces he designed and produced during his career. One may also surmise that he enjoyed creating hollowware because its size and mass allowed him greater latitude in exploring sculptural possibilities than was possible with jewelry or flatware. Although his uniquely complementary skills as a sculptor, ceramist and silversmith are discernible in all his work, they are perhaps expressed most fully and exuberantly in his hollowware. Literally and figuratively, hollowware embodied his grandest artistic statements. And these were the statements that were primarily responsible for the accolades he received and the reputation he gained as one of the very best silversmiths of his era.

One of Jensen's early hollowware forms was the so-called "Blossom" teapot, no. 2, created in 1905. The body of the teapot is a curvaceous, semi-conical form to which a gracefully curved spout is attached. The handle is ivory, and the body of the teapot rests on three short, sculpted feet, perhaps reminiscent of the feet of frogs that leapt about marshes in the vicinity of Jensen's boyhood home. The surface of the teapot is lightly hammered, imparting a shimmering effect. The teapot's most striking feature, though, is a larger-than-life stem and blossom affixed to the top of the lid that serves as the lid's handle. This piece was well received and, significantly, one example was purchased by the Danish Museum of Decorative Art.

Blossom coffee set and tray designed by Georg Jensen, 1908. Courtesy of Georg Jensen/Royal Copenhagen.

Another important hollowware piece that Georg Jensen created was a five-arm cande-labra, design no. 383. The French art critic P. Lahalle responded to this candelabra as follows:

> The sobriety of his work, which is never poverty, has the advantage that it does not permit futile fantasy to lead away from the fundamental properties of the object, its proportions, its movement and its excellent material. It is by means of a discreet hammering of the smooth surfaces that Georg Jensen's work achieves its incomparable beauty; this vibration in the silver subdues its excessive gloss, removes every thought of mechanical labor, reveals the hand of the worker — in short, his works are alive. I love this candlestick with five arms, whose massive, twisted curves drop down towards so simple and free a foot. The scintillating richness in the central stem, from which emerges a broad ring which falls well into the hand, emphasizes the pure line of these candlesticks. (Ivan Munk Olsen, *Georg Jensen*)

This appreciative review of Jensen's work was typical of the reception Jensen's work was given in France.

A silver bowl, no. 19, designed around 1910, was another stunning creation. In this composition, a deep bowl with a notched rim thrusts upward from a base by a number of vertical, leaf-like forms, thus creating the illusion that the heavy bowl is hovering weight-lessly. This piece is frequently called the "Louvre Bowl" because an example is in the collection of the Louvre Museum in Paris. Jensen's pride in this bowl is evidenced by the fact that it was frequently featured in the advertisements his firm placed in the leading American, Danish, English, French, and German decorative-arts magazines of the period.

The Louvre bowl designed by Georg Jensen, 1912. Courtesy of Georg Jensen/Royal Copenhagen.

Fruit bowl no. 263 with a grape motif, designed by Georg Jensen in 1918, is among the most popular of his hollowware designs. It was produced in four sizes and the grape motif was used on candlesticks of the same number, no. 263.

While Jensen's enthusiastic use of ornamentation is apparent in some pieces, his restraint is evident in others. A prime example of the latter is coffee pot no. 80 which he introduced in 1915. Here, Jensen's emphasis is on the form; the only ornamentation is beading around the handle mount and an ebony acorn lid. Other pieces accompany the tea pot in the same motif.

Tea and coffee servers were made in different sizes and with ivory and ebony handles. Each piece was sold individually. There is a chronological order to the pattern numbers, but there are many exceptions. In general, one should be able to assume that a piece of hollowware marked no. 80 was designed before another piece marked no. 120.

Compote with grapes no. 263 designed by Georg Jensen. Courtesy of The National Swedish Art Museums, Stockholm.

Gravy boat no. 11 designed by Georg Jensen, 1910.
Courtesy of Georg Jensen/Royal Copenhagen.

Bonbonnierre no. 87 designed by Georg Jensen,
1915. Courtesy of Georg Jensen/Royal Copenhagen.

DESIGNERS IN HOLLOWWARE

Another showcased piece was a tall bowl and cover with a handle of applied forms resembling nuts and cascading grapes. The bowl shown on page 190 as bonbonnierre no. 87, was set on four applied feet which resemble pine cones attached to leaves. This vibrant design demonstrates Jensen's use of naturalistic forms; the acorns are realistic and life size.

Leaves, flowers, grapes, berries, and acorns regularly appear in his hollowware, as do shells, fish and other natural forms. In most pieces, these elements are deftly integrated within the overall form but in a few, such as the jardiniere with grape designs, the ornamentation could be considered more decorative than integral to the form. The pedestal of the jardiniere is used itself as the main design for the bottle tray no. 229.

Original drawing of covered bowl by Johan Rohde, 1926. Courtesy of Ole Pedersen.

Original drawing of covered bowl by Johan Rohde. Courtesy of Ole Pedersen.

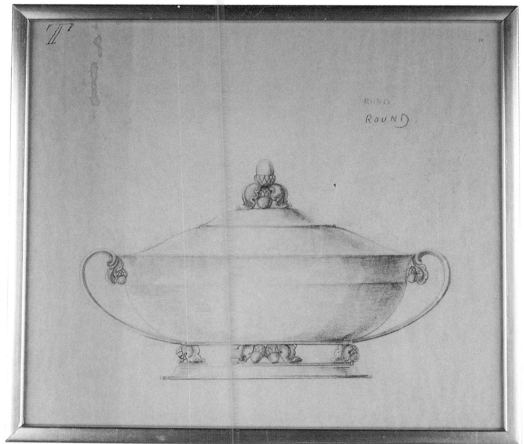

Fish server with cover designed by Johan
Rohde, 1920. Courtesy of Georg Jensen/Royal
Copenhagen.

Covered fish platter no. 335 designed by
Johan Rohde, 1919. Courtesy of Georg Jensen/
Royal Copenhagen.

Tea pot, sugar and creamer designed by Johan Rohde. Courtesy of Georg Jensen/Royal Copenhagen.

Many designers created hollowware for Jensen and he took pains to recognize their work and encourage them to explore their own artistic visions. New designs of high quality and great originality were produced. The work of Johan Rohde bore the greatest similarity to Jensen's work, but it nevertheless had a style of its own, one that successfully evolved with time. Indeed, Rohde was sometimes well ahead of his time. For example, the highly modernist pitcher no. 432, designed in 1920, was considered so advanced that Georg Jensen held it back from production until 1925.

Candelabra no. 343 designed by Johan Rohde, 1920. Courtesy of Georg Jensen/Royal Copenhagen.

Tea set designed by Johan Rohde. Courtesy of Georg Jensen/Royal Copenhagen.

Tea set designed by Johan Rohde. Courtesy of Georg Jensen/Royal Copenhagen.

Tea pot designed by Johan Rohde. Courtesy of Georg Jensen/Royal Copenhagen.

Tea caddy no. 89 designed by Johan Rohde, 1912. Courtesy of Georg Jensen/Roya Copenhagen.

Bonbonniere no. 249 designed by Johan Rohde, 1918. Courtesy of Georg Jensen/Royal Copenhagen.

Sugar bowl and creamer no. 43 designed by Johan Rohde, 1908. Courtesy of Georg Jensen/Royal Copenhagen.

The work of Harald Nielsen, who produced some of his best work during the 1930s, was in step with the prevailing Art Deco style of that period. In contrast to the highly-ornamented style Jensen developed, Nielsen and Rohde were largely responsible for creating the "Jensen modern" style. Others, many of whom also designed jewelry and flatware, added their own interpretations of this new style. They included Gundolph Albertus, Jørgen Jensen, Oscar Gundlach-Pedersen, Henry Pilstrup, Gustav Pedersen, Sigvard Bernadotte, Arno Malinowski, Henning Koppel, Magnus Stephensen, Nanna and Jørgen Ditzel, and many others.

Pair of double-armed candelabra no. 278 designed by Harald Nielsen. Collection of Ed and Lisa Guari.

Candlestick no. 604C designed by Harald Nielsen, 1930. Courtesy of Georg Jensen/ Royal Copenhagen.

Covered bowl no. 499B designed by Harald Nielsen with attached underplate. The inside of the bowl is enameled.

Tea set and candlesticks in Pyramid designed by Harald Nielsen.

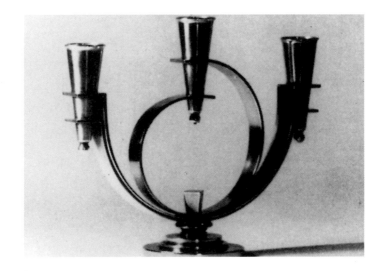

Candelabra designed by O. Gundlach-Pedersen, 1932.

Pill boxes designed by Harald Nielsen: small box no. 33E, larger box no. 33.

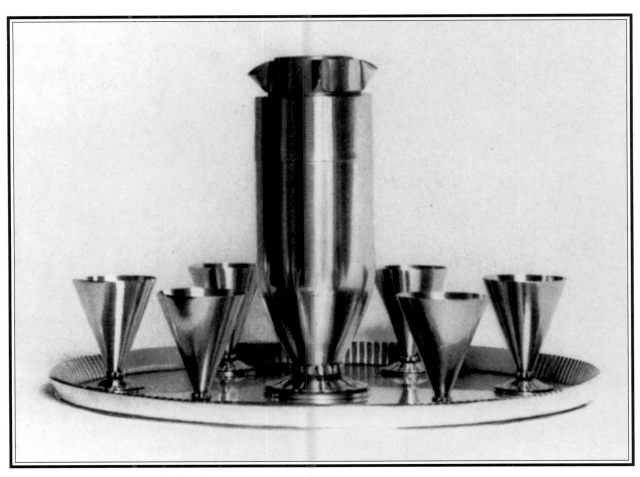

Punch set designed by O. Gundlach-Pedersen,
1928.

Chafing dish no. 1055 designed by Magnus
Stephensen, 1956. Courtesy of Georg Jensen/
Royal Copenhagen.

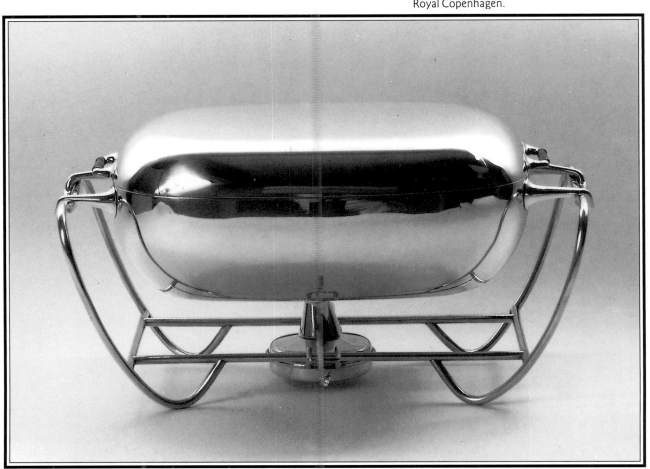

Designs by Arno Malinowski. Courtesy of
Georg Jensen/Royal Copenhagen.

Group of iron and silver (Jern/Sølv) objects
designed by Arno Malinowski. Courtesy of
Georg Jensen/Royal Copenhagen.

Group of iron and silver (Jern/Sølv) objects
designed by Arno Malinowski, circa 1944.

Objects designed by Sigvard Bernadotte.
Courtesy of Georg Jensen/Royal Copenhagen.

While every member of this group made important contributions to the advancement of hollowware design at the silversmithy, two deserve special mention: Sigvard Bernadotte and Henning Koppel. During the 1930s and 1940s, Bernadotte brought a bold new look to Jensen hollowware that emphasized line and form; ornamentation was generally linear and restrained. In the 1950s, Koppel brought in sweeping, dramatic forms that are at once functional and sculptural, and exemplify the very best of modern Danish design.

Jensen hollowware, from the earliest to the most recent, represents a cavalcade of exemplary design and craftsmanship. They are an index of the changing styles of the twentieth century, celebration of Georg Jensen's commitment to artistic excellence and freedom.

Tea caddy designed by Sigvard Bernadotte. Private collection.

Pair of double-armed candelabra no. 1050B designed by Sigvard Bernadotte.

Covered dish designed by Sigvard Bernadotte.

Punch bowl set designed by Sigvard Bernadotte. Courtesy of Georg Jensen/Royal Copenhagen.

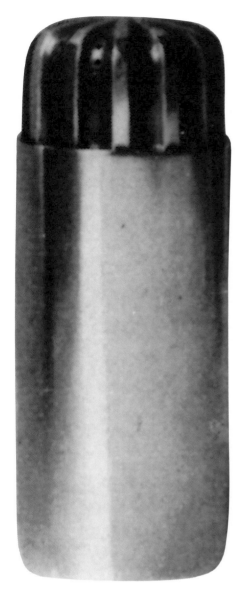

Sugar shaker designed by Sigvard Bernadotte, 1938.

Henning Koppel and the famous pitcher no. 992, introduced in 1952. Courtesy of Georg Jensen, New York.

Covered fish platter no. 843 designed by Henning Koppel, 1956. Courtesy of Georg Jensen/Royal Copenhagen.

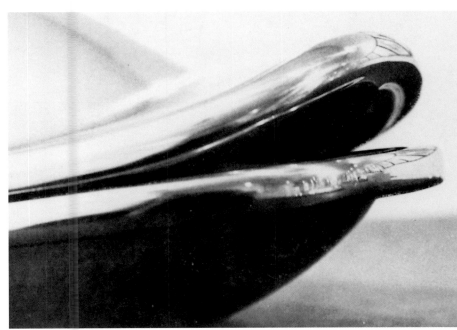

Fish dish by Henning Koppel.

Covered dish no. 1083 designed by Henning Koppel, 1960. Courtesy of Georg Jensen/Royal Copenhagen.

Serving Dishes

Bowl no. 4 with two Georg Jensen marks as
well as an assay mark.

Bowl no. 296 designed by Georg Jensen, 1919.
Courtesy of Georg Jensen/Royal Copenhagen
A/S.

Sugar basket designed by Georg Jensen.

Fruit dish no. 320A designed by Georg Jensen,
1919. Courtesy of Georg Jensen/Royal
Copenhagen.

Bonbonniere no. 10 designed by Georg Jensen, 1919.

Bowl no. 105 with unusual leaf design by Georg Jensen.

Covered dish decorated with two swans
designed by Johan Rohde, 1920. Georg Jensen
Sølvsmedie, Gennem Fyrretyve Arr, 1904-1944.

Blossom muffineer. Collection of Robert
Fredieu and Rosemary Schulze.

Dish no. 587 designed by Johan Rohde, 1930.
Courtesy of Georg Jensen/Royal Copenhagen.

Three Royal Copenhagen porcelain mustard pots with sterling silver spoons and covers in Cactus and Bernadotte. Private collection.

Sugar shaker no. 33, eight inches tall. Private collection.

Mustard pot no. 221. Collection of Janet Laws and Steve Mey.

Above: Covered dish with underplate designed by Georg Jensen.

Below: Blossom muffineer and condiment set. Collection of Robert Fredieu and Rosemary Schulze.

Dish no. 181 with octagonal base.

Beaker designed by Georg Jensen.

Covered platter no. 600B designed by Harald
Nielsen, 1931. Courtesy of Georg Jensen/Royal
Copenhagen.

Footed bowl designed by Gundorph Albertus, 1935.

Bowl with bird stem designed by Arno Malinowski, 1937.

Covered dish designed by Harald Nielsen, 1938. Courtesy of Georg Jensen/Royal Copenhagen.

Fruit bowl, 1927.

Fruit bowl designed by Harald Nielsen, circa 1936.

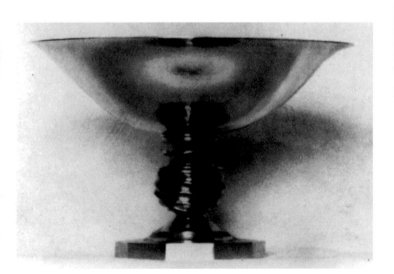

Large serving bowl designed by Johan Rohde, 1927.

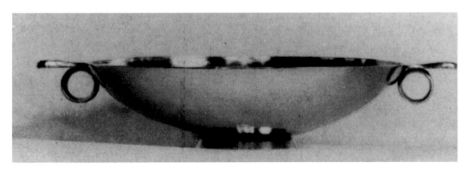

Shallow bowl designed by O. Gundlach-Pedersen, 1930.

Footed bowl. Collection of Robert Fredieu and
Rosemary Schulze.

Dish without a production number marked
GEORG JENSEN, COPENHAGEN and 830S.

Bowl no. 364.

Bowl no. 17A.

Serving bowl no. 468.

Three-section serving bowl no. 323D.

Bowl no. 197 with raised foliate bottom.

Glass jar with Blossom cover and Blossom jelly
spoon. Collection of Brenda Mixon and Thomas
Thornton.

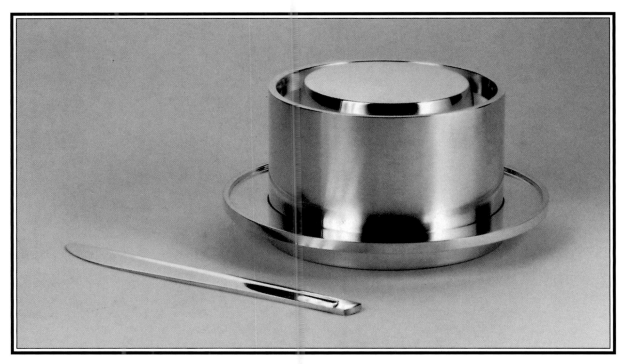

Butter dish no. 1059 designed by Søren Georg
Jensen, 1958. Courtesy of Georg Jensen/Royal
Copenhagen.

Tea and Coffee Services

Coffee set no. 1011 designed by Johan Rohde,
1906. Courtesy of Georg Jensen/Royal
Copenhagen.

Tea and coffee set no. 80 with ebony handles.

Tea kettle with warmer. Courtesy of The National Swedish Art Museums, Stockholm, Sweden.

Tea urn no. 29 designed by Georg Jensen, 1913. Courtesy of Georg Jensen/Royal Copenhagen.

Hot water kettle and stand no. 45B designed by Johan Rohde, 1915. Courtesy of Georg Jensen/Royal Copenhagen.

Coffee set no. 45 designed by Johan Rohde, 1915. Courtesy of Georg Jensen/Royal Copenhagen.

Coffee set no. 71 designed by Georg Jensen, 1920.
Courtesy of Georg Jensen/Royal Copenhagen.

Tea urn no. 182 designed by Georg Jensen, 1918.
Courtesy of Georg Jensen/Royal Copenhagen.

Tea strainer no. 1 with holder no. 40. Assay mark of Carl Heise.

Tea strainer.

Tea strainer designed by Georg Jensen.

Tea strainer in Cactus and holder.

Six piece Cosmos tea set and tray with ivory
handles. Private collection.

Coffee pot with a creamer and a sugar.
Collection of Ed and Lisa Guari.

Coffee and tea set designed by Johan Rohde,
1920.

Teapot. Collection of Ed and Lisa Guari.

Detail of the cover of the coffee pot.

Three piece coffee set with coffee pot, creamer and sugar. Collection of Dr. Barry Goozner.

Detail of open sugar.

Coffee pot designed by Johan Rohde, 1920.

Teapot designed by Johan Rohde, 1920.

Tea urn no. 179 designed by Georg Jensen, 1923. Courtesy of Georg Jensen/Royal Copenhagen.

Chocolate pot designed by Johan Rohde, 1920.

Silver tea set designed and executed by Georg Jensen.
The Studio Year Book of Decorative Art, 1922.

Original drawing of coffee pot by Johan Rohde,
1926. Courtesy of Ole Pedersen.

Original drawing of teapot by Johan Rohde,
1926. Courtesy of Ole Pedersen.

Silver tea set designed and executed by Georg
Jensen. *The Studio Year Book of Decorative
Art*, 1922.

Coffee set no. 456 designed by Harald Nielsen,
1927. Courtesy of Georg Jensen/Royal
Copenhagen.

Small coffee, sugar and creamer no. 235 on
tray.

Tea caddy no. 713 designed by Sigvard
Bernadotte, 1931. Courtesy of Georg Jensen/
Royal Copenhagen.

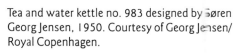

Tea and water kettle no. 983 designed by Søren
Georg Jensen, 1950. Courtesy of Georg Jensen/
Royal Copenhagen.

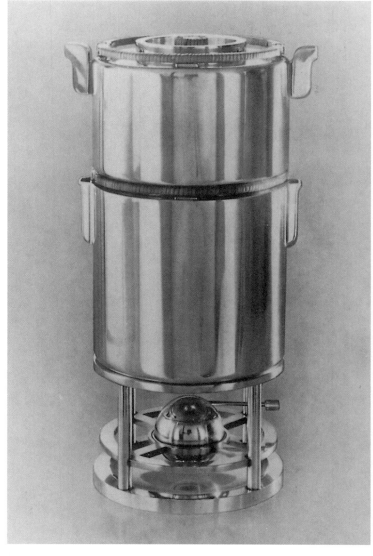

Coffee service with ebony handles designed by
Johan Rohde, 1933.

Teapot no. 1051 designed by Henning Koppel, 1952. Courtesy of Georg Jensen/Royal Copenhagen.

Tea and coffee set no. 1017 designed by Henning Koppel, 1963. Courtesy of Georg Jensen/Royal Copenhagen.

Household Hollowware:

Advertisement for Georg Jensen, Copenhagen, 1939. Courtesy of Georg Jensen/Royal Copenhagen.

Covered dresser box no. 145.

Flower vase designed by O. Gundlach-Pedersen, 1928.

Covered box no. 166A. Collection of Ed & Lisa Guari.

Pair of Pyramid candlesticks. Private collection.

Three-armed candelabra. Private collection.

Silver chandelier designed and executed by
Georg Jensen. *The Studio Year Book of
Decorative Art*, 1922.

GEORG JENSEN

HANDMADE SILVER

*By Appointment
to the King of Denmark*   *By Appointment
to the King of Sweden*

159 West 57th Street, New York

MEMBRE DE LA SOCIÉTÉ NATIONALE
DES BEAUX ARTS

Grand Prix · · · San Francisco. 1915
Grand Prix · · · · · Barcelona, 1923
Grand Prix · · Rio de Janeiro, 1923

LONDON   PARIS   NEW YORK
ATELIERS   COPENHAGEN

Advertisement for Jensen silver in New York,
1924. *International Studio*, November, 1924.

Candlestick no. 668A designed by Henning
Seidelin, 1932. Courtesy of Georg Jensen/Royal
Copenhagen.

Candelabra no. 324. Courtesy of
Georg Jensen/Royal Copenhagen.

Advertisement containing a sketch of a two-
armed candelabra designed by Georg Jensen.

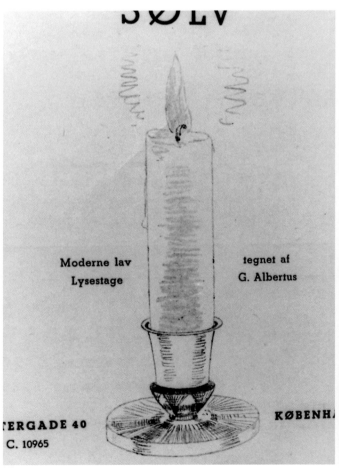

Candlestick in Cactus.

Candlestick no. 244 designed by Georg Jensen, 1918. Courtesy of Georg Jensen/Royal Copenhagen.

Candlestick no. 286 designed by Johan Rohde, 1919. Courtesy of Georg Jensen/Royal Copenhagen.

Candlestick no. 263 designed by Georg Jensen, 1918. Courtesy of Georg Jensen/Royal Copenhagen.

Candlestick no 474 designed by Johan Rohde, 1927. Courtesy of Georg Jensen Royal Copenhagen.

Candlestick no. 956 designed by Henning Koppel, 1948. Courtesy of Georg Jensen/Royal Copenhagen.

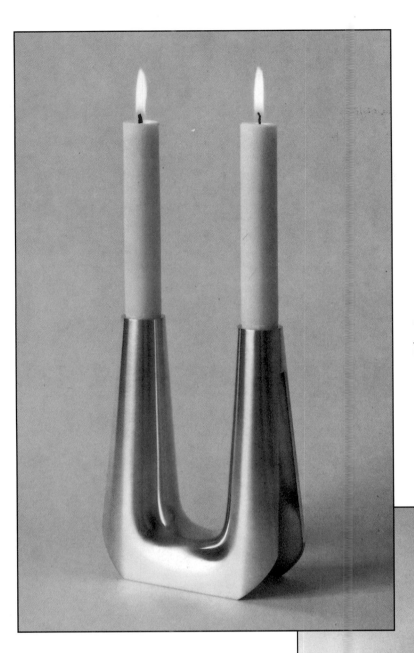

Candelabra no. 1087 designed by Søren Georg Jensen, 1963. Courtesy of Georg Jensen/Royal Copenhagen.

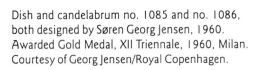

Dish and candelabrum no. 1085 and no. 1086, both designed by Søren Georg Jensen, 1960. Awarded Gold Medal, XII Triennale, 1960, Milan. Courtesy of Georg Jensen/Royal Copenhagen.

Bottle cork no. 100 in Blossom.

Decanter stopper no. 205B in Pyramid.

Glass decanter with sterling silver stopper. Private collection.

Wine goblet no. 296.

Wine goblet no. 532. Private collection.

Wine taster.

Pitcher no. 385 designed by Johan Rohde, 1923. Courtesy of Georg Jensen/Royal Copenhagen.

Beaker no. 671E.

Cup no. 60 designed by Georg Jensen, 1918.
Courtesy of Georg Jensen/Royal Copenhagen.

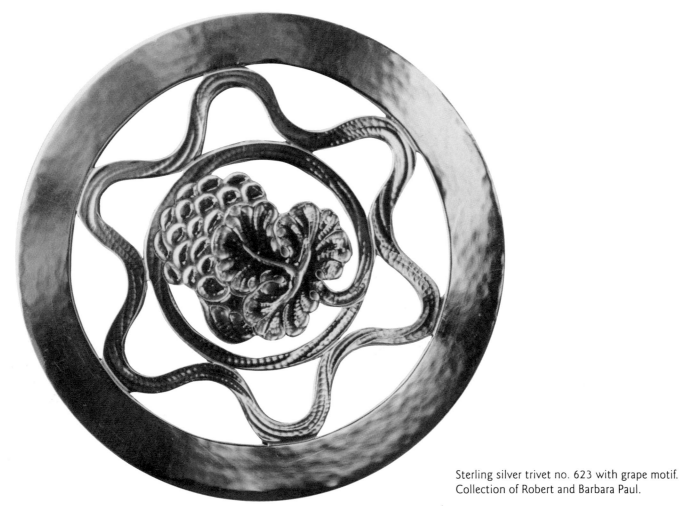

Sterling silver trivet no. 623 with grape motif.
Collection of Robert and Barbara Paul.

Wine jug no. 947 designed by Jørgen Jensen, 1948. Courtesy of Georg Jensen/Royal Copenhagen.

Wine goblet no. 309B designed by Johan Rohde with English export marks.

Wine cask. *The Studio*, February 1920.

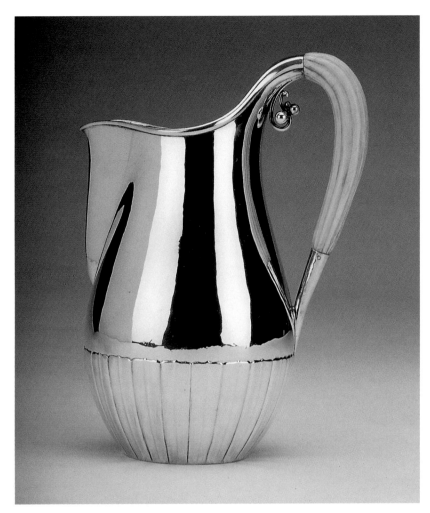

Wine pitcher with ivory handle. Private collection.

Covered box with a carnelian finial with underplate. Private collection.

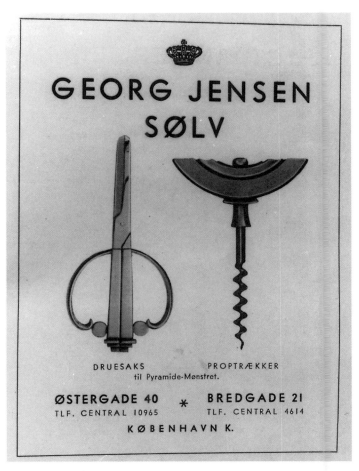

Advertisement for a corkscrew and a grape shear in the Pyramid pattern showing the addresses of the two Jensen retail stores in Copenhagen. *Samleren*, 1933.

Ice bucket with tongs and cocktail glasses designed by Sigvard Bernadotte.

Beaker designed by Arno Malinowski, circa 1937. Georg Jensen Sølvsmedie, Gennem Fyrretyve Arr, 1904-1944.

Cocktail shaker designed by Gundorph Albertus.

Pitcher designed by Johan Rohde and vase designed by Harald Neilsen.

Pitcher no. 432 designed by Johan Rohde.
Collection of Anne and Lindsay Waters.

Pitcher by Henning Koppel.

Drawing of Henning Koppel pitcher.

Flower bowl designed by Arno Mailnowski, circa 1938.

Cocktail shaker.

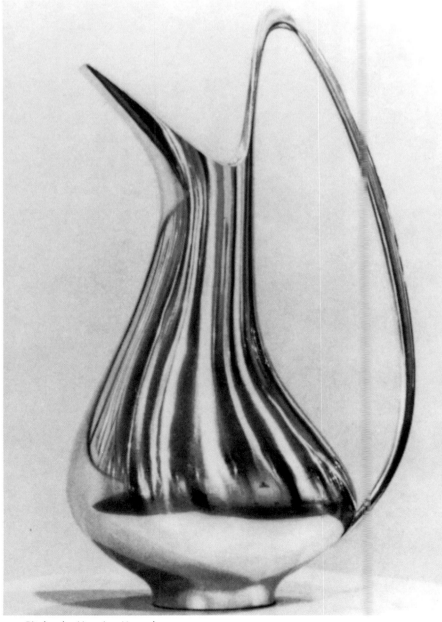

Pitcher by Henning Koppel.

Pitcher with ebony handle designed by Johan Rhode.

Pitcher no. 13 designed by Sigvard Bernadotte, 1952. Courtesy of Georg Jensen/Royal Copenhagen.

Silver ashtray designed by Georg Jensen and purchased by the Newark Museum in 1929, 4" high, 4 3/4" long, 3 1/2" wide. Collection of The Newark Museum.

Pitcher no. 407 designed by Georg Jensen, 1925. Courtesy of Georg Jensen/Royal Copenhagen.

Chocolate pitcher no. 460B designed by Georg Jensen, 1925. Courtesy of Georg Jensen/Royal Copenhagen.

A group of butter pats and salt cellars. Private collection.

Salt and pepper shakers no 1031 designed by Hans Henriksen in 1953.

Cigarette holder designed by Gundorph Albertus, 1926.

Salt and pepper shakers no. 965 designed by Soren Georg Jensen.

Bonbonniere designed by Sigvard Bernadotte, 1938.

Two rectangular covered boxes with diagonal striping.

Cherub napkin ring with blue enamel background. Private collection.

Sugar castor no. 627, 5 3/4" h, designed by Ove Brøbeck in 1931. Courtesy of Georg Jensen/ Royal Copenhagen.

Place card holders no, 102 designed by Gundorph Albertus with GJ Ltd. and English hallmarks. Private collection.

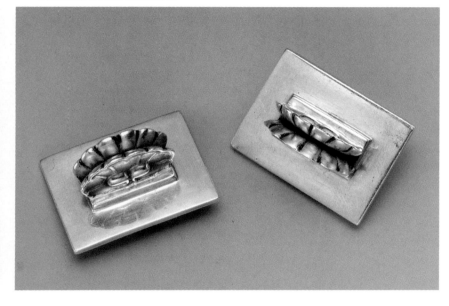

Super egg box no. 1147A and tray no. 1146A, both designed by Piet Hein, 1966. Courtesy of Georg Jensen/Royal Copenhagen.

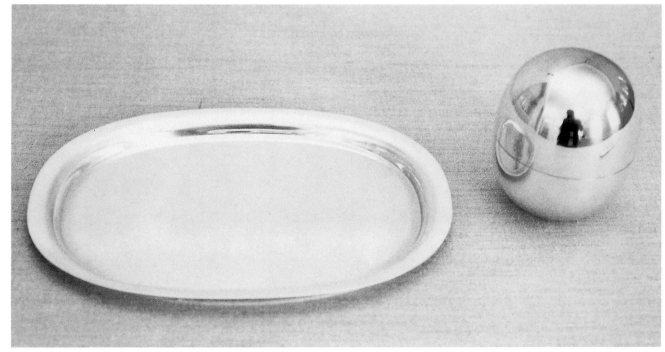

Chafing dish designed by Magnus Stephensen.
Courtesy of George Jensen/Royal Copenhagen.

Butter dish and marmalade jar no. 1059A
designed by Søren Georg Jensen, 1958.
Courtesy of George Jensen/Royal Copenhagen.

Bowl no. 980 designed by Henning Koppel, 1950. Courtesy of Georg Jensen/Royal Copenhagen.

Exhibit of Jensen table setting. Courtesy of Georg Jensen/Royal Copenhagen.

Table set with Jensen silver.

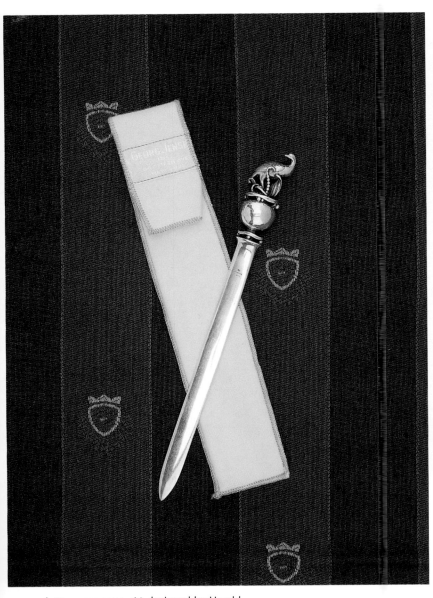

Group of three letter openers: from left, no 83, no. 202 with green agate, and no. 126 with flower form handle. Collection of Ed and Lisa Guari.

Letter opener no. 61 designed by Harald Nielsen.

Five letter openers: from left, Acorn (Konge), no. 141, no. 126 with ivory blade and silver handle, no. 127, and no. 136.

Bookmark.

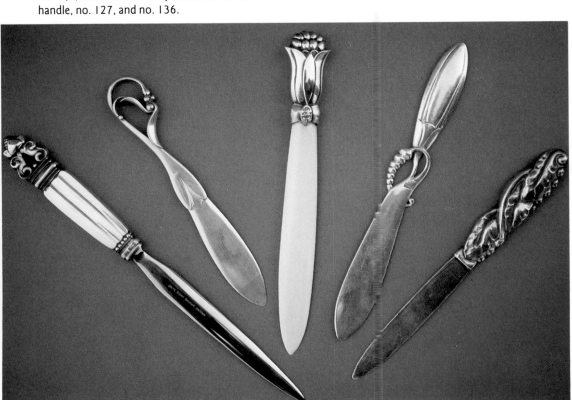

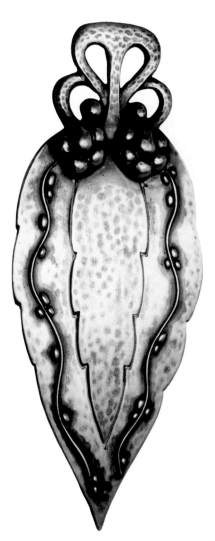

Accessories to the home, 1942. Courtesy of
Georg Jensen/Royal Copenhagen.

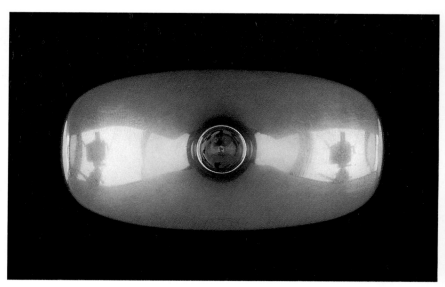

Sterling silver Mezzuzah with cabochon
amethyst designed by Henning Koppel.
Collection of the author.

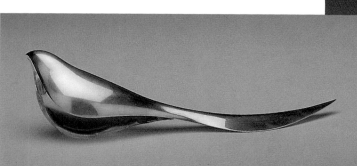

Crystal paperweight and sterling letter opener
no. 485 marked Allan Scharff.

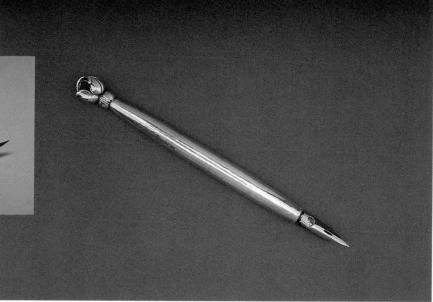

Sterling silver pen. Collection of the author.

Owl seal with coral eyes. Private collection.

Letter opener/book mark no. 198 with fish
finial and chain.

Bell push with ivory button.

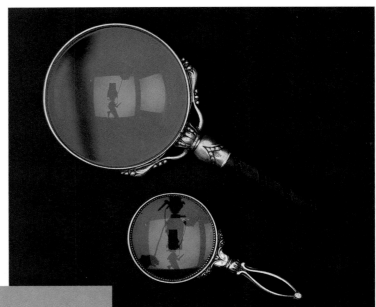

Large magnifying glass no. 74 with carved ebony handle, and small magnifying glass no.184 which can be worn on a chain. Private collection.

Bell pusher no. 108 with ivory finial. Collection of Janet Laws and Steve Mey.

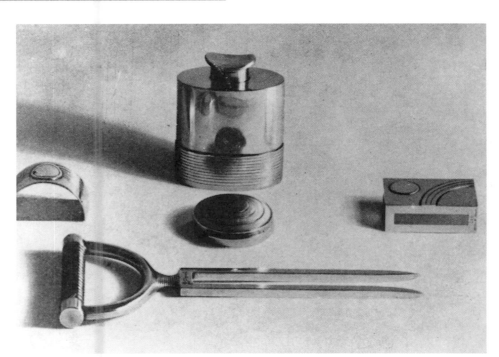

Group of desk accessories. Courtesy of Georg Jensen/Royal Copenhagen.

Ring tray no. 429B. Private collection.

Stainless steel clock designed by Sigvard
Bernadotte, 1943. Courtesy of Georg Jensen/
Royal Copenhagen.

Hand mirror no. 172A signed with the initials
of designer Harald Nielsen.

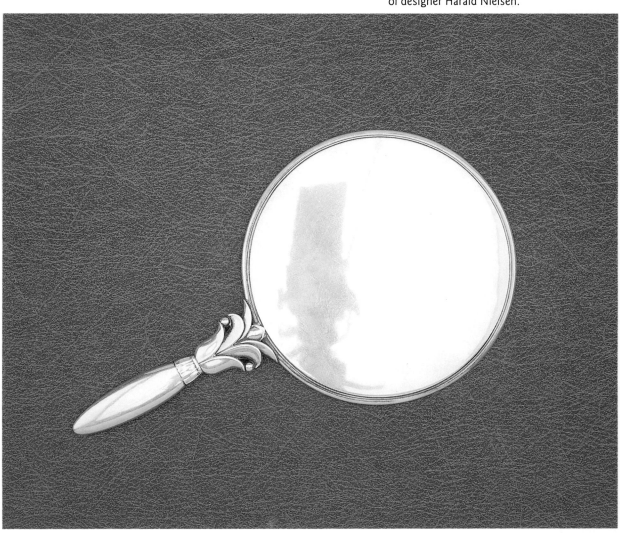

Sterling silver compact no. 231R decorated with raised dolphin. Collection of Ed & Lisa Guari.

Sterling silver primping mirror in its original fitted box. Private collection.

Square compact.

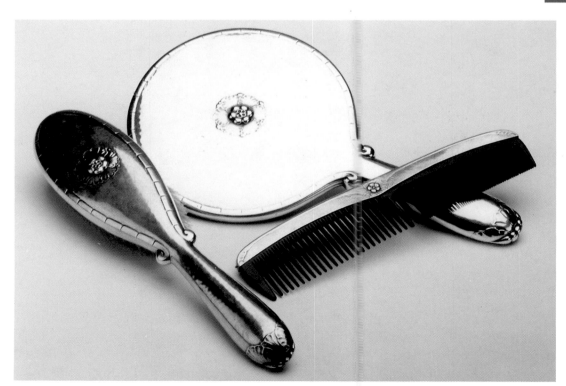

Covered box designed by Georg Jensen.

Three piece dresser set no. 79. Private collection.

Men's shaving ensemble. *The Studio*, 1936.

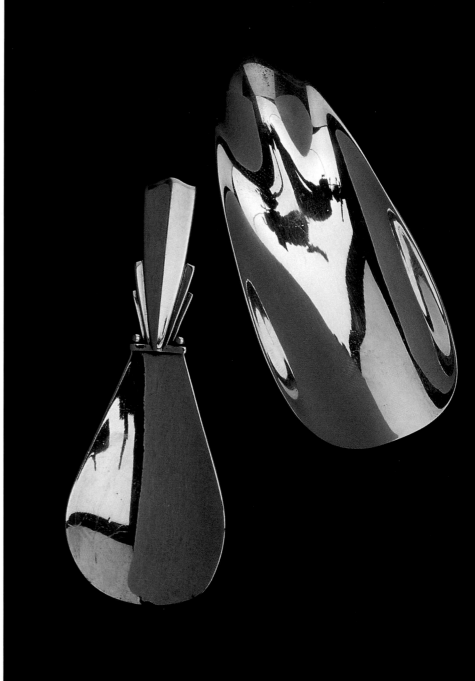

Two shoe horns.

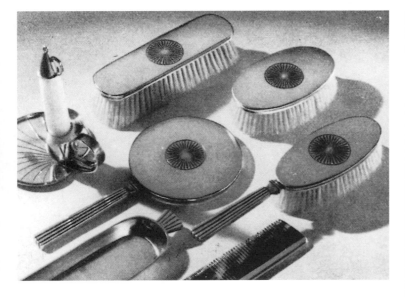

Dresser set, 1940. Courtesy of Georg Jensen/
Royal Copenhagen.

Dresser set of ebony with inlaid silver exhibited
in Kunstindustrimuseet, April, 1941. Courtesy
of Georg Jensen/Royal Copenhagen.

Silver and porcelain objects, circa 1942.
Courtesy of Georg Jensen/Royal Copenhagen.

Two cigar cutters. Collection of Barbara and
Steve Herman.

Blossom wooden matchbox holder no. 2D
designed by Georg Jensen. Collection of Ed
and Lisa Guari.

Cigarette box no. 329 designed by Johan Rohde, 1919. Courtesy of Georg Jensen/Royal Copenhagen.

Cigarette holder in Acorn.

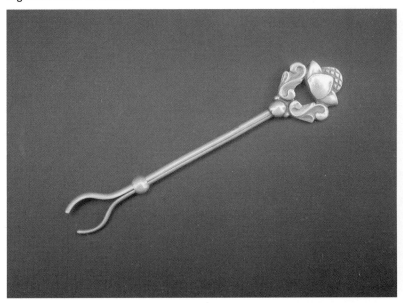

Tobacco jar designed by Jørgen Jensen. Courtesy of Georg Jensen/Royal Copenhagen.

COMMEMORATIVE SILVER:

Presentation copper box commemorating 50th anniversary and lettered "1866-1916." Marked with designer's name Johan Rohde. Private collection.

Presidential hammer with block presented to the Corporation of Copenhagen by the Federation of Sealand Agricultural Societies, designed by Georg Jensen. Georg Jensen Sølvsmedie, Gennem Fyrretyve Arr, 1904-1944.

Writing set designed by Gundorph Albertus and presented as a gift to His Majesty the King from the Ministerial Commission for the Royal Jubilee, 1937. Georg Jensen Sølvsmedie, Gennem Fyrretyve Arr, 1904-1944.

Gift from the Crown Prince to United States President Franklin D. Roosevelt. Designed by Sigvard Bernadotte, 1939. Georg Jensen Sølvsmedie, Gennem Fyrretyve Arr, 1904-1944.

Spice set, gift for the Swedish Crown Prince from his children. Designed by Sigvard Bernadotte, 1942. Georg Jensen Sølvsmedie, Gennem Fyrretyve Arr, 1904-1944.

Ski jumping trophy designed by Johan Rohde for the Lake Placid Club, U.S.A., 1928. Georg Jensen Sølvsmedie, Gennem Fyrretyve Arr, 1904-1944.

Commemorative church plate designed by Axel Hou. Courtesy of Georg Jensen, Copenhagen.

Model ship "Kronprins Frederik" executed in silver, gift from the United Steamship Company to His Royal Highness the Crown Prince, 1941. Designed by Gundorph Albertus. Georg Jensen Sølvsmedie, Gennem Fyrretyve Arr, 1904-1944.

Trophy designed by Professor Anton Rosen, 1917. Georg Jensen Sølvsmedie, Gennem Fyrretyve Arr, 1904-1944.

Chairman's bell no. 266 with ivory designed by Georg Jensen, 1918. Courtesy of Georg Jensen/Royal Copenhagen.

Chapter 8
Flatware

Georg Jensen thought of dining as a sacred ritual through which family members could share nourishment and renew bonds. For him, the table was a symbol of home and family, and he believed that beautiful flatware could enhance people's lives by making dining a more pleasurable experience. Therefore, he designed flatware for everyday use that was functional and aesthetically pleasing. His imaginative lyricism is epitomized by sugar spoon no. 2, with its graceful line and wonderful aura of softness.

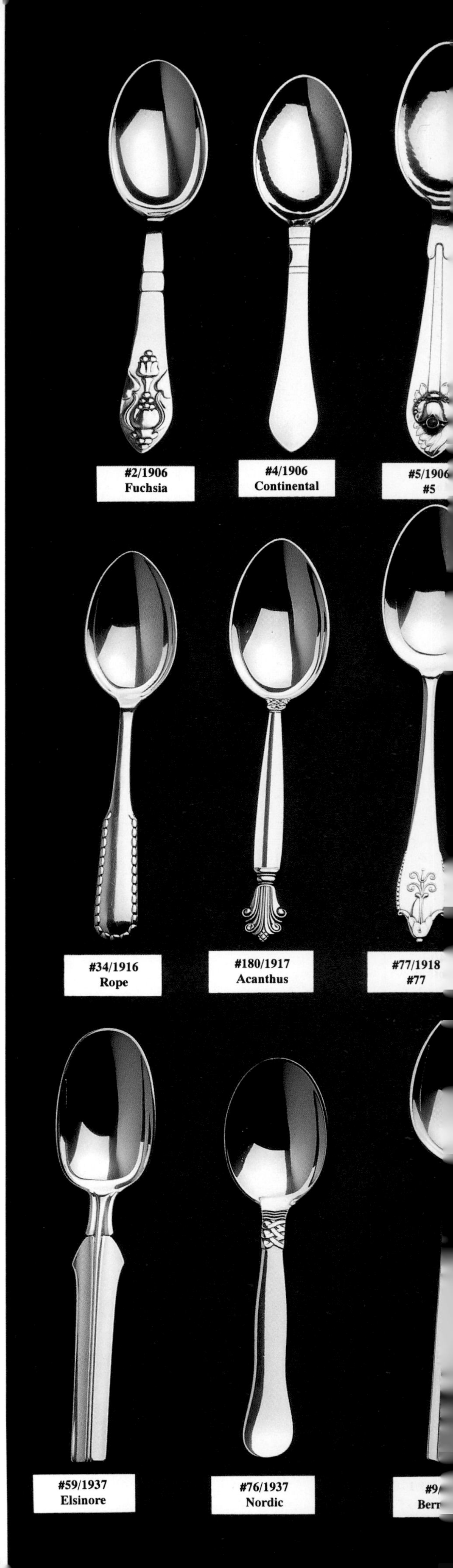

The sterling silver flatware patterns produced by Georg Jensen Co. Courtesy of Georg Jensen Museum, Copenhagen.

#2/1906
Fuchsia

#4/1906
Continental

#5/1906
#5

#34/1916
Rope

#180/1917
Acanthus

#77/1918
#77

#59/1937
Elsinore

#76/1937
Nordic

#9/
Berr

/1906
#16

#145/1910
#145

#18/1910
#18

#19/1910
#19

#3/1912
Dahlia

#1/1913
Rose

#62/1915
Acorn

#7/1916
Beaded

4/1919
lossom

#15/1926
Pyramid

#6/1927
Viking

#22/1927
Scroll

#30/1930
Cactus

#25/1931
Parallel

#46/1934
Acadia

#56/1937
Mayan

#79/1940
Bittersweet

#100/1947
Old Danish

#99/1954
Cypress

#111/195?
Caravel

#118/1961
Argo

#134/1966
Margrethe

#101/1981
Koppel

The steps toward making a serving spoon from a silver bar as displayed at the Georg Jensen Museum.

Place setting in Lily of the Valley (Liljekonval) designed by Georg Jensen, 1913. Courtesy of Georg Jensen/Royal Copenhagen.

Place setting in Blossom (Magnolia) designed by Georg Jensen, 1919. Courtesy of Georg Jensen/Royal Copenhagen.

FLATWARE BEGINNINGS

Jensen's flatware designs emerged during the first decade of the twentieth century when Denmark was enjoying an economic boom. Many Danes had the means to acquire luxury goods that had previously been out of their reach. Because it connoted affluence, sterling silver flatware was among the luxury items many coveted, and Jensen was well positioned to respond to the growing demand. His flatware patterns soon found considerable favor in Denmark, and eventually garnered international acclaim.

During the early years of the Jensen silversmithy, European flatware production was dominated by a modernist aesthetic that embraced generic forms and tended to be mechanically mass produced. In contrast, Jensen's flatware designs were highly individualistic, designed for function with beauty.

Jensen's first flatware pattern, called Antik in Danish (and Continental in English), was introduced in 1906. It has a relatively simple, restrained design characterized by surface hammering and simple, decorative grooves and notches. It was probably inspired by traditional Nordic wooden utensils, in particular a wooden spoon that was given to Jensen's wife when she was a child. Jensen's borrowing from vernacular design is not surprising; apparently endeavoring to attract middle class Danish customers, he fashioned a conservative design that would be familiar. Many of Jensen's subsequent patterns are more adventurous, exhibiting the sculptural qualities that are characteristic of his style. His Liljekonal (Lily of the Valley) pattern, introduced in 1913, features a leaf garland that traces the tapering end of the handle. Even more sculptural is the Magnolie (Blossom) pattern, introduced in 1919, which features a realistic stem and blossom design that appears to grow from the handle. This pattern, perhaps more than any other, demonstrates the sculptural quality that earned Jensen widespread acclaim.

Many of Jensen's flatware designs were inspired by natural forms: flowers that resemble lilies trace handles, entwined fish form handles of fish serving implements, a blossom with berries forms the ends of serving spoons, and leaves are engraved on a vegetable serving set. The flower on the Blossom flatware pattern also appears as a handle on the cover of the Blossom teapot, which was introduced in 1905.

Not all of Jensen's flatware designs are redolent of nature. The Antik (Continental) pattern, mentioned above, is devoid of naturalistic forms, as is the Beaded pattern, an elegant composition from 1916 that is distinguished by a simple beaded border along the lower edge of the handle. The Beaded pattern remains contemporary in design while imparting a timeless quality.

During his career, Georg Jensen designed thirteen flatware patterns; eight have names and five have only numbers, they include: Klokke (Bell), Antik (Continental), Liljekonval (Lily of the Valley), Kugle (Beaded), Rope (Pearl), Akkeleje (no translation in English), Magnolie (Blossom), Nordiske (Viking), 5, 16, 18, 119, and 145. Four of Jensen's own patterns are still in production (Continental, Lily of the Valley, Beaded, and Blossom), indicating their continuing aesthetic and utilitarian appeal.

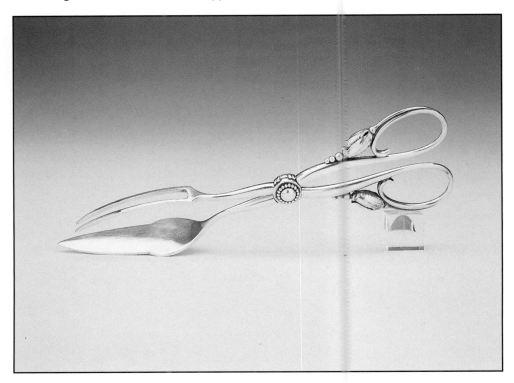

Blossom sandwich server no. 84.

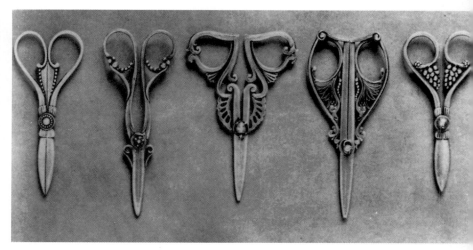

Five grape shears in different patterns by Johan
Rohde and Georg Jensen. Georg Jensen
Sølvsmedie, Gennem Fyrretyve Arr, 1904-1944.

An assortment of flatware in Acorn. Georg
Jensen Sølvsmedie, Gennem Fyrretyve Arr,
1904-1944.

Place setting in Scroll (Saga) designed by Johan
Rohde, 1917. Courtesy of Georg Jensen/Royal
Copenhagen.

Twelve other designers also created nineteen flatware patterns for the Jensen company between 1912 and 1981, as indicated on the flatware chart. Some of these patterns deserve special attention. The Konge (Acorn) pattern, designed by Johan Rohde and introduced in 1916, is probably the best known and most popular of all Jensen flatware patterns. It features a handle with a fluted, classical shaft, topped by a highly sculptural pierced finial with a stylized acorn bud supported by two scrolls. At one time, this pattern comprised 228 different pieces, from the standard knife, fork and spoon of the basic place setting to unusual specialized accessory pieces such as salad sets, mustard spoons, herring forks, and tea strainers. A photograph in volume 1 of the Danish decorative arts journal *Samleren* in 1928 shows 67 different pieces in this pattern. The size and variety of this assortment is impressive, and it rather boggles one's mind to consider that another 151 unique pieces were made as well. Currently, 80 different pieces are produced in the Acorn pattern, including table card holders, lemon knives, ice tongs, grape scissors, and strawberry spoons. Acorn is a cheerful pattern that seems equally appropriate for a casual meal or a formal dinner.

The Acorn pattern shares some characteristics with Acanthus, another pattern designed by Rohde and introduced in 1917. Acanthus also has classical motifs in the fluted column-like shaft and an acanthus leaf finial. Indeed, the two patterns appear to be variations on the same theme.

Scroll, also designed by Rohde and introduced in 1927, is a bold synthesis of two seemingly disparate elements: a large, roughly textured, S-shaped scroll in high relief (probably derived from a traditional Nordic motif) and a sleek handle in keeping with modernistic trends. The scroll, from which the pattern takes its name, is placed in the center of the handle, seemingly as a symbolic statement that the past is imbedded in the present.

The Pyramid pattern, designed by Harald Nielsen and introduced in 1926, is a marked departure from the flatware designs of Jensen and Rohde. Inspired by the popular interest in Egyptian forms aroused by the discovery of Tutankhamen's tomb, Pyramid's straight lines and stepped finial blend a historical reference with the functional look then in vogue. Nielsen's design appears to owe more to the influence of the German Bauhaus than to Georg Jensen's naturalism. Nielsen's clean, unadorned design was precisely in step with the popular Deco style of the time. Moreover, Nielsen led the way to making the firm's designs once again fresh and contemporary.

Another of Nielsen's designs is the Old Danish pattern, introduced in 1947. Far less radical than Pyramid, it has handles with undulating outlines and a pair of incised parallel lines that follow the handle's shape; the spoon bowl is rather square. Although modern in its lack of ornamentation, this pattern's overall proportions are reminiscent of much earlier flatware designs, as the name Old Danish implies.

Subsequent flatware patterns continued in the modern trend. Albertus's Cactus, which features stylized floriforms clustered above a smooth and gently curving handle, is another balanced composition in the Art Deco style. This pattern is still a favorite, particularly among people with an affinity for the American southwest.

Another of Albertus's designs is Bittersweet, in which a blossom of the bittersweet plant is at one end of an otherwise unornamented handle.

The Bernadotte pattern emphasizes long, straight, converging lines, and a crisp, clean simplicity. In its use of flat surfaces and straight lines, it is a perfect reflection of Sigvard Bernadotte's other work in silver which corresponds with the angular modernism of Wright, Gropius, Meis van der Rohe, and other titans of modern design.

Over the years, Jensen designers continued to create new patterns for flatware which captured the imagination of customers. The firm endeavored to attract customers for flatware made by combining sterling silver and stainless steel. For example, pattern no. 101, designed by Henning Koppel and introduced in 1980, combined sterling silver handles with stainless steel utensils. No. 101 thus exhibited contemporary design yet was much more affordable than patterns in all sterling silver.

Although each of these patterns, from Georg Jensen's Continental through Henning Koppel's No. 101, can be appreciated individually without regard to their relationship to the stylistic trends they reflect, nearly all are powerful, innovative, and among the best decorative art of their times. They belong among the most original designs of their periods, and when they were introduced, they each had a profound impact on flatware designs internationally.

Of the thirty-three known sterling silver flatware patterns made by the Jensen company, ten continue in production: Antik (Continental), Liljekonval (Lily of the Valley), Kugle (Beaded), Konge (Acorn), Dronning (Acanthus), Magnolie (Blossom), Pyramide (Pyramid), Kaktus (Cactus), Bernadotte, and Dobbeltriflet (Old Danish).

Cutlery pieces in Pyramid (Pyramide).
Courtesy of Georg Jensen/Royal Copenhagen.

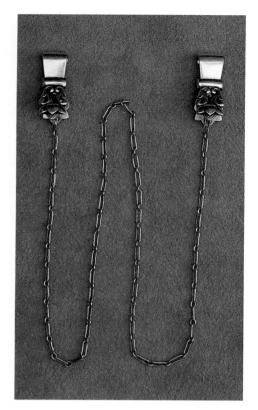

Bib clips in Acorn.

In addition, there are patterns used only for handmade serving pieces that complement the place settings, and these are referred to as "odd pieces" or "ornamental." Indeed, the complexity and delicacy of their designs could not be successful without a skilled silversmith's expert touch. Each serving piece has a number, but no name, impressed on the back of each piece. There are many such pieces, including the following: 2l, 38, 39, 40, 4l, 42, 44, 47, 53, 54, 55, 57, 7l, 72, 83, 86, 91, 93, 102, 110, 117, 122, 124, 130, 131, 132, 136, 140, 141, 153, 144, 159, and 162. Each of these patterns has different serving pieces, and many of them are intricate and highly ornamental. For example, pattern 83 includes a specialized cake knife, compote fork, compote spoon, fish knife, fish fork, fish serving set, large paper knife, small paper knife, pastry fork, salad fork, sauce ladle, serving fork, vegetable fork, and vegetable spoon. Today, there are approximately twenty-one varieties of ornamental serving pieces.

Each flatware piece in a standard place setting has the Georg Jensen Company mark impressed on the back. Serving pieces also have the maker's mark as well as the sterling mark.

Jensen flatware reflects stylistic trends as well as changing social and cultural trends over the last century. The large number and variety of flatware pieces that were common at the beginning of the century were necessary for the elaborate formality in dining that was normal at the time. Over the years, domestic dining has become much less formal and ritualized, and thus the number of flatware pieces that are felt to be necessary is much fewer. The flatware also reflects what people eat. Sardine forks and jelly spoons, for example, which were common in 1910 but seem anachronistic today, indicate a change in culinary conventions and social etiquette. Jensen also produced flatware in accordance with culinary traditions of different countries, and so cultural differences are apparent in the flatware. For example, the bowls of soup spoons exported to the United States were made smaller than the bowls of soup spoons intended for the European market.

Standard Place Settings

Many people find pleasure in using fine flatware everyday, and this carries out Georg Jensen's ideal of making quality goods, even art, a part of one's daily environment. Today, a place setting of five pieces is standard and typically it includes a dinner knife, dinner fork, dessert spoon, large teaspoon, and salad or fish fork. Many serving pieces today are intended to fulfill more than one function, so quite a bit of flexibility in selection is possible. For example, a gravy ladle can be used to dispense creamed dishes, dessert sauces, and whipped cream. A pie server can be used also for grilled vegetables, pastry, and hamburgers. Ultimately, the number and type of flatware pieces in a person's service depends on their dining aesthetic and anticipated culinary needs.

Obtaining new or vintage flatware to expand or fill in sets can be complicated because some pieces were made in a variety of sizes. Therefore, in order to make ordering as foolproof as possible, it is advisable to photocopy the exact piece needed. For pieces that are no longer in production, the second hand market must be explored.

Knife rests in Acorn. Service for twelve designed by Johan Rohde.

Jensen Sterling Silver Flatware Patterns arranged chronologically, 1906 to 1981

No.	Pattern Name American	Danish	Year	Designer
#2	Fuchsia	Klokke	1906	Georg Jensen
#4	Continental **a**	Antik	1906	Georg Jensen
#5*			1906	Georg Jensen
#16*			1906	Georg Jensen
#18*			1910	Georg Jensen
#145*			1910	Georg Jensen
#19*			1910	Georg Jensen
#3	Dahlia	Dahlia	1912	Siegfried Wagner
#1	Rose **a**	Liljekonval**	1913	Georg Jensen
#7	Beaded **a**	Kugle	1916	Georg Jensen
#34	Rope	Perle	1916	Georg Jensen
#62	Acorn **a**	Konge	1915	Johan Rohde
#180	Acanthus **a**	Dronning	1917	Johan Rohde
#77		Akkeleje	1918	Georg Jensen
#84	Blossom **a**	Magnolie	1919	Georg Jensen
#15	Pyramid **a**	Pyramide	1926	Harald Nielsen
#6	Viking	Nordisk	1927	Georg Jensen
#22	Scroll	Saga	1927	Johan Rohde
#30	Cactus **a**	Kaktus	1930	Gundorph Albertus
#25	Parallel	Relief	1931	O. Gundlach-Pedersen
#46	Acadia	Blok	1934	Ib Just Andersen
#56	Mayan	Rune	1937	Johan Rohde
#59	Elsinore	Agave	1937	Harald Nielsen
#76	Nordic	Ladby	1937	O. Gundlach-Pedersen
#9	Bernadotte **a**	Bernadotte	1939	S. Bernadotte
#79	Bittersweet	Pinje	1940	Gundorph Albertus
#100	Old Danish **a**	Dobbeltriflet	1947	Harald Nielsen
#99	Cypress	Cypres	1953	Tias Eckhoff
#111	Caravel	Caravel	1957	Henning Koppel
#118	Argo	Fregat	1961	Magnus Stephensen
#134	Margrethe	Margrethe	1966	Rigmor Andersen &
#101	Koppel	Koppel	1981	Annelise Bjørner

Key:
a -Currently in Production
* -Patterns designed by Georg Jensen only identified by numbers, no names given.
** -Pattern no.1, Liljekonval (Lily of the Valley) was called Rose in the United States when it was introduced in 1913. It was discontinued for a time and in recent years has been reintroduced as Lily of the Valley.

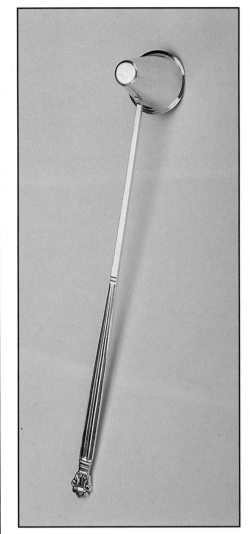

Candle snuffer in Acorn. Collection of Abby Drucker.

The numbers of the Jensen flatware patterns do not relate to the chronological order of their production. For example, the Continental pattern, the first flatware produced, is no. 4. This lack of a system for flatware contrasts with the numbering systems for Jensen hollowware and jewelry, where the numbers indicate a general chronological order of their original design. (Bracelet no. 19 can be assumed to have been designed before bracelet no. 20, although there are many exceptions.) For flatware, the silver standard mark indicates the year the piece was assayed and that, coupled with the maker's mark Georg Jensen, can be used to determine the date of production.

The flatware patterns were given American names when thier sales expanded to the United States. Sometimes, patterns were given other names that related to the country where the flatware was sold, for example in England, the Nordic pattern was referred to as Hamlet.

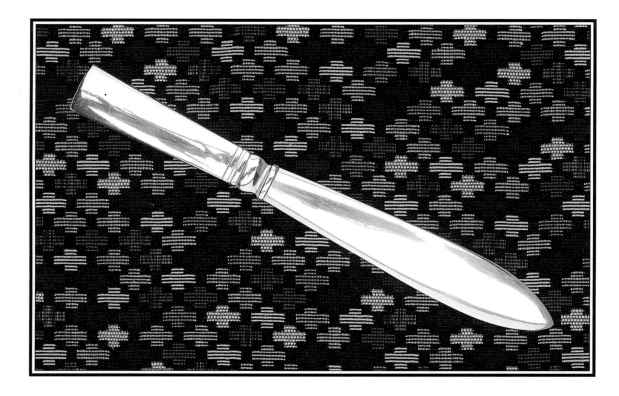

Patterns arranged alphabetically

Acadia (Blok)

Sterling silver letter opener in Acadia (Blok)
(no. 46) designed by Just Andersen, 1934.

Acanthus (Dronning)

Place setting in Acanthus (Dronning).
Courtesy of Georg Jensen/Royal Copenhagen.

Acorn (Konge)

Place setting in Acorn (Konge). Courtesy of
Georg Jensen/Royal Copenhagen.

Sterling flatware service in Acorn (Konge).
From left, fish/salad fork, luncheon fork,
luncheon knife, butter spreader, serving ladle,
dessert spoon, teaspoon, and demitasse
spoon. Courtesy of Skinner's Inc., Boston and
Bolton.

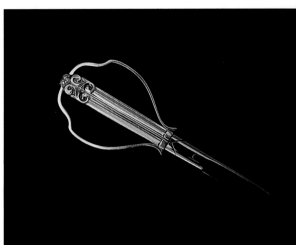

Grape shears in Acorn.

Place settings for children in Acorn and Cactus. Collection of Sarah Beth Drucker & Matthew Jason Drucker.

Argo (Fregat)

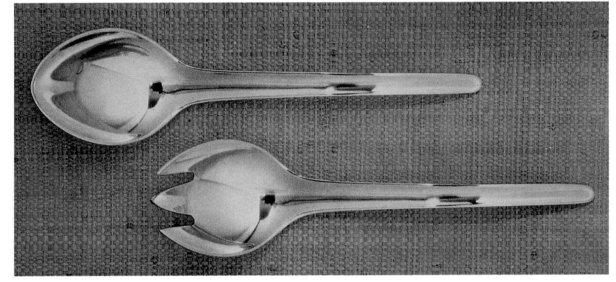

Beaded (Kugel)

Place setting in Beaded (Kugle). Courtesy of Georg Jensen/Royal Copenhagen.

Bernadotte (Bernadotte)

Place setting in Bernadotte. Courtesy of Georg Jensen/Royal Copenhagen.

Bittersweet (Pinje)

20-piece place setting of Bittersweet (no.79) designed by Gundorph Albertus, 1940. Collection of Dr. Barry Goozner.

Blossom (Magnolie)

Detail of Blossom (Magnolia) designed by Georg Jensen, 1919. Courtesy of Georg Jensen/Royal Copenhagen.

Cactus (Kaktus)

Place setting in Cactus (Kaktus). Courtesy of Georg Jensen/Royal Copenhagen.

Bottle opener in Cactus (Kaktus), designed by Gundorph Albertus, 1930. Collection of Steve Herman.

Caravel (Caravel)

Place setting in Caravel designed by Henning Koppel, 1957. Courtesy of Georg Jensen/Royal Copenhagen.

Continental (Antik)

Place setting in Continental (Antik). Courtesy of Georg Jensen/Royal Copenhagen.

Cypress (Cypres)

Cutlery pieces in Cypress (Cypres) designed by Tias Eckhoff which won the design competition held for the 50th anniversary of the founding of the Georg Jensen company. Courtesy of Georg Jensen/Royal Copenhagen.

Dahlia (Dahlia)

Fish serving set in Dahlia pattern designed by Siegfried Wagner. Collection of Marsha Ewing-Current.

Detail of finials on serving set in Dahlia pattern.

Elsinore (Agave)

Elsinore (Agave) place setting designed by Harald Nielsen, 1937. Courtesy of Georg Jensen/Royal Copenhagen.

Fuchsia (Klokke)

Six serving pieces in Fuchsia (no.2) designed by Georg Jensen, 1906. Collection of Dr. Barry Goozner.

Koppel (No. 101)

See group picture, p. 263.

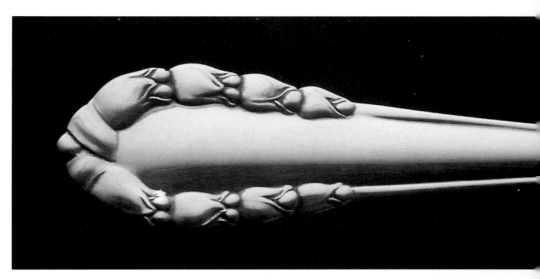

Lily of the Valley (Rose) (Liljekonval)

Detail of Lily of the Valley (Liljekonval) designed by Georg Jensen, 1913. Courtesy of Georg Jensen/Royal Copenhagen.

Margarethe (Margarethe)

Mayan (Rune)

Mayan (Rune) serving pieces designed by Johan Rohde. Courtesy of Georg Jensen/Royal Copenhagen.

Nordic (Ladby)

Nordic (Ladby) serving pieces designed by O. Gundlach-Pedersen, 1937. Courtesy of Georg Jensen/Royal Copenhagen.

Old Danish (Dobbeltriflet)

Place setting in Old Danish (Dobbeltriflet). Courtesy of Georg Jensen/Royal Copenhagen.

Parallel (Relief)

Table setting in Relief (Parallel) designed by Oscar Gunlach-Pedersen.

Pyramid (Pyramide)

Sterling flatware service in Pyramid (Pyramide). From left, cheese knife, mocha spoon, coffee spoon, cold meat fork, pastry fork, cake knife, salad spoon, salad fork, and gravy ladle. Courtesy of Skinner's Inc., Boston and Bolton.

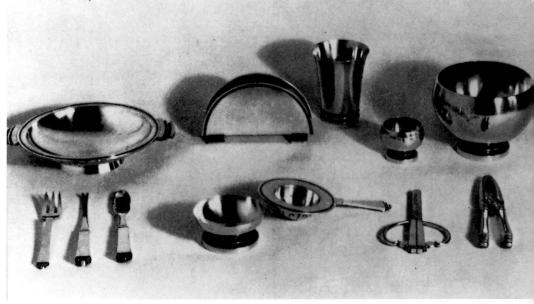

Pyramid lunch service designed by Harald Nielsen. Courtesy of Georg Jensen/Royal Copenhagen.

Rope (Perle)

A pie server in Rope (Perle). Courtesy of Skinner's Inc., Boston and Bolton.

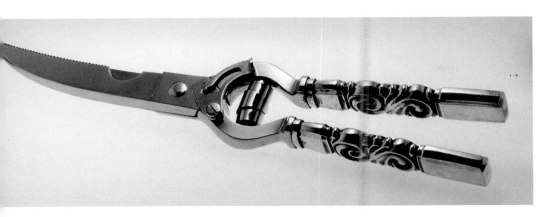

Poultry shears in Scroll.

Scroll (Saga)

Detail of Scroll (Saga) designed by Johan Rohde, 1917. Courtesy of Georg Jensen/ Royal Copenhagen.

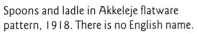

Spoons and ladle in Akkeleje flatware pattern, 1918. There is no English name.

Numbered and Ornamental Pieces

Serving set no. 35 designed by Georg Jensen, 1913.

Serving pieces, pattern no. 38 designed by Georg Jensen, 1912. Collection of Dr. Barry Goozner.

Sugar spoon, pattern no. 41, designed by
Georg Jensen. Collection of Dr. Barry Goozner.

Serving set with owl finials, pattern no. 39.

A group of no. 42 serving pieces
designed by Georg Jensen, 1918.
Collection of Dr. Barry Goozner.

Serving pieces, pattern no. 83 designed by Georg Jensen, 1914. Collection of Dr. Barry Goozner.

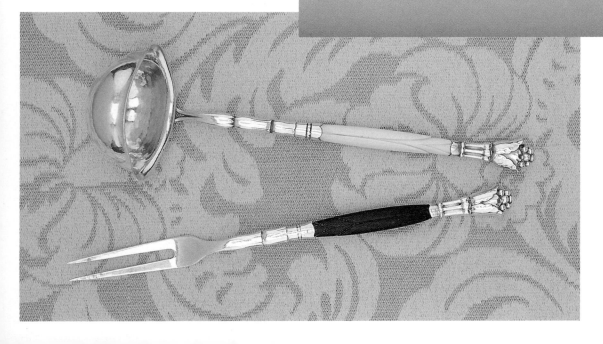

Pie server, pattern no. 91. Collection of Dr. Barry Goozner.

Sauce ladle with an ivory handle and two-tine serving fork with ebony handle, both pattern no. 93 designed by Georg Jensen, 1916. Collection of Dr. Barry Goozner.

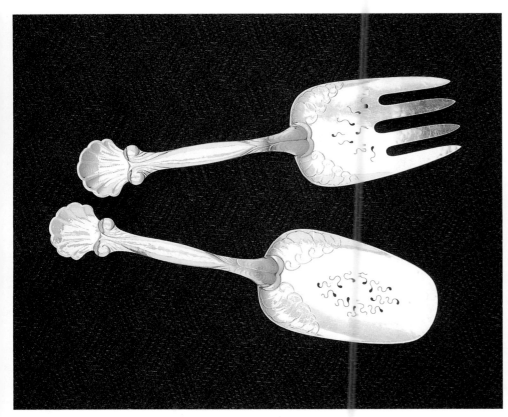

Fish set pattern no. 102. Collection of Dr.
Barry Goozner.

Ladle with two spouts, pattern no. 128.
Collection of Dr. Barry Goozner.

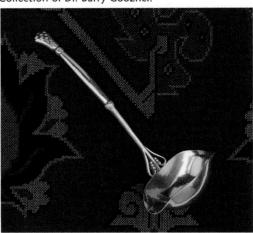

Ice tongs, pattern no. 106. Collection o
Marcia A. Ewing-Current.

Serving pieces no. 136. Collection of
Dr. Barry Goozner.

Spoons: from left to right, no. 53, two of no. 52, no. 148, and two of no. 72. Collection of Dr. Barry Goozner.

Commemorative server with inscription Concordia 1933. Collection of Marsha Ewing-Current.

Reverse of commemorative spoon.

Bread tongs.

Salad set with shell motif.

Three ornamental serving pieces in the Snail pattern designed by Georg Jensen. Collection of Marsha Ewing-Current.

Serving pieces. Collection of Marsha Ewing-Current.

Two necklaces of the same design, one by
Georg Jensen, 1917, and the other signed
Sterling Handwrought at the Kalo Shop.

Chapter 9
The Legacy
Jensen's Worldwide Influences

Like a pebble dropped into the mill pond, the impact of Georg Jensen's work radiated in expanding circles through the course of his life and beyond. There are a number of ways to assess his impact. There is little doubt that, through the excellence of his work, he played a major role in the elevation of Danish silversmithing to the highest echelons of international decorative art, in terms of both craftsmanship and design artistry. The praise he received for his splendid silver helped to bring attention to other talented Danish silversmiths and Danish decorative arts as a whole.

Jensen and his company have contributed significantly to his nation's economy. The firm accounted for substantial exports, particularly to France, Germany, Great Britain, and the United States and provided jobs, over the century, for thousands of Danes. Also, a significant number of those who served their apprenticeships at Jensen's smithy went on to establish their own workshops and make further contributions to Danish silversmithing and other decorative arts. Two prominent examples are Inger Møller (1886-1979) and Kay Bojesen (1886-1958). Møller began at Jensen's workshop in 1909, worked there until 1921 when she opened her own workshop and created distinctive high quality silver. Bojesen, another of the early apprentices, later formed his own workshop and worked with other materials as well as silver. Bojesen became an important industrial designer of a wide range of products including cutlery, hollowware, and whimsical wooden toys. Both Møller and Bojesen exhibited their work internationally and won major awards. Jensen was an inspiration for many artists and craftsmen throughout Denmark.

Georg Jensen also inspired artists outside Denmark, to lesser or greater degrees. Sometimes the influence was so apparent that the term "copying" comes to mind. One of the necklaces produced by the Chicago-based Kalo Workshop is nearly indistinguishable from Jensen's necklace no. 57. Precisely how this came to pass is not known, but the presence, in Chicago, of silversmiths who emigrated from Denmark and were employed by Kalo is a possibility. Another Jensen design, for the Tulip Bracelet, no. 93, was apparently the inspiration for a necklace and bracelet set designed about 1930 by American Frederick W. Davis (1880-1961), who worked in Mexico after 1910 where he bought and sold folk art, including silver, and eventually designed silver that was produced by Mexican craftsmen (see Berk and Morrill, *Mexican Silver, 20th Century Handwrought Jewelry & Metalwork*, p. 29). Another of Davis's designs was unmistakably influenced by Jensen's famous Dove Brooch, no. 191, which was designed by Christian Mohl-Hansen in 1906. Other of Jensen's designs can also be seen in Mexican silver, including serving spoons sold through the Mexico City store Sanborn's, where Davis worked, and in hollowware produced by various manufacturers. After World War II, American flatware manufacturers, such as International Silver, sought to take advantage of the growing popularity of Jensen designs in the American market by creating flatware patterns with Nordic-sounding names such as Royal Danish, a design obviously inspired by Jensen's Acorn pattern.

In some cases, Jensen's direct impact on other artists is more difficult to detect, especially if their work does not contain overt references to Jensen's characteristic style. American goldsmith Edward Everett Oakes was a medalist of the Boston Society of Arts and Crafts. His jewelry is predictably replete with the floral motifs emblematic of the Arts and Crafts style, but contains no recognizable quotations of Jensen's work. However, the author found a drawing of Jensen's bracelet no. 14 in Edward Oakes' studio workbox, indicating that he surely was familiar with Jensen's jewelry.

Signs of Jensen's influence sometimes surface in unexpected places. A textbook, published in 1926 in Peoria, Illinois, and presumably was used in American industrial art classes, contains photographs of jewelry attributed to the author of the textbook and others that were obviously based on Jensen designs (see Emil F. Kronquist, *Metalcraft and Jewelry*, p.46 and 92). How the designs found their way into the book is not a mystery. The Danish-born author Emil Kronquist worked in a Copenhagen silversmithy (possibly Jensen's) before emigrating to the United States and subsequently becoming an instructor of metalwork at the Milwaukee State Normal School and the Washington High School in Milwaukee, Wisconsin.

46 *METALCRAFT AND JEWELRY*

Fig. 46. Silver Work by Students—Bar Pin, Watch Fob, Shoe Buckles

Page from Emil Kronquist's *Metalcraft and Jewelry*, a textbook on metal work, showing jewelry of Jensen designs attributed to the students. The author was a teacher at the Milwaukee State Normal School, the Washington High School in Milwaukee, and the Stout Institute in Menomonie, Wisconsin, c. 1925.

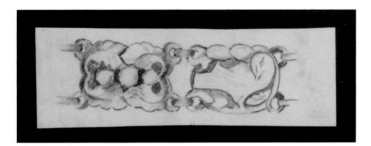

Drawing by Edward Everett Oakes of a Jensen dove bracelet. Courtesy of Oakes Studio, New Hampshire.

A photograph of a Jensen dove bracelet and a porcelain bird found in Edward Everett Oakes' files. Courtesy of Oakes Studio, New Hampshire.

Finally, Jensen's influence continues to be evident at the celebrated company he founded through the maintenance of high standards of craftsmanship and design. Public recognition of the work of Jensen company designers has continued throughout the century. In continuing the apprenticeship system, the company has perpetuated Jensen's belief in the deft combination of work done by hand and work done by machine. As a final tribute to his continuing influence, a worldwide public has validated his designs by continually purchasing a large number of his original designs, right up to the present.

These few examples of Georg Jensen's influence offer persuasive evidence of the strength, variety and diffusion of his impact on design and decorative arts in the twentieth century.

THE GEORG JENSEN MUSEUM

In June of 1982, an important addition to Danish culture and art was established with the opening of the Georg Jensen Museum in Copenhagen, located at Amagertorv 6, adjacent to the flagship Georg Jensen Store, the main Royal Copenhagen store, and the Georg Jensen Museum Shop. The museum houses the archives of the Georg Jensen Silversmithy and provides public access to stunning exhibitions, as well as photographs, design drawings and other documents that illuminate the history of the firm from 1904 to 1940. Notable displays feature rare jewelry and hollowware, flatware designs, and explanations of the processes used to produce silver at the Jensen silversmithy. Illustrations of Georg Jensen during the early days of his workshop are a large part of the display. The museum is visited by some 140,000 people annually, is an appealing venue for the casual visitor and an invaluable resource center for museum professionals, antique dealers, collectors, auctioneers, journalists, and others who are keenly interested in Georg Jensen silver. The museum's curator is Michael von Essen.

Page from Emil Kronquist's *Metalcraft and Jewelry* showing Jensen designs in jewelry attributed to Kronquist.

Appendix
Museum Collections
with Georg Jensen Silver
(Partial List)

Albright-Knox Art Gallery, Buffalo, New York,
Birmingham Museum of Art, Birmingham, Alabama
Boston Museum of Fine Art, Boston, Massachusetts
British Museum, London, England
Brooklyn Museum, Brooklyn, New York
Brohan Museum, Berlin, Germany
Carnegie Institute of Arts, Pittsburgh, Pennsylvania
Chicago Art Institute, Chicago, Illinois
City Art Museum of St. Louis, St. Louis, Missouri
Cleveland Museum of Art, Cleveland, Ohio
Corcoran Gallery of Art, Washington, D. C.
Corning Museum of Glass, Corning, New York
Cranbrook Academy of Art, Michigan
Curia Gallery of Art, Manchester, England
Dallas Museum of Art, Dallas, Texas
Detroit Institute of Art, Detroit, Michigan
Folketinget, Christiansdborg, Copenhagen, Denmark
Georg Thomas Hunter Gallery of Art, Chattanooga, Tennessee
Georg Jensen Museum, Copenhagen, Denmark
Germanic Museum, Harvard University, Cambridge, Massachusetts
Gewerbemuseum, Nuremberg, Germany
The Goldsmiths' Hall, London, England
Grass Museum, Leipzig, Germany
Isaac Delgade Museum of Art, New Orleans, Louisiana
J.B. Speed Art Museum, Louisville, Kentucky
Joslyn Art Museum, Omaha, Nebraska
Kolding Museum, Kolding, Denmark
Kunstgewerbe Museum, Zurich, Switzerland
Kunstindustrimuséet, Copenhagen, Denmark
Kunstindustrimusée, Oslo, Norway
Landesgewerbeaomt Baden-Wurtenberg, Stuttgart, Germany
Latvijus Volsts Makslos Muzejs, Riuso, Russia
Metropolitan Museum of Art, New York, New York
Musée d'Art et Histoire, Geneva, Switzerland
Musée des Beaux Arts, Cairo, Egypt
Musée du Louvre, Paris, France
Museum fur Kunst und Gewerfvbe, Hamburg, Germany
Museum of Modern Art, New York, New York
National Gallery, Melbourne, Australia
Nationalmuséet, Stockholm, Sweden
Neue Sommling (Die), Munich, Germany
Newark Museum, Newark, New Jersey
Nordenfjeldske Kunstindustrimuseum, Rundheim
Philadelphia Museum of Art, Philadelphia, Pennsylvania
Riijksmuseum, Amsterdam, Holland
Rochester Museum, Rochester, New York
Rohsska O Konstslojdmuséet, Goteburg
Vesterlandska Museum, Bergen, Norway
Victoria and Albert Museum, London, England
Virginia Museum of Fine Art, Richmond, Virginia
Walker Art Center, Minneapolis, Minnesota

Selected Artists of the Georg Jensen Silversmithy

The following designers are those whose work is most frequently encountered in the Jensen line from Denmark.

Gundorph Albertus (1887-1954)

Gundorph Albertus, who married the sister of Johanna, Jensen's third wife, joined the Georg Jensen workshop in 1911 as a chaser. From 1926 to 1954, he served as the Company's Assistant Director, and he designed the Cactus flatware pattern in 1930. He was trained as a sculptor at the Royal Academy of Arts and exhibited at Charlottenborg and at the Salon d'Automne in Paris. He was awarded a gold medal at the Paris World Exhibition in 1925 and the Diplôme d'honneur at L'Exposition Internationale in Paris in 1937, and remained with the Georg Jensen firm throughout his career.

Vilhelm Albertus (1878-1963)

Vilhelm Albertus, brother of Gundorph Albertus, worked for many years in the design department of the Georg Jensen Silversmithy.

Ibe Just Andersen (1884-1943)

While working for Georg Jensen, Ibe Just Andersen designed the Bloch flatware pattern. He established his own firm in Copenhagen in 1918 called Just Andersen Pewter.

Sigvard Bernadotte (1907-)

In 1930, when he started with the Georg Jensen firm, Count Sigvard Bernadotte, son of the king of Sweden and brother of Ingrid, queen mother of Denmark, was the first non-Danish designer for the Jensen company. As exemplified in the flatware pattern that bears his name, Bernadotte is well known for the clean lines of form introduced in the 1930s.

Vivianna Torun Bülow-Hübe (1927-)

Torun Bülow-Hübe started designing on a freelance basis for the Georg Jensen Silversmithy in 1967, after having been awarded the Lunning Prize in 1960. She trained at the National College of Art, Craft and Design in Stockholm. Torun, as she is known and as she signs her work, had her own studio in Stockholm from 1951 to 1956, in France from 1956 to 1968, in Germany from 1968 to 1978, and opened a studio in Indonesia in 1979. Torun has a very distinctive style that is clean, modern, graceful, and integrates smooth stones into her designs. An internationally acclaimed designer, her work is in many prominent museums around the world.

Nanna Ditzel (1923-) and **Jørgen Ditzel** (1921-1961)

A husband and wife team, both Nanna and Jørgen Ditzel were trained as furniture designers in Copenhagen. Nanna Ditzel started her own design firm in 1946. She won the Lunning prize in 1956 and a gold medal at the Milan Triennale in 1960. Since 1954, she has been associated with the Georg Jensen Silversmithy. Her work has been exhibited at selected prominent museums in the United States and in Europe.

Tias Eckhoff (1926-)

In the competition that was held to celebrate the 50th anniversary of the founding of the Georg Jensen firm, Tias Eckhoff won a prize for his Cypress flatware pattern. In addition, he was awarded the Lunning Prize.

Bent Gabrielsen (1928-)

Bent Gabrielsen apprenticed as a goldsmith and trained at the Danish College of Jewelry, Silversmithing and Commercial Design from 1950 to 1953. He was awarded the Lunning Prize in 1964, and a gold medal at the Milan Triennale in 1960. In addition to designing for the Georg Jensen Silversmithy, Gabrielsen was also a designer for Hans Hansen Silversmithy A/S from 1953 to 1969 and started his own workshop in Kolding in 1969.

Arje Griegst (1938-)

Arje Griesgt, trained in Copenhagen, has designed ceramics for the Royal Copenhagen Porcelain Manufactory and has worked as a designer for the Georg Jensen Silversmithy since 1965.

Oscar Gundlach-Pedersen (1886-1960)

Trained as an architect, Oscar Gundlach-Pedersen designed many prominent buildings in Denmark. His work was included in the Third International Exhibition of Contemporary Industrial Art, American Federation of Arts Traveling Exhibit in 1930-1931. He was the Manager of the Georg Jensen Silversmithy from 1927 until 1931 as well as a designer for the firm.

Poul Hansen (1902-)

Poul Hansen began to work for the Georg Jensen firm in 1922 and became the foreman of the goldsmith workshop in 1937.

Erik Herlow (1913-)

Professor of industrial design at the Royal Danish Academy of Fine Arts, Erik Herlow has designed many architectural installations and has served as artistic consultant to the Royal Copenhagen Porcelain Manufactory since 1955. Herlow was awarded gold medals at the Milan Triennale in 1954 and 1957.

Jørgen Jensen (1895-1966)

Jørgen Jensen, a son of Georg Jensen, was a siversmith for his entire life. He worked on his own in Munich and Stockholm and returned to Denmark in the mid-1930s as a designer in the Georg Jensen Silversmithy, where he stayed until 1962.

Søren Georg Jensen (1917-)

Søren Georg Jensen, a son of Georg Jensen, was educated as a silversmith and a sculptor and was the head of the design department of the Georg Jensen Silversmithy from 1962 to 1974. He is well known for his sculptural works. 1946 Gold Medal, Royal Academy; 1960 Gold Medal, Milan Triennial.

Edvard Kindt-Larsen (1901-1954)

The designer Edvard Kindt-Larsen, whose clean-lined, geometric work is still in production today, worked mostly in industrial design.

Henning Koppel (1918-1982)

Henning Koppel, one of the Jensen firm's most distinctive designers since 1945 and a major innovator of the modern Jensen style, was the protege of Harald Nielsen. Not only did Koppel design for Georg Jensen, but he also created works for Bing & Grondahl Porcelain Manufactory from 1961 and Orrefors Glassworks from 1971. As a young man, Koppel studied sculpture at the Royal Academy of Fine Arts and at the Academie Ranson in Paris. He was awarded the Lunning Prize in 1953 and gold medals at the 1951, 1954 and 1957 Milan Triennales. His work is represented in major museums throughout the world.

Ole Kortzau (1939-)

Ole Kortzau has designed hollowware for the Georg Jensen Silversmithy since 1978. He also has worked for the Royal Copenhagen Porcelain Manufactory and maintains his own design firm.

Arno Malinowski (1899-1976)

Arno Malinowski was educated at the Royal Danish Academy of Fine Art as a sculptor and engraver. Malinowski worked at the Georg Jensen Silversmithy from 1936 to 1965. Among his designs, he developed the iron and silver jewelry produced by the firm during the Second World War and the emblem Kongemaerket, designed on the occasion of the 70th birthday of His Majestry Christian X.

Christian Møhl-Hansen (1876-1962)

Christian Møhl-Hansen trained as a painter at the Royal Academy of Fine Arts and received a gold medal for textiles at the Paris Exhibition in 1925. He created various designs for Georg Jensen, including a cup designed in 1916 which was exhibited at the Smithsonian Institution's Renwick exhibition in 1980.

Harald Nielsen (1892-1977)

Harald Nielsen, the brother of Jensen's third wife Johanne joined the Jensen Silversmithy in 1909. Along with Jensen and Johan Rohde, Nielsen, a gifted draughtsman who wanted to become a painter, helped to establish the Jensen style as we know it and the firm's tradition for outstanding quality. In the 1920s, he designed jewelry, flatware and hollowware, many of which are still in production today. After Jensen's death in 1935, Nielsen became the artistic leader of the Georg Jensen Silversmithy.

Henry Pilstrup (1890-1967)

Henry Pilstrup joined the Georg Jensen Silversmithy in 1904 and remained with company until 1957. He was Georg Jensen's first apprentice and went on to design gold and silver jewelry for the firm while he was foreman of the jewelry workshop. His no. 64 cufflinks produced in gold and silver are still in production.

Johan Rohde (1856-1935)

Johan Rohde was a recognized painter when he began his collaboration with Georg Jensen 1906. He was Jensen's closest collaborator along with Harald Nielsen. Johan Rohde designed furniture, flatware and hollowware. The Acorn flatware pattern, one of the most famous ever produced by the Jensen smithy, was designed by Rohde in 1916. Johan Rohde presented design with perfect balance of material and purpose. He was keenly attuned to the goals and work of Georg Jensen and remained constantly in harmony with his ideals until his death.

Magnus Stephensen (1903-)
Magnus Stephensen, who was trained as an architect, has received several medals at the Milan Triennale and started his association with the Georg Jensen Silversmithy in 1950.

The following artists are among those who have designed for the Georg Jensen Company over the years. Their initials are sometimes used to identify their work.

Gundorph Albertus	GA	Georg Jensen	GJ
Vilhelm Albertus		Jørgen Jensen	JJ
Anne Ammitzbøll	AA	Søren Georg Jensen	SGJ
Ib Just Andersen		Bjarne Jespersen	
Knud Holst Andersen	KHA	Edvard Kindt-Larsen	EKL
Rigmor Andersen		Henning Koppel	HK
Steffen Andersen	SA	Nina Koppel	NK
Jens Andreasen		Ole Kortzau	OK
Sigvard Bernadotte	SB or Sigvard	Anette Kræn	AK
Annelise Bjørner		Peter Kristiansen	PK
Ib Bluitgen		Eva Dora Lamm	EDL
Bente Bonné		Henry Larsen	HL
Max Brammer	MB	Hugo Liisberg	HL
Ove Brøbeck		Erik Magnussen	EM
Torun Bülow-Hübe	Torun, or TBH	Arno Malinowski	AM
Jørgen Dahlerup		Andreas Mikkelsen	A.Mik.
Ibe Dahlquist	ID	Christian Møhl-Hansen	
Agnete Dinesen	AD	Jørgen Møller	JM
Jørgen Ditzel		Lene Munthe	LM
Nanna Ditzel	ND	Mikala Naur	MN
Tias Eckofff	TE	Kim Naver	KN
Flemming Eskildsen	FE	Harald Nielsen	HN
Tuk Fischer		Regitzer Overgaard	RO
Kay Fisker	KF	Verner Pantom	VP
Astrid Fog	AF	Gustav Pedersen	
Ernest Forsmann		Arne Petersen	
Kirsten Fournais	KF	Bent Holse Petersen	
Bent Gabrielsen	BG	Ole Bent Petersen	
Bertel Gardberg		Henry Pilstrup	HP
Arje Griegst		Johan Rohde	JR
Oscar Gundlach-Pedersen	OGP	Anton Rosen	
Hans H. Hansen	HHH	Stephan Rostrup	
Hans H. Hansen, Jr.	HH	Allan Scharf	ASCH
Karl Gustav Hansen	KGH	Anne Schiang	ASch
Poul Hansen	PH	Georg Schütt	
Per Harild		Henning Seidelin	
Piet Hein	PHi	Thor Selzer	
Hans Henriksen		Svend Siune	
Gudmund Hentze	GH	Gail Spence	GS
Erik Herlow	EH	Eva Stæhr-Nielsen	
Gert Holbek		Olaf Stæhr-Nielsen	
Knud Holscher		Mette Stengaard	MST
Annette Howdle	AH	Magnus Stephensen	MS
Theresia Hvorslev		Siegfried Wagner	
Ole Ishøj	OI	Ole Wanscher	
Hans Ittig		Ove Wendt	OW
Axel Jensen	AJ	Othmar Zschaler	

Marks

There are a variety of marks that have been used by the Georg Jensen Silversmithy. Since records from the earliest date of 1904 are not complete, discoveries regarding verification of production dates are made when older pieces appear in the market place. There are several categories of marks that appear in various combinations on Georg Jensen silver:

A. - company mark
B. - silver content
C. - mark of origin
D. - design number
E. - initials of the designer

A. **The Company Marks and dates of production.**

 1904-1908 G with a decorative J superimposed, G.J.

 1909-1914 GJ and GI and Georg Jensen

 GEORG JENSEN
1915-1927 Background of dots stamped in oval surrounding Georg Jensen

 1915-1930 GI 830S, GI impressed in a circle of dots.

1915-1930 Upright oval of dots surrounding GI, under that

925, beneath that the letter
S

 1926-1932 Background of dots stamped in oval surrounding Georg Jensen with a crown

 1933-1944 A rectangular box surrounding the initials GJ in a logo

1945-1951 <u>Georg Jensen & Wendel: A/S</u> This mark was used only in the years 1945 to 1951. During these years the rights to the Smithy's mark was disputed between the Smithy in Copenhagen and the Georg Jensen Inc., U.S.A. Co. in New York.

 Since 1945 Background of dots in oval surrounding Georg Jensen

End link of a necklace marked with GJ in a box, 830S and DENMARK. Example of marks of configuration of marks reflecting various years of production. The 830S mark would indicate that this piece was produced before 1932, while the GJ in a box indicates that the necklace would have been made in a later period.

Example of the back of a brooch marked GEORG JENSEN, COPENHAGEN and GI 830S without any production number.

Import mark on a fork.

B. The Silver Content

The silver standard in Denmark was revised in 1893, with the revised Danish Hall-Marking Act which required the maker to mark the silver content, in figures, as well as the company mark. The hallmarking act placed the responsibility on the retailer to meet the standards required. The minimum silver standard .826S, in use up to 1915, when the minimum was changed to .830S to correspond to the other Scandinavian countries. The assay mark, the initials of the assay master accompanied by the control mark of 3 towers and date numerals, were not necessary to guarantee the silver content by the well known companies. The increase in exporting silver to England and the United States after 1915 required additional marking to meet the import regulations of other countries. For example, Danish silver exported to England, for sale in the Jensen store was stamped with the appropriate English hallmarks.

1904-1910	826 and 826S
1911-1914	830S
1915-1930	Upright Oval of dots surrounding GI above, 830 and beath that an S.

After 1933 the Smithy went to the Sterling Standard of 925. This standard continues to the present.

Assay marks:
C.F. Heise Assay Master 1904-1932 CFH
J.Sigsgaard Assay Master 1932-1933 JS

C. Mark of Origin

1907-1914	COPENHAGEN
1915-1919	COPENHAGEN
1935- present	DENMARK

D. The Design Number

A design number was given to each piece of jewelry and holloware.Numerical order was the placement of production numbers although there are many exceptions for which the explanations are not certain. It is probable that a design number was given to a piece of jewelry and at some point the piece was not put into production, leaving a number gap. This number could have been assigned to a piece at some later time.Generally, one could expect that lower numerals mean an earlier year of production. A letter designation, e.g. A, B, C, that accompanies the design number on a piece indicates a difference: size, border, stone, etc. All pieces of jewelry and holloware are still marked with a number, except special order items.During the early years, all flatware was marked with a number. Flatware today is not marked with a number except for handmade pieces, e.g. ornamental.

E. Designer's Signature

On some items, the signature or intials of the designer can be found, sometimes in a beaded oval, below the word *Dessin*, or standing alone. Examples of some designers marks are shown below, see a more complete list on page 294.

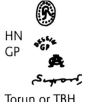

	Johan Rohde
HN	Harald Nielsen
GP	Gustave Pedersen
	Gundorph Albertus
	Sigvard Bernadotte
Torun or TBH	Torun Bülow-Hübe
ND	Nanna Ditzel
HK	Henning Koppel

EXPLANATION OF SILVER MARKS.

 Signature Mark.

 } Danish Hall Marks.

9 2 5.5 Standard Mark.

2 2 2 Registered Number of Design

LONDON ASSAY HOUSE MARKS:

 Signature.

London Hall Mark for Foreign Silver.

(925) Standard Mark.

Date Mark.

Examples of Georg Jensen's work were exhibited at the Royal Academy, London in 1923, and special exhibitions were held at the Fine Art Society, New Bond Street, London, in 1921/1923 and at the Walker Art Galleries, Liverpool in 1922/1923. In New York a choice collection, to which new examples will be continually added, is now on permanent exhibition at

159 WEST 57th STREET.

GEORG JENSEN

PRINTED IN ENGLAND.

Back page of a small catalogue of Hand Wrought Silver from the Jensen store at 169 West 57th Street, New York, indicating the marks of Georg Jensen Silver.

Chronology
Georg Jensen's Life

1866 Born August 31, Raadvad, Denmark

1872-79 Attends school in Raadvad

1879 Assists father at his job in the cutlery factory, Raadvad

1880 Moves to Copenhagen with his family; secures apprenticeship with goldsmith and attends technical school

1884 Completes apprenticeship as a goldsmith

1885-87 Works in workshop of Copenhagen goldsmith, while continuing to attend technical school

1887 Becomes student at Royal Academy of Fine Arts, Charlottenborg, Copenhagen

1889 Exhibits bust of father at Charlottenborg, Copenhagen

1891 Marries Marie Christiane Antonette Wulff, his first wife; son Vidar born; Jensen's sculpture "The Harvester" (which now stands in front of the Jensen silversmithy at Smallegade 45 in Frederiksberg, Copenhagen) is accepted for the annual exhibition at Charlottenborg

1892 Graduates from Royal Academy of Fine Arts, Department of Sculpture

1893 Participates in the annual exhibit at Charlottenborg in 1893, 1894 and 1896

1895 Son Jørgen born

1897 Wife Antonette dies; sculpture "Spring" rejected by Academy for annual exhibition, but accepted by Johan Rohde at "den Frie" Exhibit. For the first time, Georg Jensen travels outside of Denmark

1898 After he returns home, he begins collaboration in ceramics with Christian Joachim Petersen.

1899 Ceramic piece "The Maid on the Jar" chosen to be included in the Danish section at the World Exhibition in Paris (1900) and purchased by the Danish Museum of Decorative Art

1900 Wins honorable mention, with Christian Joachim Petersen, for ceramic display of work at World Exhibition in Paris; awarded travelling scholarship by the Academy for "The Maid on the Jar"; travels to Paris, Florence and Rome to study sculpture

1901 Returns to Denmark and continues his work in ceramics with Joachim; also works as silversmith in the Mogens Ballin silver workshop.

1904 Marries Maren Pedersen, called Magne, his second wife; daughter Vibeke born later in the year; opens his first workshop at 36 Bredgade, Copenhagen; exhibits silver jewelry at the Danish Museum of Decorative Art

1905 Exhibits silver at Folkwang Museum, Hagen, Germany; Folkwang Museum purchases some of his work; Belgian designer Henry Van de Velde visits Jensen's workshop; exhibits work at autumn exhibition, Charlottenborg; designs first hollowware, the "Blossom" teapot subsequently purchased by Danish Museum of Decorative Art

1906 The beginning of his association with the painter/designer Johan Rohde; the first flatware design, pattern no. 4 "Continental/Antik," is produced

1907 Wife Magne dies in January; moves, with children, from Copenhagen to Charlottenlund; marries Laura Julie Johanne Nielsen, his third wife, in November

1908 Exhibits work at Danish Museum of Decorative Art

1909 Harald Nielsen, his brother in law, joins Georg Jensen workshop as an apprentice; Jensen exhibits work at autumn exhibition, Charlottenborg; Carl Dyhr, Danish art dealer, opens Georg Jensen store in Berlin, the first Jensen store outside Copenhagen.

1910   Awarded gold medal at World Exhibition, Brussels; exhibits work in Paris and at Königliches Kunstgewerbemuseum (Museum of Decorative Art), Berlin

1911   Gundorph Albertus, a Danish sculptor, joins the workshop in Bredgade as a chaser; Albertus later became a designer for the firm and in 1918, director of the Silversmithy in Ragnagade; Albertus marries Johanne's younger sister, Inger, in 1919

1912   Daughter Lise born; moves workshop to large quarters at Knippelsbrogade, Copenhagen; opens store at 21 Bredgade, Copenhagen

1913   Exhibits work and awarded "Diplôme d'Honneur" at International Exposition, Gent, Belgium; Johan Rohde becomes a permanent designer for Georg Jensen workshop

1914   Daughter Birgitte born; exhibits work at Baltic Exhibition, Malmö, Sweden; Swedish art dealer Nils Wendel buys all works in exhibition to sell in his Stockholm art gallery

1915   World War I forces closure of Berlin shop; wins "Grand Prix" at Panama Pacific International Exposition, San Francisco, where William Randolph Hearst buys the majority of Jensen's silver

1916   Georg Jensen Sølvsmedie A/S founded as joint stock company with Jensen as president and artistic director

1917   Son Søren born; Thorolf Møller marries Johanne's sister, who was a bookkeeper for Georg Jensen

1918   Wife Johanne dies; expansion and renovation of the Bredgade store; Georg Jensen store opens in Rue St. Honoré, Paris; Knippelsbrogade worshop moves to larger factory at Ragnagade

1919   Financial problems are solved by Thorolf Møller brother-in-law of Georg Jensen, and P.A. Pedersen, together major stockholders since 1916, who again invest additional capital in the company

1920   Marries Agnes Christiansen, his fourth wife; exhibits work at Charlottenborg and Stockholm; appointed "Associé de la Société National des Beaux Arts," France; Frederik Lunning becomes manager of Bredgade store

1921   Daughter Mette born; store is opened on Maddox Street in London

1922   Frederik Lunning, manager of Bredgade store, arrives in United States to develop new markets for Georg Jensen silver; exhibits work at Anderson Galleries, New York City

1923   Wins "Grand Prix" awards at exhibitions in Barcelona, Brussels and Rio de Janeiro

1924   Frederik Lunning opens the first Georg Jensen store in New York City; in Copenhagen, P.A. Pedersen is the Director of the Georg Jensen Silversmithy and brother in law Thorolf Møller is the President of the Georg Jensen & Wendel A/S retail operation; second exhibition of Georg Jensen silver at Anderson Galleries, New York City

1925   Goes to Paris to try to establish a workshop; Jensen receives the "Grand Prix" at World Exposition, Paris; Georg Jensen store opens in Barcelona

1926   Returns to Denmark and again becomes artistic director of the silversmithy; celebrates his 60th birthday; new Jensen store opens in Berlin

1927   Son Ib born; Jensen silver is exhibited as part of the Danish art exhbit at the Brooklyn Museum, Brooklyn, New York

1929   Wins "Grand Prix" at World Exposition, Barcelona

1930   Georg Jensen store in London relocates to Bond Street; Sigvard Bernadotte joins the company as a designer

1932   Exhibits work at Goldsmiths' Hall, London

1935   The Georg Jensen store in New York moves to 667 Fifth Avenue, New York; Jensen is awarded "Grand Prix" at World Exposition, Brussels; Georg Jensen store opens in Brussels; Johan Rohde dies on February 13th; Georg Jensen dies on October 2nd.

Bibliography

Books

Battersby, Martin. *The Decorative Thirties*. New York: Whitney Library of Design, 1988.

Becker, Vivienne. *Art Nouveau Jewelry*. London: Thames and Hudson, 1985.

Becker, Vivienne. *Antique and Twentieth Century Jewelry*. New York: Van Nostrand Reinhold, 1982.

Beer, Eileene Harrison. *Scandinavian Design: Objects of Life Style*. New York: Farrar, Straus and Giroux, 1975.

Boris, Eileen. *Art and Labor: Ruskin, Morris, and the Craftsman Ideal in America*. Philadelphia: Temple University Press, 1986.

Brunn, Vibeke, Esbjørn Hiort, Richard Kjærgård and John Vedel-Rieper, eds. *Dansk Kunsthåndværker Leksikon*. 2 vols. Copenhagen: Forlaget Rhodos, 1979.

Cera, Deanna Farneti, ed. *Jewels of Fantasy: Costume Jewelry of the 20th Century*. New York: Harry N. Abrams, 1992.

Crawford, Alan. *C. R. Ashbee: Architect, Designer & Romantic Socialist*. New Haven and London: Yale University Press, 1985.

Dahlbäck-Lutteman, Helena and Marianne Uggla, eds. *The Lunning Prize*. Nationalmusei utställningskatalog no. 489. Stockholm: Nationalmuseum, 1986.

Darling, Sharon S. *Chicago Metalsmiths*. Chicago: Chicago Historical Society, 1977.

Duncan, Alastair. *Art Nouveau*. New York: Thames and Hudson, 1994.

Eidelberg, Martin, ed. *Design 1935-1965: What Modern Was*. Montreal: Le Musée des Arts Décoratifs de Montréal; New York: Harry N. Abrams, 1991.

Encyclopedie des arts décoratifs et industriels modernes au XXeme siecle: Twelve volumes documenting the Paris Exhibition of 1925, Vol. 5: "Furniture, hardware and accessories," Garland Publishing: New York and London, 1977.

Ewald, Donna, *San Francisco Invites the World: The Panama-Pacific International Exposition of 1915*, San Francisco: Chronicle Books, 1991.

Fifty Years of Danish Silver in the Georg Jensen Tradition, Copenhagen: Schønberg, 1954; New York [1955].

Gabardi, Melissa. *Art Deco Jewelry*. Woodbridge: Antique Collectors" Club, 1989.

Garner, Philippe. *Contemporary Decorative Arts from 1940 to the Present*. New York: Facts on File, 1980.

Hardie, Melissa, ed. *100 Years in Newlyn: Diary of a Gallery*. Penzance: Patten Press in association with Newlyn Art Gallery, 1995.

Hiort, Esbjørn. *Modern Danish Silver. Moderne Dansk Solv*. New York: Museum Books, 1954.

Hughes, George Ravensworth. *The Worshipful Company of Goldsmiths as Patrons of Their Craft, 1919-53*. London: The Company, 1965.

Hughes, Graham, *Modern Jewelry: An International Survey, 1890-1963*, New York: Crown Publishers, 1963.

Hughes, Graham, *Modern Silver throughout the World, 1880-1967*, New York: Crown Publishers, 1967.

Hughes, Graham. *The Art of Jewelry: A Survey of Craft and Creation*. London: Studio Vista, [1972].

Kaplan, Wendy. *"The Art that is Life": The Arts & Crafts Movement in America, 1875-1920*. Boston: Little, Brown, 1987.

Karlin, Elyse Zorn. *Jewelry and Metalwork in the Arts and Crafts Tradition*. Atglen: Schiffer Publishing, Ltd., 1993.

Komiteen for Danmarks Deltagelse i Verdensudstillingen i Paris, 1900. *Officiel Beretning om Danmarks Deltagelse i Verdensudstillingen i Paris, 1900*. Copenhagen: Nielsen & Lydiche, 1902.

Krekel-Aalberse, Annelies. *Art Nouveau and Art Deco Silver*. New York: Harry N. Abrams, 1989.

Kronquist, E. and A. G. Pelikan. *Simple Metalwork*. London: The Studio, Ltd.; New York: The Studio, Inc., 1940.

Kronquist, Emil F. *Metalcraft and Jewelry*. Peoria: The Manual Arts Press, 1926.

Manufactures and Varied Industries: Offical Catalogue of Exhibitors, Panama-Pacific International Exposition, San Francisco, 1915, San Francisco: The Wahlgreen Company, 1915.

Møller, Henrik Sten. Dansk Design/Danish Design. Copenhagen: Forlaget Rhodos, 1975.

Møller, Jørgen E. R., *Georg Jensen, The Danish Silversmith*, Copenhagen: Georg Jensen & Wendel A/S, 1988.

Møller, Viggo Sten, *Dansk Kunstindustri, 1850-1900*, Copenhagen: Forlaget Rhodos, 1969.

Morrill, Penny Chittim and Carole A. Berk. *Mexican Silver 20th Century Handwrought Jewelry & Metalwork*. Atglen: Schiffer Publishing Ltd., 1994.

Moro, Ginger. *European Designer Jewelry*. Atglen: Schiffer Publishing Ltd., 1995.

Nielsen, Laurits Christian, *Georg Jensen: An Artist's Biography*, Copenhagen: Fr. Bagge Printers, 1921.

Nielsen, Laurits Christian, *En Dansk Kunstner Virksomhed Georg Jensen Sølvet gennem 25 Aar*, Copenhagen: C. C. Petersen, 1929.

Niggl, Reto, *Thorvald Bindesbøll: Keramik und Silber*, Starnberg: Schaefer Verlag, 1989.

Olsen, Ivan Munk, *Sølvsmeden Georg Jensen*, Copenhagen: Arthur Jensens Forlag, 1937.

Raulet, Sylvie. *Art Deco Jewelry*. New York: Rizzoli, 1985.

Raulet, Sylvie. *Jewelry of the 1940s and 1950s*. New York: Rizzoli, 1988.

Renwick Gallery, *Georg Jensen Silversmithy: 77 Artists, 75 Years*, Washington: Smithsonian Institution Press, 1980.

Reventlow, Christian Ditlev, *Georg Jensen Sølvsmedie gennem Fyrretyve Aar, 1904-1944*, Copenhagen: Nordlund, [1944].

Schultz, Sigurd, *Johan Rohde Sølv.*, Copenhagen: Fischers, 1951.

Schwartz, Walter, *Georg Jensen, En kunstner, hans tid og slægt*, Kopenhagen: Georg Jensen & Wendel, Inc., 1958.

Stovenow, Åke and Christian Detlev Reventlow. *Harald Nielsen: Et Tilbageblik på en Kunstners Arbejder ved 60-arsdagen*. Copenhagen: Georg Jensen & Wendel, 1952.

Thage, Jacob, *Danske Smykker Danish Jewelry*, Copenhagen: Komma & Clausens Bøger, 1990.

The Arts of Denmark, Viking to Modern, Denmark: Det Berlingske Bogtrykkeri, 1960.

Todd, Frank Morton, *The Story of the Exposition*, Vol. 3, 217-219; vol. 4, 145-157. New York & London: G. P. Putnam's Sons; The Knickerbocker Press, 1921.

Westin, Ann, *Torun: Samtal med Vivianna Torun Bülow-Hübe*, [Stockholm]: Carlssons Bokförlag, 1993.

Articles and Special Issues

"A Gentle Revolution and a Flexible Tradition: Jensen Silver." *Interiors* 111, no. 10 (May 1952: p. 106-109.

Alexandre, Arsene. "Variations sur Georg Jensen." *La Renaissance* 12 (1929): p. 189-192.

"Art Exhibitions for the Week," *The New York Times*, Dec. 9, 1923, sect. 9, p. 7.

"Art Exhibitions of the Week." *The New York Times*. Nov. 9, 1924, sect. 8, p. 13.

[Been, Ch.] "Danske Kunstindustrielle Arbejder paa Verdensudstillingen i Paris. Udstillingen i Kunstindustrimuséet," *Tidsskrift for Industri*, 1 (1900): 25-34, 53-58.

[Been, Ch.] "Fra Kunstindustrimuséet," *Tidsskrift for Industri* 2 (1901): 249-257.

Benson, Oscar, "In Memoriam: Georg Jensen, Designer, Craftsman, Silversmith," *The Studio*, 111 (1936): 30-35.

Borchsenius, Kaj, "Danske Sølvsmede: Georg Jensen og hans Medarbejdere," *Nyt Tidsskrift for Kunstindustri*, 7 (1934): 89-93.

Borchsenius, Kaj, "Silver and Other Metals in Our Time " *Nyt Tidsskrift for Kunstindustri*, 21 (1948): 67-71.

Bröchner, Georg, "Dänische Porzellan- und Metallarbeiten," *Dekorative Kunst*, 10 (1906/1907): 109-117.

Bröchner, Georg, "Denmark," *The Studio Year-Book of Decorative Art*, 1922, edited by Geoffrey Holme, 125, 127-138. London: The Studio, Ltd., [1922].

Cary, Elisabeth L., "Danish Art in the Leading Industries: A Right Basis," *The New York Times*, Nov. 20, 1927, sect. 10, p. 11.

Christensen, Ch., "Georg Jensen," *Nyt Tidsskrift for Kunstindustri*, 2 (1929): 33-34.

"Critics' Opinion of the Danish Exhibition," *The Brooklyn Museum Quarterly*, 15 (1928): 23-30.

["Danish Exhibition."] *The Brooklyn Museum Quarterly* 15 (1928): 33-34.

"Danmark Udenlands: II. Georg Jensen Sølv," *Nyt Tidsskrift for Kunstindustri*, 22 (1949): 187-189.

Dorph, N. V., "Gesellschaft für Dekorative Kunst in Kopenhagen," *Dekorative Kunst*, 7 (1903/1904): 81-88.

Dyhr, Carl, "Georg Jensen," *Nyt Tidsskrift for Kunstindustri*, 8 (1935): 161.

"Exhibitions of the Week," *The New York Times*, Nov. 9, 1924, sect. 8, p. 13.

Gelfer, Mirjam, "Skønvirke-Jugendstil," *Nyt Tidsskrift for Kunstindustri*, 41 (1969): 89-96.

"Georg Jensen 1866-1966," *Mobilia*, special issue, nos. 131-132 (June-July 1966).

"Georg Jensen, Danish Silver Sculptor, Dies," *New York Herald Tribune*, Oct. 3, 1935, p. 20.

"Georg Jensen Dies; Danish Silversmith," *The New York Times*, Oct. 3, 1935, p. 25.

"Georg Jensen Sølv," *Samleren*, special issue, 15, no. 11 (Nov. 1938).

"Georg Jensens Nordiske Konkurrence," *Nyt Tidsskrift for Kunstindustri*, 39 (1966/1967): 22-24.

Gerfalk, Axel, "Modern Danish Metalwork," *The Studio*, 91 (1926): 24-27.

Grosch, H., "Die Nordische Kunstausstellung in Krefeld," *Dekorative Kunst*, 6 (1902/1903): 111-120.

Gundlach-Pedersen, O., "'Der Laante Fjer,'" *Nyt Tidsskrift for Kunstindustri*, 3 (1930): 9-13.

Gundlach-Pedersen, O., "Georg Jensen Sølvsmedie og dens Plade i den Moderne Udvikling," *Nyt Tidsskrift for Kunstindustri*, 4 (1931): 75-79.

Guralnick, Margot, "The Silver Standard: Georg Jensen's Designs Remain the Hallmark of Twentieth-Century Excellence," *House & Garden*, 165, no. 3 (March 1993): 132-137.

Hannover, Emil, "Moderne Dansk Kunsthaandværk paa Udstillingen i Kunstindusrimuséet og paa Kunstnernes Efteraarsudstilling paa Charlottenborg," *Tidsskrift for Industri*, 5 (1904): 219-233.

Hannover, Emil, "Rundskue over Europas Kunsthaandværk paa Verdensunstillingen," *Tidsskrift for Industri*, 1 (1900): 175-208.

Hiort, Esbjørn, "Brugskunst på slottet: Nanna Ditzels Udstilling på Lerchenborg," *Nyt Tidsskrift for Kunstindustri*, 43 (1972): 218-222.

Jacques, G. M., "Les bijoutiers modernes à l'exposition," *L'Art Décoratif*, 2 (1900): 173-211.

Janneau, Guillaume, "Ce que sera l'exposition de 1935," *La Revue de L'Art*, 45 (1924): 316-322.

Janneau, Guillaume, "La section Danoise," *La Renaissance*, 9 (1925): 420-430.

Jensen, Georg, "Af et Tres-Aaright Kunstnerliv: Erindringer fra min Barndom og Udvikling," *Samleren*, 3 (1926): 168-171.

Jensen, Georg, "Kunstneren Johan Rohde," *Samleren*, 8 (1931): 150.

Johansson, Gotthard, "Dansk Silver och Dansk Hemkultur," *Nyt Tidsskrift for Kunstindustri*, 2 (1939): 24-27.

Jörgensen, Johannes, "Mogens Ballin's Werkstatt," *Dekorative Kunst*, 5 (1901/1902): 244-250.

Klint, P. V. J., "Aabningsudstilling af 'Skønvirke': og Nogle Betragtninger Desangaaender," *Tidsskrift for Industri*, 8 (1907): 265-278.

Koppel, Henning, "Lidt om Sølv," *Nyt Tidsskrift for Kunstindustri*, 43 (1972): 248.

Krohn, Pietro, "Det Danske Kunstindustrimuseum," *Tiddskrift for Industri*, 2 (1902): 31-44.

Krohn, Pietro, "Muséets Indkjøb paa Verdensudstillingen i Paris, Aar 1900," *Tidsskrift for Industri*, 2 (1901): 50-63.

Krohn, Pietro, "Verdensudstillingen i Paris Aar 1900," *Tidsskrift for Industri*, 1 (1900): 4-14.

Kyster, Anker, "Thorvald Bindesbøll i Hans Forhald til Haandværket," *Tidsskrift for Industri*, 9 (1908): 208-215.

Lassen, Erik, "Georg Jensen," *Nyt Tidsskrift for Kunstindustri*, 38 (1965/1966): 133-135.

Lassen, Erik, "Mindeudstilling for Johan Rohde Sølv," *Nyt Tidsskrift for Kunstindustri*, 29 (1956): 214.

"M. Georg Jensen: A Great Danish Silversmith." *The Times*, Oct. 4, 1935, p. 16.

Malinowski, Arno, "Om Smykker," *Nyt Tidsskrift for Kunstindustri*, 16 (1943): 38.

Malinowski, Arno, "Om Smykker og Deres Funktion," *Nyt Tidsskrift for Kunstindustri*, 29 (1956): 35.

Malinowski, Arno, "Sølvtoj," *Nyt Tidsskrift for Kunstindustri*, 26 (1951): 3.

"Moderner Schmuck," *Dekorative Kunst*, 6 (1902/1903): 174-181.

Møller, Henrik Sten, "Henning Koppel, Arbeider gennem 25 år," *Nyt Tidsskrift for Kunstindustri*, 43 (1972): 49-52.

Møller, Svend Erik, "Henning Koppel som Sølvkunstner," *Nyt Tidsskrift for Kunstindustri*, 38 (1965/1966): 37-41.

Møller, Thorolf, "Enfaringer fra Georg Jensen Sølvsmedie, især om Fremmed Skik og Brug," *Nyt Tidsskrift for Kunstindustri*, 1 (1928): 89-95.

Møller, Thorolf, "En Kunstindustri-Virksomheds Tilblivelse i Anledning af Georg Jensen Sølvsemdie 25 Aars Jubilæum," *Nyt Tidsskrift for Kunstindustri*, 2 (1929): 34-36.

Møller, Thorolf, "Georg Jensen Udstilling," *Nyt Tidsskrift for Kunstindustri*, 11 (1938): 194.

Møller, Viggo Sten, "Arno Malinowskis Sølvarbejder," *Nyt Tidsskrift for Kunstindustri*, 16 (1943): 6-7.

[Møller, Viggo Sten,] "Danmark Udenlands: III. Lunning i New York," *Nyt Tidsskrift for Kunstindustri*, 23 (1950): 37-38.

Møller, Viggo Sten, "Jern og Sølv: Nye Arbejder i Anledning af et 40 Aars Jubilæum," *Nyt Tidsskrift for Kunstindustri*, 17 (1944): 56-57.

Møller, Viggo Sten, "Sigvard Bernadottes Sølvarbejder," *Nyt Tidsskrift for Kunstindustri*, 15 (1942): 36-37.

Mørch, Ibi Trier, "Inger Møller på Kunstindustrimuséet," *Nyt Tidsskrift for Kunstindustri*, 39 (1966/1967): 57.

Mørch, Ibi Trier, "Ske, Kniv og Gaffel," *Nyt Tidsskrift for Kunstindustri*, 33 (1960): 175-182.

Mørch, Ibi Trier, "Smykket," *Nyt Tidsskrift for Kunstindustri* 33 (1960): 42-53.

Mørch, Ibi Trier, "Sølv fra seks smedier," *Nyt Tidsskrift for Kunstindustri*, 30 (1957): 91-94.

Mørch, Ibi Trier, "Sølvet og Smykkerne på Årsudstillingen." *Nyt Tidsskrift for Kunstindustri*, 34 (1961): 92-99.

Mørch, Ibi Trier, "Torun Bülow-Hübe: En Sølvkunstner er kommet til Danmark," *Nyt Tidsskrift for Kunstindustri*, 41 (1969): 115-117.

Mourey, Gabriel, "La section Danoise," *Art et Décoration*, 48 (1925): 147-156.

"Museum Notes," *The Brooklyn Museum Quarterly*, 15 (1928): 96-103.

Nielsen, L. C., "Georg Jensen Sølvet: 1904-1929," *Samleren*, 6 (1929): 63-64.

"Nye Modeller Hos Georg Jensen: Prins Sigvards Sølvarbejder," *Samleren*, 8 (1931): 32.

Olsen Ivan Munk, "Kunstneren Johan Rohde," *Samleren*, 12 (1935): 45-48.

Olsen, Ivan Munk, "Nye Arbejder fra Georg Jensen Sølvsmedie," *Samleren*, (10 (1933): 163-164.

Olsen, Ivan Munk, "Sølvsmeden Georg Jensen." *Skønvirke* 12 (1926): 49-62.

[Olsen, Ivan Munk,] "Sølvsmeden Georg Jensens Nye Arbejder," *Samleren*, 5 (1928): 91.

Olsen, Ivan Munk, "The Art of Denmark: 4. Glass and Metalwork." *The Studio*, 111 (1936): 264-267.

Oppermann, Th., "Johan Rohde: I Anledning af Hans 75 Aarige Fødselsdag," *Nyt Tidsskrift for Kunstindustri*, 4 (1931): 161-164.

Pedersen, Johan, "Georg Jensen Sølvsmedie A/S 1904-1954: Jubilæumsudstilling i Kunstindustrimuseet," *Nyt Tidsskrift for Kunstindustri*, 27 (1954): 78-81.

Rambosson, Yvanhoé, "L'exposition des arts décoratifs: la participatiuon étrangère: II. Japon, Belgique, Angleterre, Italie, Russie, Yougoslavie, Espagne, Luxembourg, Suisse, Grèce, Danemark, Turquie," *La Revue de L'Art*, 48 (1925): 156-178.

Rambosson, Yvanhoé, "L'exposition des arts décoratifs: les pavillons de la province et de l'étranger: quelques aspects," *La Revue de L'Art*, 48 (1925): 30-40.

Schultz, Sigurd, "Dansk Sølvindustri," *Nyt Tidsskrift for Kunstindustri*, 2 (1929): 161-169.

Schultz, Sigurd, "Dansk Sølvstil," *Nyt Tidsskrift for Kunstindustri*, 2 (1929): 1-8.

Schultz, Sigurd, "Den Kongelige Porcelainsfabriks Udstilling i Berlin," *Nyt Tidsskrift for Kunstindustri*, 1 (1928): 45-52.

Schultz, Sigurd. "Georg Jensen Sølv." *Samleren* 11 (1938): 203-228.

Schur, Ernst, "Die Dänische Ausstellung in Berlin," *Dekorative Kunst*, 14 (1910/1911): 221-232.

Schwandt, Jörg, "Dänisches Silber des 20. Jahrhunderts. Teil I: Der Weg zum Jensen-Stil," *Weltkunst*, 57 (1987): 3412-3415. Schwandt, Jörg, "Dänisches Silber des 20. Jahrhunderts. Teil II: Funktionalismus, dreißiger und vierziger Jahre," *Weltkunst*, 57 (1987): 3590-3593.

Schwandt, Jörg, "Dänisches Silber des 20. Jahrhunderts. Teil III: Fünfziger und sechziger Jahre," *Weltkunst*, 57 (1987): 3686-3689.

Sedeyn, Émile, "L'orfèvre Georg Jensen," *Art et Décoration*, 35, no. 7 (July 1914): 15-21.

Skawonius, Sven Erik, "Ande och materia: Torun Bülow-Hübes smycken," *Nyt Tidsskrift for Kunstindustri*, 33 (1960): 218-221.

Slomann, Vilh, "Johan Rohde," *Nyt Tidsskrift for Kunstindustri*, 8 (1935): 49-51.

Teevan, Bernard, "Georg Jensen's Silver," *International Studio*, 30 (1924): 160-162.

"Udstillingen af Kunsthaandværk i Industriforeningen April-Maj," *Tidsskrift for Industri*, 9 (1908): 107-127.

Wacker, Leonhard, "Der Wert der Künstlichen Farbstoffe für die Bestrebungen des Modernen Kunstgewerbes," *Dekorative Kunst*, 6 (1902/1903): 182-195.

Wanscher, Vilhelm, "Fra de Sidste Udstillinger," *Tidsskrift for Industri*, 11 (1910): 125-137.

Wanscher, Vilhelm, "Haandværk og Kunst," *Kunstbladet*, (1909/1910): 323-325.

Wanscher, Vilhelm, "Thorvald Bindesbøll som Kunstner," *Tidsskrift for Industri*, 9 (1908): 195-207.

Werner, B. E., "Der Dänischer Silberschmied Georg Jensens Neue Arbeiten," *Dekorative Kunst*, 32 (1929): 101-103.

Westheim, Paul, "Dänische Kunst," *Kunst und Handwerk*, 61 (1910/1911): 255-261.

Value Reference Guide

The values that appear here are derived from compiled sources and were not supplied by the author or by the people acknowledged in the credit lines. The prices were conscientiously determined to reflect the market at the time this work was compiled. No responsibility for their future accuracy is accepted by the author, the publisher, or the people credited with the photographs. Values vary immensely according to an article's condition, location of the market, parts of the country, materials, and overall quality of design. While one must make their own decision, we can relate estimates from our survey of different markets.

Auction Results KEY:
Year-Month-Day Auction House City $ auction bid DESCRIPTION

JEWELRY

92-05-15 Skinner, Inc. Bolton, MA $550 FOUR GEORG JENSEN SILVER BROOCHES THREE FOLIATE DESIGNS WITH BLOSSOMS AND BEADS, IMPRESSED "GEORG JENSEN DENMARK," AND A LEAF DECORATED BAR WITH OVAL SEAL MARKED "GEORG JENSEN HAND WROUGHT STERLING."

92-05-21 Butterfield & Butterfield, San Francisco, CA $330 COLLECTION OF TWO GEORG JENSEN STERLING SILVER BROOCHES #256 & #178.

93-12-08 Christie's East, NY $1495 THREE GEORG JENSEN SILVER BRACELETS, #3, #57, -.

90-01-20 Skinner, MA $220 GEORG JENSEN OVAL STERLING SILVER PIN.

90-01-20 Skinner, MA $220 GEORG JENSEN STERLING SILVER AND MOONSTONE RING, no. 3.

90-01-20 Skinner, MA $495 GEORG JENSEN ROUND STERLING SILVER PIN, no. 283.

90-01-20 Skinner, MA $412.50 GEORG JENSEN STERLING SILVER PIN AND EARRING SET no. 91.

90-04-21 Skinner, Bolton, MA $303 GEORG JENSEN STERLING SILVER PIN 305.

90-07-21 Skinner, Inc. Bolton, MA $165 GEORG JENSEN STERLING SILVER PENDANT, COPENHAGEN, POST 1945, DESIGN NO. 337A.

90-07-21 Skinner, Inc. Bolton, MA $93.50 GEORG JENSEN STERLING SILVER RING, COPENHAGEN, POST 1945, DESIGN NO. 130.

90-07-21 Skinner, Inc. Bolton, MA $110 A PAIR OF GEORG JENSEN STERLING SILVER EARRINGS, COPENHAGEN, NO. 116B.

90-01-20 Skinner, MA $495 GEORG JENSEN ROUND STERLING SILVER PIN NO.283.

90-04-21 Skinner, Bolton, MA $303 GEORG JENSEN STERLING SILVER PIN.

92-05-15 Skinner, Inc. Bolton, MA $660 GEORG JENSEN SILVER AND PANSY BRACELET #29.

92-05-15 Skinner, Inc. Bolton, MA $412.50 GEORG JENSEN JEWELED CIRCLE PIN 4B.

92-05-21 Butterfield & Butterfield, San Francisco, CA $1540 COLLECTION OF TWO GEORG JENSEN STERLING SILVER BRACELETS #89.

92-06-22 Skinner, Inc. Bolton, MA $715 TWO GEORG JENSEN STERLING SILVER BRACELETS.

93-07-23 David Rago Lambertville, NJ $600 GEORG JENSEN 18K GOLD PENDANT WITH SAPPHIRE IN A FLORAL AND LEAF DESIGN 750/18K/32.

94-06-16 Butterfield & Butterfield San Francisco, CA $4.0 COLLECTION OF STERLING SILVER DRESS SETS, GEORG JENSEN ONE PAIR OF HORSE HEAD CUFF LINKS #63 AND MATCHING TIE BAR #65; ONE PAIR OF VIKING SHIP MOTIF CUFF LINKS AND MATCHING TIE BAR #50; TOGETHER WITH ONE BUFFALO TIE BAR #71.

90-04-21 Skinner, Bolton, MA $468 GEORG JENSEN STERLING SILVER AND GREEN ONYX PIN, 236A.

94-04-22 Sotheby's London $1537 GEORG JENSEN PENDANT, CIRCA 1920 SILVER COLORED METAL WITH OPAL AND LABRADORITE #4 AND WITH THE JENSEN MARKS FOR 1915-27 AND 1915-30.

93-03-19 Sotheby's New York $1840 SILVER AND LABRADORITE NECKLACE AND TWO SILVER BROOCHES, GEORG JENSEN SILVERSMITHY, COPENHAGEN, 1933-44 AND AFTER 1945.

94-03-08 Skinner, Inc. $230 TWO STERLING SILVER PINS NOS. 111 AND 101.

HOLLOWWARE

93-06-12 Christie's New York $2,300 A PAIR OF DANISH SILVER MUSTARD POTS PEPPER CASTERS, AND SALT CELLARS.

93-06-10-Sotheby's New York $25,300 A PAIR OF DANISH SILVER FIVE-LIGHT CANDELABRA, GEORG JENSEN NUMBERED 383A, DESIGNED BY GEORG JENSEN

95/03/17 Sotheby's New York $5,462 A DANISH SILVER BONBONNIERE AND COVER, GEORG JENSEN SILVERSMITHY, COPENHAGEN, AFTER 1945, NUMBERED 262.

95/03/17 Sotheby's New York $4,312 A DANISH SILVER COVERED BUTTER DISH ON STAND SET WITH AMBER, GEORG JENSEN SILVERSMITHY, COPENHAGEN, NUMBERED 44, AND A MATCHING BUTTER DISH, ALSO NUMBERED 44.

94-12-09 Christie's New York $6,900 A PAIR OF PEWTER DOORS FOR GEORG JENSEN INC., NEW YORK.

92-01-25 Christie's New York $9,900 A SILVER COMPOTE DESIGNED BY GEORG JENSEN, MADE BY GEORG JENSEN SILVERSMITHY, 1925-1932, #196.

92-01-25 Christie's New York $14,300 A PAIR OF SILVER TWO-LIGHT CANDELABRA DESIGNED BY GEORG JENSEN IN 1920, MADE BY GEORG JENSEN SILVERSMITHY, POST-1945 #244.

92-12-12-Christie's New York $3,520 A DANISH SILVER COVERED CANISTER DESIGNED BY GEORG JENSEN IN 1926, MADE BY GEORG JENSEN SILVERSMITHY, 1933-1944 #530.

92-12-12 Christie's New York $17,600 A DANISH SILVER PITCHER DESIGNED BY HENNING KOPPEL IN 1952; MADE BY GEORG JENSEN SILVERSMITHY, 992.

92-12-12 Christie's New York $6,600 A DANISH SILVER FRUIT DISH DESIGNED BY GEORG JENSEN IN 1919; MADE BY GEORG JENSEN SILVERSMITHY, 1919-1927 #320.

93-06-27 Dunning's Elgin, IL $7700 PAIR OF GEORG JENSEN STERLING SILVER TWO LIGHT CANDELABRA #324.

92-01-25 Christie's New York $48,400 A RARE PAIR OF SILVER FIVE-LIGHT CANDELABRA DESIGNED BY GEORG JENSEN CIRCA 1935, MADE BY GEORG JENSEN SILVERSMITHY, POST-1945 #740.

93-01-02 Skinner, Inc. Bolton, MA $385 GEORG JENSEN STERLING COMPACT AND A LIPSTICK CASE.

95/06/09 Christie's New York $3,220 A DANISH GRAPE-PATTERN SILVER COMPOTE DE-SIGNED BY GEORG JENSEN IN 1918; MAKER'S MARK OF GEORG JENSEN SILVERSMITHY, POST-1945 #263B.

94-06-11 Christie's New York $4,600 A DANISH SILVER GRAPE-PATTERN COMPOTE DE-SIGNED BY GEORG JENSEN IN 1918; MAKER'S MARK OF GEORG JENSEN SILVERSMITHY, #264.

94-06-11 Christie's New York $9,200 A LARGE DANISH SILVER GRAPE-PATTERN COM-POTE DESIGNED BY GEORG JENSEN IN 1918, MAKER'S MARK OF GEORG JENSEN SILVERSMITHY, # 264B.

94-06-11 Christie's New York $13,800 A DANISH SILVER GRAPE-PATTERN TUREEN AND COVER DESIGNED BY GEORG JENSEN IN 1921, MAKER'S MARK OF GEORG JENSEN SILVERSMITHY, POST-1945 #408A.

94-06-11 Christie's New York $12,650 A PAIR OF DANISH SILVER GRAPE-PATTERN CANDLESTICKS DESIGNED BY GEORG JENSEN; MAKER'S MARK OF GEORG JENSEN SILVERSMITHY, POST-1945 # 263B.

94-06-11 Christie's New York $2,530 A DANISH SILVER BOWL DESIGNED BY GEORG JENSEN IN 1912, MAKER'S MARK OF GEORG JENSEN SILVERSMITHY, #19A.

94-06-11 Christie's New York $4,830 A DANISH SILVER ROSE BONBONNIERE DESIGNED BY GEORG JENSEN IN 1918; MAKER'S MARK OF GEORG JENSEN SILVERSMITHY, 1918-1927 #262.

94-06-15 Sotheby's New York $3,162 A DANISH SILVER COVERED BOWL, GEORG JENSEN SILVERSMITHY,# 72.

94-06-15 Sotheby's New York $5,175 A DANISH SILVER THREE PIECE COFFEE SET AND A CIRCULAR TRAY, GEORG JENSEN SILVERSMITHY, COPENHAGEN, CIRCA 1932, NUM-BERED 80A AND 519B, COMPRISING: COFFEE POT, COVERED SUGAR AND CREAMER.

94-12-09 Christie's New York $23,000 A RARE DANISH SILVER MANTEL CLOCK DESIGNED BY JOHAN ROHDE IN 1919; MADE BY GEORG JENSEN SILVERSMITHY, 1945-1951 #333.

94-12-09 Christie's New York $9,775 A DANISH SILVER GRAPE-PATTERN CENTERPIECE BOWL DESIGNED BY GEORG JENSEN IN 1919; MAKER'S MARK OF GEORG JENSEN SILVERSMITHY, 1925-1932 #296A.

94-05-06-Robert Eldred Co. MA $852 BOWL ON STAND BY GEORG JENSEN #6.

90-12-04 Christie's New York $52,800 SILVER BLOSSOM-PATTERN EIGHT-PIECE TEA AND COFFEE SERVICE AND A LARGE TRAY DESIGNED BY GEORG JENSEN IN 1905; MADE BY GEORG JENSEN SILVERSMITHY, POST-1945, THE IVORY HANDLES FLUTED; THE OVAL TRAY WITH TWO OPENWORK HANDLES SET WITH BLOSSOMS.

90-12-04 Christie's New York $18,700 A LARGE SILVER TWO-HANDLED TEA TRAY DE-SIGNED BY GEORG JENSEN CIRCA 1912; MADE BY GEORG JENSEN SILVERSMITHY, 1919-1925.

90-12-04 Christie's New York $20,900 A SILVER BLOSSOM-PATTERN TEA-TRAY DESIGNED BY GEORG JENSEN CIRCA 1905; MADE BY GEORG JENSEN SILVERSMITHY, POST-1945.

90-12-04 Christie's New York $44,000 PAIR OF SILVER FIVE-LIGHT CANDELABRA DE-SIGNED BY GEORG JENSEN IN 1920; MADE BY GEORG JENSEN SILVERSMITHY, 1925-1932.

90-12-04 Christie's New York $18,700 A LARGE SILVER TWO-HANDLED TEA TRAY DE-SIGNED BY GEORG JENSEN CIRCA 1912; MADE BY GEORG JENSEN SILVERSMITHY.

92-01-25 Christie's New York $49,500 CENTERPIECE DISH DESIGNED BY HENNING KOPPEL IN 1956, MADE BY GEORG JENSEN SILVERSMITHY, POST-1956 ELONGATED OVAL, WITH TAPERED AND FLARED ENDS, THE DOMED COVER WITH UPTURNED HANDLES, MARKED 1054.

92-01-25 Christie's New York $28,600 COVERED MEAT-DISH WITH FIGURAL BIRD-FORM HANDLE DESIGNED BY HARALD NIELSEN CIRCA 1931, MADE BY GEORG JENSEN SILVERSMITHY, POST-1945 600S.

92-01-25 Christie's New York $15,400 A MATCHED SET OF FOUR SILVER SAUCE BOATS AND FOUR SAUCE LADLES, ON THREE STANDS DESIGNED BY GEORG JENSEN, CIRCA 1920, MADE BY GEORG JENSEN SILVERSMITHY, # 177.

92-01-25 Christie's New York $15,400 A SET OF FOUR SILVER GRAPE-PATTERN CANDLE-STICKS DESIGNED By GEORG JENSEN, MADE BY GEORG JENSEN SILVERSMITHY, POST-1945 #263.

92-01-25 Christie's New York $10,450 A SET OF EIGHT SILVER GRAPE-PATTERN WINE GOBLETS DESIGNED BY GEORG JENSEN IN 1919, MADE BY GEORG JENSEN SILVERSMITHY, POST-1945 MARKED 296A, 3 3/4 IN. HIGH (58 OZ.)

92-01-25 Christie's New York $6,600 A SILVER GRAPE-PATTERN WINE COASTER 289A, 3 3/4 IN. HIGH.

92-01-25 Christie's New York $11,000 A PAIR OF SILVER GRAPE-PATTERN SMALL OVAL BOWLS MARKED 296C, 2 3/4 IN. HIGH, 7 7/8 IN. WIDE (30 OZ.)

92-01-25 Christie's New York $18,700 A SILVER GRAPE-PATTERN OVAL CENTERPIECE BOWL 1925-1932 marked 296.

92-01-25 Christie's New York $11,550 A COVERED AMBER-SET SILVER BUTTER DISH DE-SIGNED BY GEORG JENSEN IN 1912, MADE BY GEORG JENSEN SILVERSMITHY, 1925-1932 #44.

92-05-06 Christie's New York $3,850 A SILVER WATER PITCHER DESIGNED BY JOHAN ROHDE IN 1920; MADE BY GEORG JENSEN SILVERSMITHY, POST-1945 #432C.

92-05-06 Christie's New York $9,350 A PAIR OF SILVER TWO-LIGHT CANDELABRA DE-SIGNED BY GEORG JENSEN IN 1920; MADE BY GEORG JENSEN SILVERSMITHY, 1920-1927 MARKED 244, 8 1/8 IN. (20.6 CM.) HIGH (85 OZ.)

92-11-07 Sotheby's New York $17,600 A DANISH SILVER SIX PIECE TEA AND COFFEE SET WITH MATCHING TWO-HANDLED OVAL TRAY, GEORG JENSEN SILVERSMITHY, COPENHAGEN, 1919-AFTER 1945, 2A, 2B, 2D, AND 2S.

92-11-07 Sotheby's New York $6,050 A DANISH SILVER DISH, GEORG JENSEN SILVERSMITHY, COPENHAGEN, AFTER 1945, NUMBERED 2E, DESIGNED BY GEORG JENSEN.

92-11-07 Sotheby's New York $1,980 A DANISH SILVER CIRCULAR VEGETABLE DISH AND COVER, 290A.

93-03-19 Sotheby's New York $18,400 A PAIR OF DANISH SILVER FIVE LIGHT CANDELA-BRA, GEORG JENSEN SILVERSMITHY, COPENHAGEN, 1945-1951, NUMBERED 474, DESIGNED BY JOHAN ROHDE.

93-06-10 Sotheby's New York $10,350 A DANISH SILVER FIVE-LIGHT CANDELABRUM, GEORG JENSEN NUMBERED 383A.

93-06-10 Sotheby's New York $24,150 A RARE AND IMPORTANT DANISH SILVER PITCHER, GEORG JENSEN SILVERSMITHY, COPENHAGEN, DESIGNED BY HENNING KOPPEL, CIRCA 1956, NUMBER 1052.

93-06-12 Christie's New York $3680 A PAIR OF DANISH SUGAR BASKETS DESIGNED BY GEORG JENSEN IN 1917, MAKER'S MARK OF GEORG JENSEN SILVERSMITHY, POST - 1945 235B.

93-06-12 Christie's New York $23,000 DANISH SILVER COVERED TUREEN DESIGNED BY GEORG JENSEN, MAKER'S MARK OF GEORG JENSEN SILVERSMITHY, POST-1945, 408A, MARKED UNDER BASE -7 1/2IN. (19CM.) HIGH, (87OZ.)

93-09-17 DuMouchelles Detroit $32,000 GEORG JENSEN STERLING TEA SET FOUR PIECES: #45C, TOTAL APPROX. 68 TROY OZS. PLUS A GEORG JENSEN STERLING SILVER TRAY WITH EBONY HANDLES, #251C, APPROX. 85 TROY OZ.

93-03-19 Sotheby's New York $1,035 A SET OF FOUR DANISH SILVER SALTS AND FOUR MATCHING PEPPERS, 741 AND 110, DESIGNED BY JOHAN ROHDE.

94-04-22 Sotheby's London $2,733 HARALD NIELSEN FOR GEORG JENSEN VEGETABLE DISH AND COVER, DESIGNED IN 1928, 546A.

FLATWARE

92-11-07 Sotheby's New York $15,000 A DANISH SILVER FLATWARE SET, GEORG JENSEN SILVERSMITHY, COPENHAGEN, 1933-1944, DESIGNED BY GEORG JENSEN, CONTINENTAL PATTERN, 256 PIECES.

90-06-08 Christie's New York $20,900 A 246-PIECE PYRAMID PATTERN SILVER FLATWARE SERVICE IN FITTED MAHOGANY SERVING TABLE DESIGNED BY HARALD NIELSEN IN 1926, EXECUTED BY GEORG JENSEN SILVERSMITHY.

90-12-04 Christie's New York $38,500 A 291-PIECE SILVER PYRAMID-PATTERN FLATWARE SERVICE DESIGNED BY HARALD NIELSEN IN 1926; MADE BY GEORG JENSEN SILVERSMITHY, POST-1945.

95/01/31 Sotheby's Arcade New York $3,450 A SET OF TWENTY-FOUR DANISH SILVER DESSERT FORKS AND KNIVES, GEORG JENSEN SILVERSMITHY, IN THE ACORN PATTERN.

95/03/17 Sotheby's New York $2,070 A PAIR OF DANISH SILVER FISH SERVERS, GEORG JENSEN SILVERSMITHY, COPENHAGEN, AFTER 1945, NUMBERED 55, DESIGNED BY GEORG JENSEN IN 1914.

94-11-18 DuMouchelle's Detroit $750 GEORG JENSEN "BLOSSOM" PATTERN STERLING SILVER SERVING PIECES, PIE SERVER AND CAKE SERVER #84 84.

Index

C

D